Tales from the Milestone

Tales from the Milestone

◆

My Life Before and During 1940-1945

Ben Wajikra

iUniverse, Inc.
New York Lincoln Shanghai

Tales from the Milestone
My Life Before and During 1940-1945

iUniverse, Inc.

For information address:
iUniverse, Inc.
2021 Pine Lake Road, Suite 100
Lincoln, NE 68512
www.iuniverse.com

ISBN: 0-595-30611-X

Printed in the United States of America

Contents

DEDICATION AND ACKNOWLEDGMENT

This manuscript is lovingly dedicated to the memory of my parents, Max Leviticus and Sera Leviticus-ten Bosch, may they rest in peace, to my wife Rose, to our children and grandchildren, and all the children of the world. I hope all of you may find it interesting and valuable to read a little of my history during World War II.

I want to thank my wife Rose for her support, her help in editing and correcting of my Dutch-English syntax and for putting up with my disappearing into the basement almost every night. Thanks also go to Mrs. Amy Tuttle for her remarks on the first revision and especially to Dr. Ann Wyatt-Brown and Miss Tami Davidson, whose suggestions prompted me to revise my work and without whose constructive efforts this manuscript would not have been published.

My sincerest and deepest gratitude to Karel and Rita Brouwer, the Van der Pol family and to Mr. Van der Kieft (a.k.a. Moltjes Veer) and his family. The Brouwers took me into their family and cared for me during and immediately after the war. I am still their "eldest son" The Van Der Pols took me in on a fateful day and gave me shelter despite the imminent danger to themselves. Mr. Van der Kieft assisted and cared for my family when we had to go into hiding and he looked after us until we were caught. His selfless efforts were unable to save my parents, who were murdered in Auschwitz in 1942.

PROLOGUE

This manuscript, a collection of my memories, derives its name from the house where most of the events took place during WWII—the house where I lived from December 1942 until 8 months after the end of WWII. The house was called *"De Mijlpaal"*, which is the Dutch word for *"The Milestone"*. What we knew as a "Mijlpaal" was a low square, stone roadside mileage and place name marker, resembling a toadstool in shape, many of which were found all over the Netherlands. The Mijlpaal became a beehive of illegal activity during the time of the German occupation. It literally became a "Milestone" on the road of the life for me and many other persecuted people during WWII. Being there saved my life and so were the lives of many others who either lived there, passed through or were helped in some other way.

The house was built around the 1920's and became, from mid-1942 onward a center for underground activity until the end of the German occupation in May 1945. Many people, Jewish and Christian were helped by the head of the household, Mr. Karel Brouwer, his wife Rita and Karel's colleagues in the underground organization, which was called the TD-group. Some people actually passed through the house on their way to other addresses, others were helped while living in different locations. Most of those people survived, albeit not always easily.

I am one of the survivors. My personal story of adventures and escapes from disaster started about eight months before I came to live with the Brouwer family. To me they were Oom (uncle) Karel and Tante (auntie) Rita. This is mostly my story, but I have included a few stories of others, who lived in or passed through the house or were involved and connected to me, the Brouwers or the Mijlpaal.

The name I have used **"Ben Wajikra"** is a pseudonym consisting of two Hebrew words. The word **"Ben"** means "son" or in this sentence "son of"; **"Wajikra"** is the Hebrew name of the book of Leviticus, the third of the five books of the Torah. Thus the name means Son of Leviticus and is a homage to my parents, Max and Sera Leviticus, whose son I am.

I think it is important to tell my story today. There are few Holocaust survivors left to talk about WWII to this generation and to those of the future. It is important from a moral and historical point and also because of the fact, that there are still many Nazi sympathizers and pseudo-scientists alive who say that no

Holocaust ever occurred. But primarily it is important for me as a person to tell these stories as I remember them and before my brain starts to forget.

It took me a long time before I was willing and able to tell my story. My first experience of speaking about it was in the late 1990's during a visit by an interviewer from the Steven Spielberg Foundation. During that visit I told part of my story to Dr. Benjamin Nachman, the interviewer, but after I saw the videotape I was dissatisfied with my "performance". It wasn't anything Dr. Nachman did or didn't do but I thought that during that interview I appeared rather matter-of-fact and cold and I also felt that in the two hours of taping I was able to relate only a tiny fraction of the many things that happened during those five years of war and certainly was not able to express my feelings about them.

Some time later I was asked to talk about some of my experiences to a philosophy class at Nebraska Wesleyan University in Lincoln, Nebraska. That first time, it was very difficult for me to open my soul to this group of young people who were total strangers. There was a certain moment, when I talked about the last time I saw my parents, that I became quite emotional in public and I think it was that moment that the "wall of my silence" was really breached. Those in attendance understood what I felt, and I had heard and read about the same feeling from other Holocaust survivors. I had finally begun the process of putting to rest the memories of my parents, grandparents, uncles, aunts, cousins and other family members, my friends and schoolmates and my pains and sorrows and the demonic feelings of hatred and of guilt. I gave voice to my anger and distrust. I heard myself making statements which I had never made before. I understood that I had to continue to purge myself of the bitterness, the sadness, the guilt of being alive, the guilt for what I did to stay alive, and all the other feelings which I accumulated as a young boy and had kept hidden. Another reason for writing is to document my history in order to help refute those who try to deny the Holocaust. There was a Holocaust and it was perpetrated by the Nazis and their collaborators and I am one of the few lucky ones who survived! Don't tell me it was a dream!

Why is it so difficult for survivors to tell their stories? For me, as a young boy, it was a painful period full of hate, fear and distrust and as I grew older, I wanted to forget all the sadness and misery. But in reality I always lived with it. I also asked myself why anyone else would want to know about my story. Some of my experiences seemed too fantastic to be true. I wondered if people would believe what I told them. Maybe they would think that I was making it all up, or showing off (in Dutch it is called "opscheppen" or "shoveling manure"). My story would show weaknesses of character of which I was not proud. To confess to weakness in public is not easy. I am sure, that I am not alone in the fear of having people think less of me if they knew more of the truth about me. Therefore, we, the survivors, often kept quiet until we were old enough or mature enough to understand that we should speak up and never mind what some dummy may say or some shrink may think. Some of us never speak up, and important human history lessons are lost that way.

Unfortunately I had no written record of the events during the war, and was forced to rely for many details, such as dates, on books and on my memories and those of friends, my protectors and family I spoke with these last few years. I soon found out that memory isn't always reliable and that some of my recollections had become distorted by time, by my own perceptions and feelings. Mr. Brouwer, whom I shall call Karel from now on, and I had quite different recollections of some of the same events. Harry Theeboom, another Jewish survivor, with whom I spent much of the war, remembers some things differently from both Karel and me. In addition, when we talked about some of the events, we were often reminded of some other event and its details, which we had totally forgotten. Practically every time we talk about the past, we are reminded of something connected to another event and we say; "I had forgotten that......". And then we have to correct our memories again.

In the course of writing this manuscript I often had to backtrack on events because I found that things did not fit the sequence in which they occurred. Many phone calls and visits to Karel and Rita in the Netherlands as well as visits and talking to Harry Theeboom, before he became ill and passed away, and Elly Duits, both about five years my seniors and with whom I spent much time at the Mijlpaal, have helped sort out some of my confusion. Still, I wake up sometimes in the middle of the night and suddenly remember another fact "That's it! This is the way it was!"—and then I stay awake for a short time, thinking how I could have forgotten, and how I should write about it.

The perspectives with which Karel, Harry, Elly or I saw things are different. I was nearly nine years old in 1940 when the Germans invaded, eleven years old when I became an orphan and came to the Mijlpaal and fourteen just after we were liberated. At that age kids tend to live on a day to day basis and to consider many events, even the frightening ones, as adventures. Karel Brouwer was a married man of twenty-four in 1942, with a family of his own. Rita, his wife, was then twenty-one. During the war Karel was responsible for saving the lives of a large number of people who had gone in hiding or worked for the underground movement, and he was waging a continuing battle to keep one step ahead of the German occupiers and their Dutch collaborators. Harry and Elly were the same age and five years older than I was. The age difference between us made a lot of difference in our understanding of life. All of us had hiatuses in our memory, though Karel's wife, Rita, has helped us remember many things we had forgotten. Tension and fear seems to wipe out or alter certain parts of the memory, maybe because they are too unpleasant to remember or we are afraid to remember them.

I decided not to write a single story but divide it into a number of separate chapters. The main reason for this is that it is difficult for me to remember the events between major happenings. Sometimes events were overlapping and I was in a quandary how to write them down in a lucid manner. In the end, I arranged the stories in the sequence which made the most sense to me and which is chronologically correct and I hope the reader will understand and be able to follow along.

In order to provide a little mor background on the activities in and around the Mijlpaal I included a chapter on the organization, which Karel established with his friend Dr. Adolph Hendriks (Dolf) and his colleague Bob van der Heijden. In it I have tried to explain the reasons why and how things were done. I knew many of the details from the day to day goings-on in the Mijlpaal and have learned more from talks with Karel and from books, all of them written in Dutch, about the TD resistance group. It is unfortunate that Dolf died in 1989. I had left the Netherlands a long time before while he was still alive. By the time I was finally ready to talk with him about the past he had passed away.

Karel, Bob and Dolf established an organization which became known as the *"TD group"*, which was probably one of the more successful underground organizations in the Netherlands, working to thwart the German attempt to exterminate Jews and other undesirables. The group developed a system, which also helped hundreds of Dutch non-Jews, who were in danger of being deported as slave labor for work-camps in the Netherlands and Germany [Arbeitseinsatz], where they were coerced into "cooperating" with the war effort.

Some of my stories are raw and shocking, but they truly happened. The truth during a war is never nice and pretty. My children and grandchildren will learn something about me and my past from the book. They may even say or think "how could he do this?" Apart from my escapes, will they understand why I stole like a common thief and even killed? I can't help them with that but I hope they will forgive Grandpa for his sins and shortcomings.

My narrative does not have the sensitivity nor the flow of Anne Frank's diaries. She had a great talent, a wonderful sensitivity and maturity, which touches the heart of the readers of her diary. I have never been able to express my feelings like she did. I have found that she and many other women, who wrote about this period, were able to put more of their own inner feelings in their tales and their observations and language were more acute. My story is the product of a boy's experience of events as seen through the eyes and memory of an older man, who has a rather prosaic mind-set. Apart from that, I am a scientist, an engineer. I am thus more used to writing reports about facts. However, I am convinced that, after some 60 years, these stories should be told, so that the world may never forget what humans do to other humans if propaganda and the hatred which it produces are given free rein.

I apologize to the readers who may be shocked by some of my revelations. This was my life during the war and I have tried to tell it as it unfolded, without excuses or justifications. Generally, you will not find deep emotions. Those were suppressed for many years and forgotten, probably as a weapon of self-preservation of my sanity. Then, too, I was pretty young, and the young sometimes do not realize the full extent of horror—unless they are exceptional people like Anne Frank.

You will find anger and hatred directed against the Germans and the Dutch in my stories. Those were my true feelings at that time and for a long time afterwards. I remember them very well. Over time the hatred has diminished and it has enabled me to establish and maintain good, friendly working relations with a number of German scientists and engineers I have worked with and met over the years. However, they were all younger than I was and could not possibly have been involved in what I see as the actions and culpability of the German people as a whole during those Hitler years. I cannot and do not believe that the Germans didn't know what was going on, just as I know that the Dutch people knew and saw what was going on and, except for a minority, stood by and did nothing about it.

The writing of these stories rekindled some of the anger while I wrote them and rewrote them, but most of the anger went away as soon as I had finalized the story. So this has been, for me, a purging of my soul even though I will never totally lose my feelings with regard to certain situations and the injustices to which I and many others like me were subjected. Rereading the stories still stirs a certain amount of anger and resentment in me.

PART I
Who Was I

Chapter 1
BEFORE THE WAR

PART 1—EARLY MEMORIES

I have many memories, some vivid, others less clear from my life before the war. I have tried to record them in more or less chronological order...Several of them are from a time when I was still very little.

I was born on July 4th,1931, in the small Dutch village of Aalten, where my grandparents, Izak and Bertha Ten Bosch, and my uncle Jaap (my mother's brother) and his family lived. Aalten is located in the central-eastern part of the Netherlands, very close to the border with Germany. In 1931 the country was in the middle of the depression. Similar to the conditions in the rest of Europe and the US, many people, among them my father, were out of work and were living from hand to mouth. My mother had therefore gone to Aalten in order to give birth to, what turned out to be, a healthy son, me, and had left my dad in Amsterdam where he wandered from job to job whenever he could find one. I really don't know anything about that time in his life. He never talked about those hardships because at that time I was too young to be interested or under-stand. Unfortunately we didn't have each other in later years to talk about it. My maternal grandparents' and uncle's families, who were in the grocery, butchery and cattle trading business were affected also by the economics of the times, but apparently to a lesser degree. Generally, the rural food producing areas of the country were less affected by the joblessness caused by the depression because it was not industrialized and food was still needed.

Some of the earliest memories I have are from my being in my grandparents's home. I remember being on the potty one day and holding my little penis down so that I wouldn't pee over the rim. My grandmother came in, saw me and told me not to touch myself there and I let go, promptly peeing over the rim of the potty. I don't remember if she laughed or scolded me. To me it seems funny now but for the life of me I don't understand why I remember that particular incident.

Another memory from that time: I was in my little bed, which stood in my grandparents' bedroom. It was late and probably I should have been sound asleep when Oma and Opa went to bed. This time I was awake and Opa was already in bed and snoring like a chainsaw. Oma came in from the hallway and lifted the covers to get into bed—and there was Opa's big bare behind staring us both in the face. I must have made some sound because Oma turned around and said "Shhh…." and she giggled and shook her finger at me. Then she pulled on the cord and switched off the light.

I remember being often ill with terrible colds, flu, bronchitis, middle ear infections, measles, mumps and all the other regular children's ailments. Not only that, but I tended to develop very high fevers and even hallucinate and have fever nightmares. The doctor was called often to our home. As a result I positively hated all of them and would yell at them and curse them like a stevedore whenever they hurt me. My mother would be red in the face with embarrassment and say that she couldn't understand where I learned such language. It was true, I didn't learn those expressions at home, but I always seem to have had a knack for picking up those swear words and can today say bad things in a number of languages. My parents, although liberal and "modern" for those days, were very proper and refined. I don't remember ever hearing a "bad" word at home. I think, that going through all those fevers and diseases, I was immunized for my later life, especially during the war, when medical care was sparse and there were many more illnesses going around. I wasn't seriously ill during the war nor afterwards. I still remember being in bed in my grandparents' house with high fever and a steam making machine, which used to sputter and spit hot water all over the place from time to time. I can remember the awful nightmares I used to have when I had those fevers. The dreams sometimes made me afraid to go to sleep and my parents would alternate sitting with me and reading to me until I fell asleep. In short, I was quite a hand-full as a child and my parents must have worried quite a bit about me. Dr. De Vries-Robles, who lived on the *"De Lairess-estraat"* in Amsterdam was our primary care physician. He was a very nice and distinguished looking, soft-spoken, man and certainly didn't deserve the invective I hurled at him when he had to pierce my ears due to a middle ear infection or give me an injection with a syringe, with, what looked to me, an unnecessarily huge needle.

Twice I had my tonsils "cut" as it was called then. That was not a nice experience at all and I still remember it. A day would be set aside at Dr. Siemens's Nose-Throat-Ear clinic for "doing the tonsils on the kids". I remember the dark hallway, a dark, colorless waiting room which would have been a somber place to visit without it being a doctor's office. The strong smell of medicines and anaesthetic was everywhere. The chairs and benches were filled with kids, some sniffling, some crying, their nervous mothers trying to hush them. Not a smiling face in the room. Every now and then a door would open in another part of the gloomy house and a child could be heard crying in pain, as well as a mother's voice trying to quiet the child. Not very encouraging! Periodically the door to the waiting room would open and a sturdy male nurse, clad in a white rubber apron with a few blood stains, would call the next victim's name. Some stood up quietly, looking as if they were led to their execution, others started crying and some tried to get away. Then the male nurse, and I can still see him with his mustache and reddish short-cropped hair, would step forward and expertly pick the kid up, immobilize the arms and legs and carry the screaming child out of the room. When it was your turn, the world came to an end......

I am not going to go into details of the treatment, which was done with a little local anesthesia which never had any effect on me. I had the procedure performed on me twice and I can tell you that it was frightening and painful and unforgettable. Begeer, that's what we had to call the male nurse put you on his lap and pinned your arms, legs and head (how he managed it I don't remember) so you couldn't move. The frightening looking instruments were right in front of you on the table. The doctor approached with a mirror with a little hole in the center on his forehead and the torture began. It felt as if lasted a very long time, but it probably was over quite quickly. I talked about this fairly recently with some friends, who went through the same procedure during those years and everyone is unanimous in saying "Don't remind me". We all agreed that the only good thing about those tonsillectomies was the ice cream which we were fed for several days afterwards.

Until I was about four or five years old we lived on the *Haarlemmermeer Straat* in the western part of Amsterdam. Strangely, I even remember the number—it was 127 and we lived on the 2nd floor. I slept in a bed with little openings in the railing—I still have a photograph of that crib with me in it, looking unhappy. That crib always terrified me because at night all kinds of devils, mostly looking like faces from the Punch and Judy shows, used to stick their heads through the openings and make faces at me. I also remember an evening when my parents and a bunch of their friends had a big, noisy party. My room was fairly dark and I saw my father coming into the room with a pretty lady in, what we now know as a flapper's dress and they were kissing and caressing each other. That lady was not my mother!. Apparently they thought that I was asleep and, in the semi-darkness did not notice my wide-open eyes. My dad and that lady had a real good smooch, but I never uttered a peep! I wish he had been alive long enough for me to ask him who the lady was.

I often visited our downstairs neighbors. The husband was a tailor and had his workshop in a back room of the house. Fittings were done in the living room. He let me sit on the table and sow pieces of cloth together with what he called "the blind stitch" which is, as he told me, a way of sowing where the stitches do not show. I did my best, had a number of bloody fingers but wasn't really cut out to be a tailor. He was a jolly type with protruding teeth, a walrus mustache and thick glasses (maybe that's why he used the "blind" stitch) and his wife was a very thin lady who looked a bit like the wicked witch in the Wizard of Oz, which I hadn't seen yet then, but she wasn't wicked at all—in fact she was very nice. She gave me plenty of cookies and sweets whenever I had bloody fingers. There were two other tailors there. They all were very nice to me. I often stayed there for lunch and, being devout Catholics, they would pray before and after the meals. Never did I feel any hint of anti-Semitism and I prayed happily with them. My parents knew but didn't mind.

The house was then close to the big airport, Schiphol, which has since moved further west and has greatly expanded. We often used to go and see planes take off and land. My greatest joy however was to see the huge German airships come in. They generally passed over our street, very close to the roofs, or so it seemed. Those huge droning cigars, the Graf Zeppelin, the Hindenburg and others, whose engines you could hear coming for several minutes, would lumber into view over the rooftops and pass overhead and you could see the people in the cabin. We used to wave at them and sometimes they would wave back. In the meantime, our financial situation had improved a lot because my father had found a well-paying position as accountant and foreign correspondent for the Boers Company, a firm which was one of the largest recycling companies in the Netherlands. We could suddenly afford some luxuries.

One of my best memories from that time was when my parents and I flew to Paris in a Fokker Tri-motor plane, which was one of the early KLM (Royal Dutch Airline Company) planes. The weeks before the flight were full of anticipation and preparations. I think I was jumping up and down all the way to the airport on the seat of the taxi which took us there. The plane was waiting; a set of steps was ready to receive us at the open door. We sat down and after a short while the engines were started. The noise was deafening, the plane trembled and vibrated, the take-offs and landings (I think we landed in Brussels or Antwerp as well) were terrifying for my mother, who had gone white the minute the engines started, but wonderful for my dad and me. I think it took about five hours, not including the stopover, of being tossed about before we arrived at Le Bourget in Paris. We had been given big fur wraps to protect us against the cold. We flew through some rain, flew under, over and through clouds and looked at the countryside which was moving below us at an astonishing speed. Later, my mother returned by train from Paris. She flatly refused to go through that experience again. Since my mother wasn't a good traveler anyway she was train-sick on the way back from Paris and vowed never to move from Amsterdam again either by train or by plane. In the end, we did go on trips, but that was later with our own car. She didn't get sick in the car, but we had to make frequent stops.

I can remember two cars we owned. The first was a "Minerva", the second a "Citroèn". I don't remember where the "Minerva" was made, but it wasn't much good for my dad, who was a small man and the car had evidently been designed for big people. It was really a huge car with a big engine under the long hood and my dad didn't get along with it. I remember him fulminating at the dash and the steering wheel being too high and too far especially when he had a near disaster driving. I don't know what prompted him to buy that vehicle. The inside of it was big enough for a horse. Mom called it a hearse. The Citroèn was more our and his size and also held the road better. This car had one of the early front-wheel drives in the world. It rattled and shook more than the "Minerva", but it got us everywhere without mishaps, except for a punctured tire now and then. I always enjoyed listening to my father muttering under his breath at the jack, the wheel nuts, or any other part of the car he had to wrestle with. He was definitely not technically inclined.

The person I remember best from my youth was my paternal grandmother. She was, like the rest of my father's family, small of stature, but a giant lady to me. And she really was a lady, always dressed beautifully but conservatively in mourning black (for my grandfather), wearing a hat with a veil and a golden pince-nez, an old-fashioned type of glasses which were held onto her nose with a spring and hung from a gold-linked chain. When she took the glasses off there were always two imprints, one on each side of her nose, to show where the nose pieces of the glasses had been. When I was very little she used to bounce me on her knee and sing all sorts of funny songs and rhymes. I even remember some songs even though I must have been very little. She had a nervous "tic" of shaking her head from time to time, which I found wonderful and fascinating. I was her only grandchild and she spoiled me rotten—anything I wanted she would buy me. It was lucky that she lived in The Hague with her brother and sister in law, because this way she couldn't spoil me every day but only on one of her frequent visits.

She had the greatest influence on my appreciation of literature, arts and music. She taught me how to listen to music by taking me to concerts and even to the opera—the first one I saw was Bizet's "Les Pecheurs de Perles" (The Pearl Fishers). She also gave me a radio—an unheard of luxury for kids in those days. The radio was a cable radio, similar to today's cable TV, and I would listen to stations from foreign countries—the BBC from London and Coventry, Radio Diffusion Francaise, Radio Luxembourg, the German radio stations from Leipzig and Dresden, etc. It was with her that I had my first of many trips to the *Rijksmuseum* to see the beautiful Rembrands, Vermeers and other Dutch masters and learned how to look at and appreciate them and their use of light, colors and shadows. The paintings also showed me the differences between men and women without their clothes on, but it never was an important issue. Grandma just said "this is what a woman looks like; men and women look different with their clothes on—so why not when they are naked". It never occurred to me to ask more questions.

Grandma Francine exposed me not only to our western art and culture. She was also very interested in the Far East, having a brother who was an army general in what was then the Dutch East Indies. Amsterdam had the famous East Indies Institute, a museum with one of the greatest Far-Eastern art collection from what is today Indonesia and other Asian countries. Concerts were given there with wonderful evocative Eastern music such as Gamelan and the Wajang Wong puppet shadow plays which were marvels of story telling and puppetry accompanied by Javanese or Balinese music. I also saw the dancers from the island of Bali there and from Japan and from, what is now Malaysia and Thailand. The exposure to the arts of the far east and especially the music gave me the appreciation and understanding of the tonal complexities and rhythms of eastern music. Strangely enough neither of my parents were very musical and neither could carry a tune. As far as I can remember they seldom went to concerts. I remember that I used to break up in giggles and yell at my father to stop when he tried to whistle or hum a tune. I also remember nearly bursting from suppressed laughter when both of them were murdering the Dutch national anthem when the occasion arose—despite their dirty looks at me.

As a result of my father's new position, we moved, when I was about five or six years old, to the newer southern part of Amsterdam and lived in the *"Rivierenbuurt"* the River-Quarter, where all streets were named after rivers and streams in the country. Our new address in the *Gaaspstraat 36*, where we occupied the two top floors (3 and 4), was opposite the Trompenburg garage, where our car was serviced and parked. I never knew it, but we also lived opposite Miep Gies, the heroic woman who took such wonderful care of Anne Frank and her family. The block next to ours was a neighborhood playground and sports center, which was called a *"speeltuin"*. This playground was restricted to members who paid a monthly fee. Thus only families who could afford it sent their kids there. It was a good place because all the activities and sports were supervised. My parents felt that it was safe for me to be there because I didn't have to associate with "street riffraff" when I was on the playground. Fighting and coarse language were not allowed and if you did transgress those rules you were thrown out and/or suspended for a day or longer. Almost all of us, at least the kids I associated with, had their brushes with "the laws of the playground".

We played all sorts of games there, did exercises and had athletic competitions; played field hockey, soccer, hand-ball, softball and a Dutch version of basketball; there were sing-alongs and dances which were led by the beloved "street bands" which were paid to come into the fenced-in grounds. I usually could be found there after school and on free afternoons (Wednesday and Saturday) There were no activities on Sundays as far as I can remember.

PART 2—MUSICIANS, GAMES, MISCHIEF

I want to provide a little more detail about our life in Amsterdam. Probably the most wonderful traditions were the street musicians and the street organs. These were groups of musicians who went from street to street, from neighborhood to neighborhood and played their music for pennies which were thrown from windows and which were caught expertly by the musicians and their helpers in the street. One of the most famous groups was called *"de Volendammers"*, a group of six or seven folk musicians dressed in the traditional garb of Volendam, a small fishing village North of Amsterdam. Today it is a tourist attraction. I remember that they had a good tenor singer and I can still see and hear him sing, a very big man with a huge tummy, accompanied by accordions, trumpet, tuba and drums and some other instruments. They came into a street, set themselves up in a strategic location and start playing. All the kids as well as some adults would soon gather around them. They were good musicians and it was a pleasure to listen to them play popular tunes, songs and light classics. When enough kids had gathered around, one of the band members would arrange us kids in a circle, the band would step inside the circle and we would do games accompanied by the music. Everyone loved it and the contributions flowed in and thus the musicians loved it. Some mothers would bring out cakes and coffee for the musicians as well. It was always a festive day when they came, and often we would follow them around to their next stop and do it all over again.

Another great musical treat was the visit of the big mobile pipe organs. They were called "Pierement" and Amsterdam is famous for those organs which can still be seen today. Because it was heavy to move and to operate (turning the crank for a whole overture was a tough job) there were always three or four people with it. They spelled each other of at the big crank and otherwise ran around with small steel nickel catchers to garner the coins being thrown from the windows. The kids used to gather in front of the organ, as close to it as possible and see the moving puppets play the drums or put a trumpet to their lips whenever the music called for it. We also went to the back of the organ where you could see the folded music book go through the rollers and see the mechanism which operated the pipe valves which made the organ produce its beautiful music. The melodies which were played ranged from classical overtures like William Tell to current popular songs from operas and operettas. When the time came for the turner of the crank to be relieved, another man would step in at the correct moment and take over the cranking without the music being affected.

I can still remember sitting in class one sunny afternoons when I yearned to get out and play in the sunshine. The whole class would be a sort of dormant stupor, drowsily going through the class routine. Suddenly, through the open windows, the music of an organ filtered in. It was still quite far away but we all could hear it clearly. I still remember the shiver which went through my spine and the whole class, including the teacher, seemed to wake up and smile. That was a real magical experience.

Of course we also did a lot of naughty things in the streets. There was the old game of ringing doorbells and then running away and waiting at a safe distance to see if you had been successful at making someone come to the door. We used to hide around a corner or in a vestibule (hallway) of a neighboring house. The people would come to the door, stick their heads out and look around with a puzzled look on their faces. After they shut the door, we would creep back and do it again, and again, if the homeowner was silly enough to come to the door every time. Sometimes we were ambushed and caught and received a good beating or they would take us to our parents and complain. None of us ever complained about the beating because we all knew that we deserved it. We made sure not to repeat this trick at the same addresses and so we would target a new street every time we decided that it was time to play the trick again.

There was another piece of mischief, quite ingenious at that. This one was carried out at dusk and in the evenings. It was called "window tapping". For this devilry we needed a big strong needle, a spool of black thread, some chewing gum or putty and a little stone. We put the thread through the needle's eye, stuck the little stone to the needle eye with the putty or chewing gum and crept to the intended victim's house. We always chose a house where the curtains were drawn shut and where enough light showed through to indicate that people were in the room (frugal Dutch would never leave a light on in an unoccupied room). We stuck the needle in the wood close to the glass pane so that the stone rested against the glass or against the wooden frame. The preferred location was in a corner of the window. We then crept silently away, unrolling the thread from the spool until we reached a hiding place or a safe distance. Then, by giving small tugs on the thread, the stone would tap the window. The people in the room would come to the window and look out to see who was tapping. Because it was fairly dark and the needle was in a corner, they couldn't see the needle nor the thread. We sat in the shadows and saw the person behind the window turning his head back and forth and laughed our heads off. Baffled, they let the curtains fall back. We waited until we felt they had sat down again and repeated the procedure. After the second time the homeowner usually stood waiting behind the curtain and would tear them open at the first tap but......nobody was there. With a "successful" case we could get the homeowner come roaring out of the house in three repeats. Sometimes they guessed what was going on and went to another room, shutting the lights. We knew then that they were wise to our tricks and we just gave a good tug on the line and the needle came out of the window sill. Once, as we were sitting behind a fence, a bicyclist came out of an alley and tore the whole setup apart. He disappeared with our needle and the spool of thread. He must have wondered later what he had become entangled with, unless he had played the same game himself. Only once was I caught by a homeowner who had come out of his back door into a connecting alleyway. He grabbed me and my buddy by the collar and took us to his hallway through the front door. We begged him to let us go and swore we'd never do this again, but he held on and we were handed over to the police. The police pretended to take our "disturbing the peace" very seriously and took us to the nearby station. We went by tram and I remember feeling very "criminal" with the policeman holding us both by the arm and all the other passengers looking at us. I was about seven or eight and my buddy Paul and I were brought into the station, asked our names and addresses and kept in adjacent "solitary" cells for about two hours. A bowl of water was all they gave us and we sat on the hard bed in the cell. A policeman came now and then and looked sternly at us. Everybody looked serious and stern. We were released in the care of our parents after we tearfully promised never to get into trouble again. It wasn't a promise we kept, I can assure you. My dad had tears in his eyes when he told Grandma about it on her next visit. I entered the room and heard him tell her the last part of the story, but neither could wipe the grins of their faces fast enough. I saw them!

Another popular street game was called, if I remember correctly, "pinking". It may have had a different name, but somehow that one has stuck with me. The game was only played in the middle of the street. Why, I have no idea, but that was the rule. It was always played with the "base" being a round manhole cover. The rules were similar to softball with a bit of cricket thrown in to make it more complicated. The "pink" was a piece of wood, preferably with a square or round cross-section, which had been whittled down at both ends to form a point, much like a pencil. The pink was positioned on the rim of the manhole cover so that one end was hanging over the cover itself. The "batter" then struck the pointed end of the pink with sufficient force so that it twirled up into the air. Then he had to hit the pink in full flight into a direction where none of the opposing team of fielders were located. While the field team was scrambling for the pink the batter ran rounders like in cricket. The catchers had to get the pink back to base as quickly as possible. The team which scored the most rounders was the winner. There were numerous variations of the rules of the game in Amsterdam and disputes and fisticuffs would often result from disagreements amongst the players as to which street's game rules we should use. When traffic, such as trams, buses or other vehicles had to pass we waited on the sidewalks and then resumed our play. There were sometimes casualties in the game. Bystanders could get hit by the pink or by youngsters running at full tilt, who would crash into them or into other roadside obstacles. Occasionally a window would be broken and then everyone scattered before we could be apprehended by the homeowner or a helpful passer-by. We usually made sure that we were playing in a street where people didn't know us.

"Marbles" was another favorite game. There were about as many different games and rules in marbles as there were people playing with them. It was a favorite game during morning and afternoon recess at school. I suppose every country in the world knows some different versions of this game. In the Netherlands the most popular game types were those which used a shoe-box with different size holes cut in the rim. Each hole was a different size and was given a different point value. The shoe-box was inverted on the sidewalk and we were supposed to roll our marbles from a certain distance into the holes. The owner of the box, the "banker", would award a prize to those who reach a certain number by rolling their marbles through the holes. The smallest hole had the highest value and it was the banker's task to set up the game so that it was practically impossible to get the highest score. It was a typical "chumps" game, just like those which are run in today's ritzy casinos. Another variant of the game was played using larger glass marbles and larger heavy ones made from lead. Balls from ball bearings could also be used and you were the envy of your mates if you had one. The game is similar to the French game of "Boules" or the Italian "Boche" and the trick is to keep your opponent's lead balls away from the glass marbles and reach a "target" at the end of a lane. Again, rules differed and were often changed or challenged in the middle of play when the strongest kid was losing the game and then a bit of shoving and struggling would occur, which was broken up by one of the teachers, a passer-by or by the school bell ringing the end of recess.

PART 3—SPORTS

Soccer was, and still is today, the main field sport in the Netherlands. Also, in those days, field hockey and handball divided popularity with a game called "Korf Ball" which was similar to basket ball, except that a reed basket (a "korf" in Dutch) was mounted on a tall pole. Since I was far too short to participate in korf-ball, I don't even remember the rules. Field hockey was another popular sport and I did participate in it from a very early age. It was played on grass and we played mostly on the same field where we played soccer. Unlike Ice-hockey as it is played today, there was no body-checking and you were not allowed to lift the stick higher than your shoulders. Still, we all got hurt from time to time. One day, as I was trying to get at the ball, one of the boys from the opposing team hit me, accidentally, in the forehead and opened quite a gash. Blood flowed like water and I was sure that I was going to bleed to death right there on the spot. I screamed bloody murder but was consoled by the fact that I got a few stitches and a lovely white bandage on my head. My mother was, of course very worried and for a few days I was a battle scarred and important person at home and at school. I loved the attention I got from the girls. The boys were jealous of my bandaged head.

The winter sport was skating and on days when the ice was good and the temperatures bearable you would see literally thousands of skaters, from the very young to the very old, on the canals, rivers and ponds in Amsterdam and the rest of the country. The municipality kept large areas in several parts of the city clean of debris and swept it regularly to clean the shaved ice off. The area was always arranged in the form of a large oval. People skated only in one direction and it was beautiful to see this mass of humanity sliding gracefully on the track together, the only sound being the hum of voices and the scraping of the skates on the ice. The slowest skaters had to skate on the inside, the faster skating lanes were on the outside. The center area was reserved for figure skaters. We usually had wooden skates with steel blades, which were tied onto your shoes with laces made from pig-or-cowhide. There were steel skates as well, but the majority were wood frames with inserted steel blades. The same ones can be seen on paintings from the 17th century by Dutch landscape painters. The youngest skaters, no more than three or four years old, came onto the ice holding onto a chair which they pushed around while scratching the ice with frantic short strokes. Falling frequently and having bumps was a rite of passage for all of us. It was a great achievement when you could let go of the chair and yell "Dad, Mom, look at me" while flailing your arms to keep your balance. My mother went with me to the ice, but never skated. She couldn't swim and was afraid of the ice cracking. Each year there were accidents with breaking ice and wherever we were skating, we kept an ear open for the ominous creaking. When that happened most of the skaters would scatter to the shores and the ones who stayed had a wonderful time for a while skating on a nearly deserted area. Gradually we would all filter back until the next creaking would make the whole crowd scatter again.

Races were held in many parts of the country. These took place between cities, especially in the province of Friesland and the radio reports on the famous "Eleven-Cities Race" were listened to as avidly as the Super-Bowl or the Olympics today. I participated as a child in the junior races during the first few years of WWII (when Jews were still allowed to participate) and later when I was living under an assumed name. I also skated after the war in local races in and around the town of Hilversum where the orphanage I then lived in was located. The races were not without some danger, since the courses included many large and small canals in the countryside. There might be weak places in the ice and a skater could fall through. The smaller canals were not deep but I remember hearing of people drowning. Another danger lay in passing underneath bridges which crossed many canals. Many of these connected a farm with the road alongside the canal. Most, but not all, farmers used to raise the bridges when a race was on. Some of the bridges were rather low and if you misjudged the height or did not see a beam underneath you were in real trouble when you hit a bridge at full speed. I, being a little runt, didn't have many problems, but grownups often had to clamber out of the canal and cross to the other side. That made them lose time, and sometimes tempers flared. Also, walking on the ground was bad for the knife-edges on the skates. The canals were not swept and we often had to skate over grasses or other debris which had frozen into the ice surface. It took quite a bit of skill to remain skating in such areas—when your skates struck a piece of grass or reed, your speed was very abruptly reduced as if you had pushed on the brakes. Most of us went sprawling, but nothing was hurt except our pride. The trips showed us a lot of interesting things we otherwise would not have seen. Geese and ducks would be sitting on the ice near an open water area. As we approached they would get up noisily and either try to go to the open water or fly off. In both cases they had to start running and it was always a laugh to see them slide around on their webbed paddle-like feet. We found it fascinating to see fish frozen in the ice. Once we found them, we used to keep an eye on them all through the winter, but when the spring thaw came, the fish miraculously disappeared into the deeper waters again. Once we found a duck whose legs were frozen into the ice. The poor thing was weak—it had probably been there for some time. We undid our skates and ran to a nearby farm to get some tools or help to free the animal. The farmer came with us with a hatchet and a knife, but to our horror he cut the animal's throat in front of us and chopped the legs out of the ice. He only grinned and said: "This will do well in mother's soup". We started crying while he walked away and I will not repeat the names and curses we screamed after him. None of us had ever seen or experienced such cruelty before.

PART 4—SCHOOL

I was five or six years old when I started grade school. I don't remember many details of pre-school except of playing somewhere in a sandbox and one of the little boys pooping in his pants. The things I do remember—what's wrong with me! Going to grade school was a new and wonderful experience. By the time I started I had been reading for several years, prompted by my grandmother and the books she always brought with her on her visits and the reading of stories from children's literature, which my family had always done. But I remember very well how they taught us the alphabet at school. We learned to read with a "Spelling Board". Each pupil had his own rectangular board with three rows of about ten pictures. Below each row was a narrow ridge, similar to those used in the "Scrabble" game, on which we were supposed to put letters matching the title on the picture. Then the whole class had to repeat in unison the words which we had spelled out. The pictures were not alphabetical. For instance, the first picture was a monkey (*aap* in Dutch), the second picture showed a walnut (*noot* in

Dutch), the third one a girl named Mies. I still can remember a large part of the sequence of pictures on that Reading Board.

Writing we learned in those days with a *"Lei en Griffel"*. The *"Lei"* was a rectangular piece of slate, about the size of a regular 8"x10" page which was framed in wood. The *"griffel"* was a thin, round, hard chalk pencil, much thinner than a regular pencil. This pencil had to be sharpened frequently with a sharpener akin to a regular pencil sharpener. The sharpener and griffels were kept in an rectangular wooden box with a sliding cover—at least that's the one I had. In order to clean our slates after writing we used a small wetted sponge and we dried the slate with a small flannel rag. The sponge and rag were kept by each pupil in a special container. This container was a short round cylinder, about 2.5–3 inches in diameter and about 4 inches long. It had a rounded cover on each end and was divided into two parts. One end contained the wet sponge—the other end contained the flannel. The boxes were usually made out of metal or bakelite. The metal ones tended to rust and cause problems (sometimes the cover would rust onto the box)—but they were a lot cheaper.

I hated those writing materials. Apart from the difficulty of holding the thin griffel it was a messy system and we were all glad that we were promoted to the pen and ink system, although the fibers from the paper, which often caught in the nibs would cause smeary letters and were often the reason to have to repeat a whole page. It all had to be absolutely perfect—otherwise bad marks, notes to home, repeats of the work were unavoidable. Another problem was that the pens and the ink tended to dry out. We did have a pen-cleaning rag, but I always had problems keeping the pens clean and the rag dry. Threads from the rag mysteriously found their way in between the two halves of the nib and caused big smears. The rag would somehow land on my page or on my desk, or it somehow touched my clean shirt. Even today dirt seems to jump at me from a distance.

For our studies of biology we used to put a few beans or peas on the sponge and then we waited until they sprouted after which they were transplanted into pots. The pots were put on the window sill in the classroom. Each of us had to take care of their own plants and we would receive extra credit for good "farming practices". We also wrote a daily report on the progress of our horticultural endeavors. This project generated quite a lot of rivalry, some disappointments and jealousy, the latter sometimes resulting in plant sabotage!

Twice a week, for one hour, we had physical exercises in a special, fairly small and badly equipped, gymnasium. We did mostly calisthenics and sometimes, as a special treat, a ball game. None of the schools in those days had sports fields and few, if any, had a special sports teacher. Our regular teachers were also our gym teachers. I don't know how it was at private schools, which were called academies. On rare occasions we would go with the class to a nearby sports field or to a municipal swimming pool, and swim, play water polo, soccer or hockey. The boys liked the swimming classes best because that was the only time that boys and girls exercised in the same place and we liked to see the girls in bathing suits. Needless to say, this system was quite different from the schools of today here in the US where competitive sports, for better or for worse, are an important part of the curriculum.

In many of the modern schools, individualism and do-it-yourself disciplines are emphasized. When I went to school it was the whole class who studied and repeated in unison the multiplication tables, the lists of verbs and their various forms, the lists of provinces (12 in the Netherlands) and their capitals, foreign countries and their capitals and main rivers, mountains, oceans etc. etc. The modern school psychologists say this was a wrong method. Well, sorry learned people, I don't agree with you at all. I still remember those countries and their capitals, I still know where they are, I still can manipulate numbers in my head without being a math whiz and I still know the Dutch language better than today's kids which have grown up under the new systems. The same is true for foreign language studies. In grade school, those of us who wanted to learn French, were taught the same way in a special class for one year. By the time I went to High School my French skills were pretty good, even though there had been a break of a couple of years during WWII.

From 1937 till 1941 I stayed at the same school and loved it. In the spring of 1941, when I was nearly 10 years old and in the fourth grade, the German occupiers decreed that Jewish children could not be educated with the Gentile children. We were separated from our old friends and teachers and put into different schools with different teachers. More about that later.

Chapter 2
ANIMALS

PART 1—MY FRIENDS

I have always loved animals and have never been afraid of them. Animals apparently realize that and give you their undivided loyalty and friendship when you give it to them. My relationships with animals have often eased the pain of other events and have helped me to cope with occasional bad times. No animal ever treated me badly. On the other hand, the war taught me that people did and that it was often dangerous to trust people. Therefore, later in life it was difficult for me to get close to and trust people and I couldn't make friends easily.

But back to my relations with animals. One example goes back to a time, several years before the war, when my mother and I were visiting some second cousin in Amersfoort. They had a large Alsatian. The dog was reported to be unfriendly to strangers and especially toward children. I must have been about three or four years old and, despite the fact that the dog was as tall as I was, I was not afraid. After being warned that the dog would bite if I came near it, I sat down in a chair with a little game I was given and paid no attention to the animal. Ultimately the dog was curious enough to approach me. I stayed in my chair and didn't move but I let my hand dangle by the side of the chair and the dog sniffed it several times. I said a few words to her (it was a female) and she didn't growl at me. After a short time she licked my hand and then let me stroke her. Our cousin was astonished. The dog and I became good friends in a very short time. I still have a picture of me holding the dog on the street in front of their butcher shop. Till this day dogs have never treated me as if I was a potential enemy—they usually come up to me wagging their tails. My wife maintains that they think that I am another dog.

Whenever I was visiting my grandparents in Aalten, I would go and visit a farm where I knew the people well and would ask if I could go and see the horses, goats, sheep or whatever animal was available. If I was warned to stay clear of a certain animal I would just stand there and talk to them until I saw that they were relaxed. Still, I heeded the warnings, but most of the animals let me approach and stroke them after a short time. One farmer had two horses—a nice one which you could touch and a nasty one, to stay away from. They were both in the same stable. The first few times I went only to the nice horse and petted it and rubbed its neck. I never went near the other one. It laid its ears back and looked shifty-eyed every time I approached the stable. I always talked to both of them and brought them something to nibble on and one day, while I was petting the friendly horse, the other one came over, sniffed my hand and made it very obvious that I was to scratch her too. I did, being ready to withdraw my hand quickly, but nothing happened. The horse just stood there swinging her upper lip in delight while I scratched her neck.

After that episode, the farmer knew that he could trust me with his animals and let me help feed them and groom them. Others heard the story and they also welcomed my visits and occasional help around the farm such as driving the cows to the milking shed or bringing hay to their troughs. My mother didn't really like me to go and visit those farms because I always managed to accumulate unusual amounts of manure and dust on my clothes and shoes. Moreover she disliked the farm smells even though she had grown up in Aalten. But when I was on my own with my grandparents there were no problems. They were far too happy that I wasn't moping about the house and/or getting into mischief with the village kids by teasing the church beadle. Here are a few stories about some other encounters with animals, some from before the war, others during the war.

PART 2—THE ZOO

When I lived in Amsterdam, the city's zoo was called Artis. To me it was huge and beautiful, a giant paradise, full of exotic animals and plants. My father, who was a nature lover and outdoorsman, often took me there. He was ardent environmentalist—always outside, walking, cycling, motoring to forests, protesting city expansion at the cost of cutting down forests. We often went for long walks and bicycle rides in nature and he enjoyed his visits to the zoo as much as I did, although he didn't like to see animals in the restrictive cages. We had an annual family pass or something similar which enabled us to visit as often as we wanted. In those days children were quite safe from molestations and abductions on the streets of Amsterdam and I was allowed to visit the zoo on my own from about age six. I went probably once a month on average and, being the frequent visitor that I was, got to know the caretakers there and had the opportunity to hold little newborn lion cubs in my arms and to see many animals close up on special days. I was allowed to stroke and hold some of the snakes; I liked the feel of their skin, their slow sinuous movements and the way they smelled with their forked tongues flicking back and forth. According to my maternal grandmother, who once came with me, I once fell down because a heavy snake I was holding shifted its coils and threw me off balance. Skinned my knee, she said, but I didn't let go of the snake or maybe it was the other way around. I don't remember that incident at all and have had to take her word for it.

Once I had a less pleasant experience in the monkey enclosure. There were several young Orangutans in the zoo and on nice days they would be in their outdoor enclosure playing around with balls, sticks and tires and swinging on ropes and swings. Several zoo-keepers kept them busy and many spectators stood around the large oval pen. I was among a few kids who came regularly and who were sometimes allowed to go into the fenced-in area to interact with them. Usually everything went well and it was great fun. We tossed balls at the young orangutans and they tossed them back, we walked with them "hand in paw", and played with sticks and we quickly learned to appreciate how immensely strong these young animals were. When they threw a ball, it was with great force. They behaved just like normal kids, but you had to be careful not to frighten them with loud noises or sudden movements. Then they could get panicky, bare their teeth and start screaming and sometimes even bite the person nearest to them. When one started screaming and became panicky, the others would often follow suit and the keepers had a tough time quieting them down.

One day, as I was walking around the enclosure with one of the youngest apes, he got it into his (or her) monkey-head to start doing somersaults. Now, if you've ever seen orangutans do that, you know that they are excellent athletes and they can roll around like balls. Well, this one didn't let go of my arm, I had to follow and after the first two tumbles we did together, my arm was out of its socket. I screamed with pain and the monkey got frightened and screamed even louder, but luckily it let go of my arm. I was quickly hustled out of the pen by the keepers. I screamed again a bit later when the zoo doctor put my arm back into its socket. For a few days I strutted around proudly with my arm in a sling. But I soon forgot all about that incident and went back into the enclosure, but, just to be safe, I kept my distance from that particular monkey.

I also loved to visit and feed the big parrots, cockatoos and macaws. They could be pretty ornery and ferocious and could inflict a painful bite if you weren't careful how you approached them. One of their keepers taught me how to talk to them and calm them down. Often they were nervous or frightened and would react negatively to people getting too close, especially if they had been teased. They would start screaming and make threatening moves with their beaks. Some were real meanies and you always kept your distance from those. Generally, if you were careful and didn't make sudden movements, nothing would happen, and I spent many free afternoons in the large aviaries or near their perches, which were placed along the bird path, talking to them and feeding them.

One of the birds, a nice green and red macaw from South America was my special friend. This one had learned a few words from his keepers. I always had a grape, a piece of dried fruit or nut for him. When he saw me approach he used to flap his wings and yell enthusiastically some sound like "Halloo!" at me. Then he would say something like "Kra?", which meant apparently that he wanted his present. He would eye the delicacy in my hand, grasp it ponderously but gently in one claw, look at it suspiciously from all sides and look at me questioningly with another "Kra?". I would then say, in Dutch of course, "Yes, Lorre, go ahead and eat it, it's good!". Then he would slowly peel and eat, stopping from time to time to look at me with a pensive "Kra" which always made me giggle. After he finished eating, he would say something which sounded like "Koppie Krauw", which meant that he wanted me to scratch his head. He would bend down as far as he could and I would stretch up and scratch his head slowly. He would pivot his head around so he could get it thoroughly scratched and give soft sighs of utter delight. Then he would lower himself from his perch, using his beak and claws, and settle on my shoulder. While I went on scratching him, he would nibble at my hair, my ears, my eyebrows, which were quite heavy even then, and my cheek. He never touched my eyes or bit me, although he could fly into a terrible rage when people teased him. Once I arrived when he was being teased and I had to talk to him a long time before he calmed down and let me touch him again.

I used to go about twice a month and even in the winter would go in and see the animals in their winter quarters. There was always something new to see, especially when a young animal was born. All of this wonderful experience came to an end sometime during 1941 when the German occupiers prohibited Jews from entering public places, among them the zoo. I have often wondered what happened to my ponderous old friend Lorre the Macaw and all the other animals I loved and knew so well.

PART 3—JULIE

My dad had bought us a dog because I got on so well with animals (that was his excuse, but he liked them too). I was about four years old when he came home with something huge like a Great Dane. I have no idea what sort of a dog it was, but she was beige colored, had a silly face and was very big. I think dad bought her because one had to smile when you looked at her head, which had some sort of a perpetual smirk. We called her Julie. It was an unusual name for a dog, but then she was a very unusual dog. My mother felt that she was too big for me and for our family and she was probably right. That animal ate a lot and took up a lot of space, especially when we had to get her in our little Citroen car. She would half sit half lay over me because it wasn't a big car. When we had the top down she used to sit straight up and everyone who saw us coming had a laugh at seeing that silly old head of Julie sticking out of the top and seeming to drive the car. Like all dogs, she loved to go for a drive and whenever my dad and I came out of our door to go for a walk with her, she tried to cajole us to go to the garage opposite and to go for a ride. She towered over me, but never used her strength when we were playing together. She used to lie on the floor in my room while I was reading or playing with my trains. She didn't move, but followed me everywhere with her eyes. At night she slept on the landing in front of my door. When I yelled because of a dream, she would push the door open and inspect the situation.

When I came home from school, she was all over me, sniffing my hands, face and neck and digging her nose in my belly which always made me scream because it tickled. My dad said that she thought I was her puppy and she was checking me over after I had been out of her sight for several hours. One lick of her tongue was quite a wash! I always had to go and clean myself up after one of her greetings. Mother hated it when the dog licked me but I just loved it, so in the name of peace she relented.

Dad and I used to take Julie for long walks in the parks on the outskirts of Amsterdam. There she would run and cavort with other dogs. She was bigger than many, but never used her full strength or her weight. She was playful and great with other people and especially children. Because of her size, many kids didn't dare approach her or were warned off by their parents, but Julie always approached everyone with that great big whip of a tail wagging like mad from side to side. We had to stay at a good distance from the many canals and the Amstel river, for any time there was water in the area, she'd make a beeline for it and jump in, even when she was on a leash. If you didn't let go, she would pull you in with her. I remember that once she jumped into a big fountain pond at the "Van Heutz" monument in south Amsterdam and upset all the sailing boats of the children who were playing there. Dad had to take off his shoes and socks, roll up his pants and wade into the pond to get her out because she was having far too much fun to listen to any commands. Then Dad had to fish out all the capsized boats and apologize to the families while I was holding Julie, tears in my eyes and weak and hiccuping with laughter. Dad glared at me when he finally scrambled out of the pond, Julie shook herself with great energy and made the rest of him wet as well.

She sometimes seemed to see and hear things no one else heard. My mother, who was interested in ESP and spiritualism, felt that Julie was psychic and that she saw and heard beings or ghosts, which were invisible to humans. It frustrated her (my mother) because she had no idea what the dog saw or heard. Neither did anyone else and Julie couldn't tell us.

My parents and I would double up with laughter when she would suddenly jump up, dance around stiff-legged and bark at the sofa or slink away growling from a corner of the living room, looking, as it were, back over her shoulder at something which was there. Imagine the situation, when there was a visitor sitting on the sofa or in the room. I used to laugh until I was weak and had tears rolling out of my eyes and for days afterward I used to break into peals of laughter when I remembered the visitor's terrified look and the crazy antics of Julie. I still laugh when I remember her today.

The end of 1941 or in the beginning of 1942 brought one of the saddest days in my young life when Julie was taken away by the Dutch authorities. A Nazi neighbor had complained that his wife was frightened of having such a big dog near her house although she had lived there for years. They had also asked why a Jew should have a dog like that anyway? I cried and cried for many days and was inconsolable and heartbroken. I wanted to die. At just about that time the schools were segregated and I was sent to an all-Jewish school where I met the love of my young life, Anita. I was then 10 years old. She made up for the loss of Julie until she, too, was taken away from me.

PART 4—HORSES

A horse is an animal which can make a person feel great and on top of the world. This is probably due to the fact that you are looking down on the rest of humanity when on the back of the horse, but it is not just that. You don't feel that way when you sit on top of a double-decker bus. There is something about the horse which is undefinably beautiful and noble. It is alive and there is a special relationship which, I suppose, only horse lovers realize. It is a different feeling than the love of a dog. A dog is part of the family. A horse is not. He is an independent friend.

The feeling between horse and owner is one of mutual affection and respect. Here is this great warm body, and you and it become one when you ride it. How wonderfully soft is the muzzle of the horse when it nuzzles you. What a wonderful feeling it is when you can warm your hands on a cold wintery day on the horse's flank and it gives you an affectionate nibble. If it wanted to it could kick you from here to kingdom come, but if you show it respect and love it deserves, it will return them.

I am a horse lover and whenever I have a chance to get close to one I will. Horses know instinctively when you love and respect them and when you are afraid of them or don't like them. In Amsterdam, before and during the war, most of the transport was done by horsecart. I used to feed every horse which came to our street pulling a cart. I always had something—a slice of bread, a bad apple or potato which I kept for that purpose, or sugar cubes, which I stole from my mother's sugar container. Some of the horses were skittish and some laid their ears back and had that strange look in their eyes when you approached them. But after a number of encounters during which I always spoke soothingly to them and kept my distance, I could approach and touch nearly all of them. When we went on trips to places where you could ride horses, I could always be found atop one.

I learned that they liked to be rubbed and where they liked it best. I noted how they would purse their upper lip in enjoyment and look back questioningly when I stopped. Some even used to turn their heads and gave my arm or clothes a grateful nibble. That, to me, was the best compliment I could ever receive.

Later, during my time in hiding on the farm in Hoevelaken and after December 1942, when I was living in Leusden in "the Mijlpaal," I often went with the local milkman to deliver milk in the town of Amersfoort. He let me drive the cart and deliver the milk to the houses; I fed the horse and the animal knew me after a while. When we returned home, I was the one to take of the harness, lead the mare to the water trough and who put him in the stable and fed her. Then I used to give her a good brushing and combing. She loved that and awarded me with a soft nibble on my arm or my hair. Needless to say, I always smelled of horses after such outings. My mother would have sniffed, wrinkled her nose and sent me immediately to the shower, but by that time I had already lost her.

When milk was to be delivered in the neighboring town or in the city of Amersfoort, and I came out of our garden gate to meet the milkcart, the horse always whinnied in recognition. I would pat her neck, give her a kiss on the nose and give her something to nibble on. Then we went on our way. In the center of town, I was always proudest when I was allowed to take the horse by its halter and lead her around from house to house, steering around corners of narrow streets while the milkman was changing bottles or filling milk cans brought out by the housewives.

On the other side of the street from the Mijlpaal were several pastures which had cows and horses in them at different times. The fields belonged to neighboring farmers, and I was soon one of their regular visitors, helping them whenever I had some free time, haying, tilling the fields, spreading manure, harvesting grain and, above all, taking care of the animals.

The farm nearest to the Mijlpaal belonged to a brother and sister, the Hartmans. Both were unmarried, which was no surprise because they were both very big people, raw-boned with big heads and weathered and rather ugly faces, but they seemed to have taken a fancy to me. Mr. Hartman taught me to plow and drive the team and wagons to and from the field, take the horses for shoeing etc. I soon learned that there are some horses whom you cannot trust and you had to keep an eye on them, or they could bite or kick or run off with the wagon. Hartman showed me that each horse has its own character and moods, just like humans.

One of the horses the Hartmans had was a big handsome black Oldenburger mare. She was "as mean and as black as the devil" Mr. Hartman used to say. One morning, a miracle happened. A beautiful foal was born to the mare. The foal stood swaying in the stable, close to her mother's big flanks, and took those wonderful little staggering steps newborn animals take. She sniffed and snorted and looked around in great astonishment at the new world into which she had been born. The mare was very defensive, and three men were needed to keep her under control when the vet came to check up on the foal. I visited every day and soon the foal used to come over to me to be fed, talked to and scratched. This never lasted long. After a few minutes mamma used to turn her head, lift it high, walk towards me and show her teeth and that meant that it was time for me to leave. She didn't have to spell it out. She was one protective mamma!

When the foal was in the pasture opposite our house, I often went to visit. When the mother was at a safe distance I would venture into the pasture and rub the foal down with grass or hay, which she loved. But when mamma was close by, I stayed behind the fence. One time when I was in the pasture she turned on me which such ferocity that I ran for my life. I was too far from the gate and so I went straight for the nearest ditch, which was full of water. Because of the soft sides of the ditches in Holland I couldn't push off and jump far enough and so landed with a splash in the middle in the smelly, stagnant, muddy water leaving one of my wooden shoes stuck in the mud on the side where the mare was standing bristling and snorting. Farmer Hartman, who had seen the episode from the farm yard was doubled over and slapping his knees with laughter. I glared at him, but that only made him laugh harder. Only the next day, when the mare was not there did I dare go back to retrieve my clog.

Towards the end of the war, in the winter of 1944—1945, after an escape from a German raid on the Mijlpaal. I stayed in hiding for several months with a farmer, Peel van den Hengel, near the town of Achterveld. Peel owned a large farm there and also had a large number of children—sixteen, in fact. I slept in the horse stables on a ledge underneath the brick and cement feed trough. There were four big plow horses in that stable and they soon became my friends and I always felt protected by them. I still enjoy the smell of a well-maintained horse stable, although some people will crinkle their noses at it. To me it is a smell associated with safety and warmth.

The four horses in that stable were all Zeelanders. A Zeelander is a variety of the heavy Belgian horse, a huge strong animal, used mostly for heavy draft work. They are generally gentle giants and I felt very warm and safe in my bed. Sometimes I would wake up in the middle of the night with one of the horses nuzzling my hand or my cheek as if it was trying to make sure that I was OK. I remember also waking up sometimes on the straw-covered floor of the stable. The alcove wasn't very deep and I must have fallen out of my straw and potato-sacking bed. They never stepped on me. Today I realize that I must have smelled like a horse myself, because in those days a bath in the kitchen tub was available only once a week. The rest of the time you washed as much of yourself as you felt like at the outside pump, and that water was always cold and absolutely freezing in winter!

There came a day in the early spring of 1945 when we were warned that German soldiers were rounding up horses and men for the war effort. They had big trucks and guns but no fuel and heavy draft horses were just what they were looking for. Any able-bodied men they would catch in the process of rounding up horses were taken prisoners and used for building the concrete fortifications and trenches on the defense lines. Quickly we packed food and blankets, took the horses out of the pasture and galloped toward a nearby forest to hide. I rode one of the Zeelanders and had a second one in tow.

Now if you've ever seen the back of such a giant, you know there is no way you can encircle that huge back with your legs. Moreover, there weren't any saddles for such horses. So, off I rode bareback on the galloping giant, trying to hold the rein with one hand, the second horse with the other, and jumping up and down like a mad circus rider on my knees. It was a miracle that I didn't fall off the horse. After about twenty minutes we reached the safety of the forested area and stayed there for two days, keeping the horses quiet, standing watch at night and sleeping the rest of the time. I made my bed on top of the most docile horse. I could curl up there and keep warm all night. I fell off only once when the horse suddenly moved. Even though I fell about two meters, I wasn't hurt much. I rubbed my leg and side and somehow in the dark clambered back on the horse and fell asleep again almost immediately. After two days one of the farmer's daughters came to get us. The Germans had come and gone, finding no horses. Only the youngest son was at home, but he was slightly retarded and had thick glasses and so they had not taken him away to "work on the fortifications".

Finally the day came when the war had ended and I left the farm to go back to the Mijlpaal. I went to the stables to say a last farewell to my friends. I kissed them on their big soft noses, rubbed their necks and talked to them. It was very hard for me to go; tears were running down my cheeks and I couldn't speak very well. They somehow knew I was going. They seemed to look at me differently and sadly with their big eyes, and when I finally walked out of the stable all four heads were turned toward me, and they whinnied a soft and throaty goodbye.

PART 5—HEDGEHOGS

When I was living at the Mijlpaal during the war years, I frequently caught hedgehogs, who always received the name of Pietje (little Pete). Once I had two and they were both "Pietje". It didn't matter because I couldn't distinguish between them anyway. They lived in fields and backyards, underneath woodpiles and thorny hedges and under porches. They would wander out in search of food and would roll up in a ball when people or dogs came near. It was always quite a funny sight when a dog found one and tried to get at it. The dog's antics were hilarious. When I found one, I would put it in my handkerchief, in a box or even in my shirt. I would bring it home and put it in a nice roomy cage which I had built and which had twigs, hay and pieces of wood for them to hide under. I put a small saucer of milk close to the little shelter and waited patiently for the hedgehog's inquisitiveness and love of milk to get the better of its caution.

After a few minutes it would start to unroll. It would roll itself up again when it saw me, but it wasn't long before the tantalizing smell of the milk overpowered its fear. I kept quiet. Sniffing around with its little nose, it would soon bury it into the milk. That was the sign for me to start talking, using the name "Pietje". Of course, it would roll itself up immediately when it heard my voice and saw me but I didn't stop talking, and it didn't stay rolled up for long. That milk was a powerful attraction. It was difficult to keep from laughing, because that little whiffing nose was painted white with milk and looked funny. So did the animal's efforts to lick it off with its long tongue. My barely suppressed laughter often made it roll itself up again.

After a while the hedgehog would roll up only partially when it realized that I was sitting there, but not as tightly as before. It appeared to be looking at me in its semi-ball state. You could see the glint of its eyes in the V-shaped gap between its head and rear. After repeating this sequence a few times, the hedgehog became used to the sound of my voice and to my presence. It would only cower a bit and was ready to roll up, but didn't. The milk was more important. I usually left after a few minutes of this interaction and a few hours later we repeated the procedure. I also brought in other food, worms, bugs, lettuce and whatever else I thought it might eat. Also, I never stopped talking and saying "Pietje, Pietje, Pietje......".

After one or two days, I would start to touch the animal's body through the holes in the chicken wire, generally without it rolling itself into a ball. If it did roll-up I had to get my fingers out quickly and many a time I was stung by the spines. But after a few such "escapes" the hedge-hog became used to my hand as well. In about three to four days I would call its name and it would come waddling out from its hiding place and look up at me as if to say "Well, I'm here, where is the milk?" I could rub its nose and even its belly, by sliding my finger underneath its body which it seemed to like. The next step was to open the cage and let it roam free in the garden. Most of the time they returned to the cage after their foraging, because they knew that the milk would be there and there would be someone to rub their tummies. It was a lot of fun and the animals were free to come and go as they wanted. Ultimately, nature prevailed and they disappeared, probably having found an irresistible partner of the opposite sex. I was never sorry about that, although I used to go around in the yard for at least two more days calling for Pietje. I must have had six or seven of them in the three years of my stay at the Mijlpaal. I wonder if they ever met and talked about me.

Chapter 3
ABOUT MY BIRTHPLACE

Aalten, the village where I was born on July 4th, 1931, is located in the eastern province of Gelderland. The only auspicious fact about my birth date was that on that day there was a big fire raging in the village and, according to what my mother told me, they were afraid that they might have to evacuate the house. The whole region was called the "Achterhoek", which means "rear corner", because it was considered a far-off place in those days. It was also a sort of derogatory term, meaning "backward area". The majority of the population in 1940 was quite poor and considered less educated than the more developed and "civilized" western part of the Netherlands. Most farms were small and in many cases were little more than subsistence farms. Today, with all the industrial development going on in Europe, it is no longer backward. Until well after WWII, Aalten was a rural and conservative village.

The village is only a few kilometers from the border with Germany and many of its inhabitants, like my grandfather, had relatives on both sides of the border and used to cross over quite often. The population in the area was in general religious, with a Catholic majority, but at the same time people were quite tolerant of other religious groups. There were about 1800 inhabitants at the beginning of WWII and about 5% were Jewish. Most of the Jews were in trades and manufacturing. My maternal grandfather, Izaak ten Bosch, was a butcher and greengrocer. His son, my uncle Jacob, was a butcher and horse-trader.

I was born in my grandparent's home on the second floor of a house that stood on the corner of Main Street and the square, right opposite the big Catholic church and above my grandfather's butcher and greengrocery store. The house is still there and so is the church. During the depression years of the early thirties, it was a difficult time for everyone. My father, Max Leviticus, had been laid off from work, and apparently went from job to job. When my mother, Sera, became pregnant she left him in Amsterdam and came to her parents' house to give birth. I am not sure how long we stayed in Aalten. However, before the war and later until we went into hiding, I visited my grandparents frequently and stayed also with Uncle Jaap and his wife, Aunt Jans, and their daughter Hettie, who was about six years younger than I was. I still remember the warm drowsy summer days trying to catch sticklebacks with neighbor kids in the shallow, clear, fast-flowing stream which ran through town. Sometimes we were lucky enough to catch a young gar. We kept them in glass jars but I never understood why they didn't stay alive more than a day. My memories of those days are pleasant ones.

Another favorite, and forbidden pastime I remember was "riding the gate" at the church opposite my grandparents' house. The church was located right in the center of the town and stood on a little higher ground. It had a huge wrought-iron gate and we would climb on it and push off with our feet. We could get quite a speed on it and we jumped off before it slammed against the brick pillars of the fence. It made quite a racket and drove the church beadle crazy. He used to come out of the chancellery waving his stick at us and we would run away, and then stand laughing and jeering at a safe distance. He used to complain to my grandfather about me and then grandpa would give me a totally deserved paddling or some other appropriate punishment. When I returned to Aalten in 1993 for a short visit with my wife Rose and two friends, I showed them how we used to do it—the old gate was still there, but it didn't look as big now as it did then. Needless to say, I didn't let it slam into the wall and the old beadle didn't come running either.

Aalten was a conservative, deeply religious, but "tolerant" town and was very intent upon the proper behavior of all its inhabitants and visitors, whether Christian or Jewish. The Christians had their Sabbath on Sunday and Jews had their Sabbath on Saturday and no Christian or Jew ever did any work on their Sabbath, nor was he expected to unless it was an emergency. There is an interesting story typifying the Aalteners' code of proper behavior. One day a Jewish salesman from Amsterdam came to town on a Saturday and went into one of the non-Jewish stores to peddle his wares. When the owners found out that he was Jewish, they threw him out of the store, sample cases and all, and told him to go to the Synagogue because that's where he was supposed to be on the Sabbath. The story does not say if he did.

According to the Sabbath laws Jews are not allowed to switch on lights or make fires during the Sabbath and so, every Friday night at sunset, local non-Jewish boys and girls used to go to Jewish homes to switch on the lights and put coal or wood on the fireplaces. They or their parents returned later to turn the lights off, and some stayed overnight and arose early to put coal or wood on the fire to keep the house warm in the winter. They were generally paid for their services, but there are stories of Christian families who refused payment, either because they felt it was their duty to let people with other religions practice their beliefs or because they believed that Jews were God's chosen people and that one should not take money from them.

There always remained, however, a separation between Jewish and Christian population. The children mixed at school but generally did not play together outside of school. There was rarely open anti-Semitism unless there were some problems about kids getting in trouble, money or shop hours. The anti-Semitic actions usually originated from a small group of people who were uneducated and poor and envied the relative prosperity of the Jewish shop-owners. In the history of the town, which goes back to about 1630, Jews were never elected to public office, such as the municipality and the council. However, the Jews were always very active and accepted in social, cultural and other public affairs and organizations.

We had relatives on my mother's side of the family in Aalten itself and in many of the nearby towns such as Winterswijk, Varsseveld, Deventer, Zutphen and others, so we did a great deal of visiting in the days before the war and during the first year of occupation. I vaguely remember some of my cousins, although I never could figure out the exact family connections. It was all pretty complicated, and at my age I wasn't interested in knowing all those things. It was sufficient that they were all family. As a result, most of my playmates were either relatives or other Jewish children. We were a normal bunch of kids and managed to get ourselves in plenty of trouble from time to time.

The most famous (or infamous) story about my cousins and me is the one which concerned an uncle who had a big textile business adjacent to his house and he also had several trucks in which he sometimes took us out for a short ride. Every one of us had sat on the front seat and watched my uncle or his eldest son drive, so driving seemed easy. I had also had plenty of opportunity to see my dad drive our car we had in Amsterdam. One day about three of us kids—I was about seven or eight and my cousins were the same age range—were playing together and climbed into the cab of one of the trucks. We started fooling around with the knobs and handles and suddenly the engine started. We looked at one another and then one of us pushed the clutch in while another engaged a gear and released the brake and suddenly we were lurching forward. My elder cousin and I grabbed the steering wheel and somehow the truck lumbered to the end of the long driveway, which ran alongside the factory. I can remember thinking: "How do we stop this thing." At the end of the driveway we had to turn to the right or to the left because the canal was straight ahead. But this was a truck; it was big and in those days there was no power steering. Try as we might, and with all those four hands on the steering wheel pulling in different directions, we kept on going straight toward the canal and plunged into it. The engine went under water and died immediately and the truck became hung up on its belly. We started hollering for help and pressing the horn, which was still working and everyone came rushing out of the house to see what had happened. My uncle took us one by one into the machine shed and gave us a well-deserved hiding with a cane. His boys received some extra punishment, because they should have known better than to show off to me. When I came back to grandpa's home in Aalten, he gave me more of the same medicine, grounded me and I had to stay with him in the store for three days and help him. I actually enjoyed that part of the punishment. Serving customers was fun and when he saw that I was enjoying it he sent me to grandma to help with the housework. I didn't like the housework, but enjoyed the cookies she slipped me.

In the course of the war, several Jewish families from Aalten went into hiding in the eastern region. Some had good identity papers which allowed them to live and work and lead more or less, normal lives but others had to stay hidden till the end of the war. My grandparents and uncle and aunt also went into hiding in the area. People tried to seek shelter in the area because the local dialect, which was very typical, might arouse suspicion if they went to another region in the Netherlands. The records show that on July 13, 1942, there were about seventy-five Jews in Aalten left out of a total of 90 at the beginning of the war. Fifty-one died during the war, one died of natural causes, two more were shot by the Dutch Underground for being traitors (yes, there were also Jewish traitors) and the rest died in concentration camps. I have not been able to trace the fates of any of our other relatives, except my uncle and aunt, because I was too young to know their family names. Most of them did not survive the war years, otherwise we would have found each other by now. My grandparents changed their hiding place several times during the war, but did survive. They did not return to Aalten after the war, but lived with my mother's sister and her family in Amersfoort.

The two people who were shot by the Underground movement, Fritz Landau and his German-born wife Amalia Landau-Lorch, had apparently betrayed several people who were in hiding, among them my Uncle Jacob and Aunt Jans who were hiding in Halle, a town not far from Aalten. Uncle Jacob and Aunt Jans were murdered in Auschwitz, the camp where my parents died. They never met my parents in Auschwitz because my parents were killed in November 1942 (mother) and December 1942 (father), and my aunt and uncle in December 1943 and March 1944 respectively. The Landau couple certainly got what they deserved. They were not the only cases of Jews becoming willing and cruel tools in the hands of the Nazis. There are unfortunately many examples of cruelty of some Jewish supervisors against other Jewish prisoners, judging from the stories which came out of the concentration camps. Simon Wiesenthal, the famous Nazi-hunter, once said that the crime of the Germans was even greater than just murder, because they made some of their victims become monsters like themselves.

On October 4 of 1942 the "work-camps" set up by the Germans were emptied and their inhabitants transported to Germany. Some residents from Aalten were in those camps. My father, who had also been in such a camp, had managed to escape before the transportation. People now started disappearing with greater frequency from Aalten. Some went into hiding; others were rounded up and sent to Westerbork, the infamous transfer camp or "the gateway to extermination" in the Netherlands. By November 1942 only 28 "legal" Jews, those who had special passes, were left in Aalten.

The German authorities then issued a proclamation that by April 1943 the whole province of Gelderland had to be *"Jüdenrein* (cleansed of Jews)" and most of the Jews who were not in hiding, but were living with "passes and permits", were rounded up and transported to Vught, which was one of several penal camps in the Netherlands. From there they disappeared into the concentration camps in Germany, Austria and Poland, most of them never to return.

There are a few stories of miraculous escapes. One of them was told by a young boy who was only six years old in 1943. My grandparents were good friends of his parents and I knew his older brother quite well and played with him often. Neither the boy's parents nor his brother survived the holocaust. Here is the boy's story, as he told it after the war. They are the words of a nine year old boy, which I have translated from Dutch (P. Lurvink—pp265):

> *My parents had found an address of a farm where I could stay—however there was place only for one child and I had to say good-bye to my parents and my brother. After some time I felt that the farmer and his wife were my parents. One day a pilot was hidden on the farm and police came and surrounded the farm. They didn't find the pilot but they found me. When they pulled down my pants* [something which was done regularly by the Nazis and their Dutch helpers to identify Jews, which were practically the only people who were circumcised in the Netherlands] *they saw that I was a Jew. The farmer was sent to a punishment camp* [Vught] *and they took me to the police station. I cried and was very afraid. The told me to shut up and slapped my face. I did not cry anymore. After three weeks at the police station, I was taken by the police to Arnhem* [a city not far from Aalten].

*When I arrived in Arnhem I was taken to a building where I saw hundreds of Jewish children and police guard. I then knew that I'd never see my parents again and I thought about ways to escape but it was impossible. After three weeks all of us were taken by train to Amsterdam. In the train station I saw that all the children were loaded into big brown train cars without windows (*cattle cars*). Every 15 minutes there was a new car filled with Jewish children. I thought: "None of us will ever come back" and looked around for an escape. I decided to hide under the skirt of a nun who was standing nearby on the station platform. She told me to keep quiet and stand on her feet and then we walked slowly down to another platform from where we took a train back to Arnhem.*

I stayed in Arnhem for six months but had to leave because it became too dangerous; a German officer had been quartered in a neighbor's house. The lady with whom I lived took me by train to Aalten. My "auntie" as I called her didn't know that I had lived there. When the ticket collector came he wished us "a good voyage" and I could see in his eyes what he was thinking. That must have been a "nice" Dutchman.

In Aalten a lady was waiting for us with a bicycle and a glove in her left hand. We left the station together. Suddenly we were passing by our former home where other people now lived [probably Dutch Nazis] and I said to my auntie: "That is our house". My auntie became very nervous and told me not to talk. Then we arrived at the doctor's house and I said : "But that is our doctor!" My auntie was shaking with fear. She left me with the doctor. The doctor brought me back to the house where I had been picked up six months ago. The farmer was still in Vught but he came back later.

As a footnote to this story, after the war the boy was inan orphanages for war orphans. The nun was located after the war. Her name was Sietske Hoekstra. She was one of the many who helped when there was a need, but unfortunately there were not enough of her kind.

PART II
The War Years

Chapter 4
War arrives—the first days

I was nearly nine years old in May 1940 when World War II came to the Netherlands. It took the Germans only five days, from May 10 till May 15, to occupy our small country. From the beginning it was an uneven match. The Germans had the latest technology in tanks, artillery and planes, and used paratroopers. The Dutch army was a peace-time army, equipped with World War I weapons, which were outdated and inferior, an army more for show than for fighting and certainly unable to oppose the German "Blitzkrieg".

A major part of the Dutch defense strategy was to flood large areas of land on the assumption that the invaders would be unable to cross. But the German paratroopers were dropped by the thousands on the other side of the flooded land and behind the Dutch defenders, where they surprised the overwhelmed Dutch army. In other areas, which had not been flooded, the Germans simply drove in and occupied the land. They had good tanks and heavy artillery and their cavalry was motorized, as opposed to the Dutch, who were on foot, on bicycles or on horses. Despite all that, there were a number of places where there was strong resistance and where the fighting was heavy. This was especially along the "Grebbe-line" and in the southwest, in the province of Zeeland, where very strong resistance was mounted and in particular near the area of the strategic port of Rotterdam. When the Germans found themselves "behind schedule", they sent an ultimatum to the commander of Rotterdam to cease resistance or else they would bomb the city. Before the deadline passed, the treacherous Germans became impatient and started their bombing anyway with several hundred Heinkel 111 bombers. They dropped their bombs only on the densest civilian housing areas, taking care not to destroy any port and industrial facilities. The attack leveled the old populated center of Rotterdam. Seventy-eight thousand homes were destroyed in one night. About one thousand civilians and hundreds of Dutch soldiers who were garrisoned in the city were killed and tens of thousands were wounded. The German command made it clear that they would do the same with other cities if the resistance wasn't stopped and the Dutch Chiefs-of-Staff decided to capitulate in order to save civilian lives. Still, a few days later, the center of the city of Middelburg on the island of Walcheren in the province of Zeeland, where fighting had continued for three days after the official capitulation, was also indiscriminately destroyed. The seat of the Government, the Hague, had efficient anti-aircraft defenses and they were a bit luckier. The city and surrounding area were attacked by about 900 bombers of which 250 were shot down.

There were attacks on Amsterdam as well and I remember huddling with mother, our maid and neighbors under the stairs on the ground floor while our building shook and rattled. At that time I thought that it was all rather exciting, what with the sirens sounding and the anti-aircraft guns firing away. Then, and later during the war, I always wanted to see what was going on outside and to look at the searchlight and see the flashes of exploding ammo in the air. Sometimes I was even "lucky" enough to see an airplane caught in the convergence of two or three searchlight beams. After the capitulation, the country became of course a target of the British and, after Pearl Harbour, both the British and American air attacks.

During the four days of actual war, the Dutch army lost over two thousand soldiers, more than 2700 were severely wounded. Of these about 850 remained disabled. The civilian population lost 2600 dead and many thousands were wounded in the bombardments of the cities. The Germans, naturally, never published their losses, but it is said that they were considerable.

The first mobilization in the Netherlands had taken place in 1939 when England and France declared war on Germany. At that time, only men born after 1904 and older than twenty years were called up. My father was not among them since he was born in 1896 and had served in the Dutch army during WWI. He never saw any combat then, because The Netherlands had remained neutral during that war. He was an officer and therefore was called up to serve several weeks before the May 1940 invasion and my mother and I had no idea where he was. Before the invasion on May 10 he often wrote to us or managed to come and see us on some of his free days. I was very proud of him in his uniform and, when he came home for a short furlough, I constantly nagged him to go with me for walks through the neighborhood, so that I could "show him off" to my friends, the neighbors and the shopkeepers. My father wasn't the only one to be called up, but he had these impressive master sergeant's chevrons and medals, showing that he had been in WWI, which made him so magnificent in my eyes and I wanted to show him of all the neighbors in our area, many of whom were just privates, corporals or plain sergeants.

In preparation against air attacks, my parents and I, like everyone else, had put sticky paper strips on the windows to prevent glass from being scattered around in case of a bombardment. We had also bought rolled blackout paper and installed it in accordance with instructions from the authorities. Every house had blacked out windows, though not everyone had used the sticky paper strips. Those who didn't or had been delaying putting it on soon found out how dangerous it was because serious damage and injury would occur, caused by the flying glass every time there was an explosion of bombs nearby.

On that first night of the war, May 10th, the whole city was pitch-black and only the fires of the petroleum tank depot in the north and occasional stars peeking through the clouds gave some light. I don't remember if there was a moon or not. There had been blackouts before, but they were not always complete and did not always include the public transport. This time it was for real and my mother and I, as well as many others, went outside to see this new, dark Amsterdam and see the fires in the north of Amsterdam where the Germans had dropped bombs on the oil refineries. It was really eerie; no light came from the houses; there were no streetlights; trams, buses, cars and bicycles drove around with dimmed slits of bluish light and the people were barely distinguishable specters. That night Amsterdam was a city of ghosts, but nobody stayed outside long because everyone wanted to get back inside and listen to the latest war news on the radio. Unfortunately, it was never good news as it was mainly news of pullbacks, defeats despite heroic resistance, numbers of casualties, death and destruction and other bad news from Belgium and France. We feared for my dad—I remember both of us trying unsuccessfully to reassure ourselves and the other. Our school was also closed during those first days of war.

Before the war started, we had already been through several air-raid drills at home and at school. At school it was sort of fun having to crouch under the benches and telling the girls that you could see their panties. That always elicited screams, the teacher darting toward the source and the culprit being punished accordingly. "Write fifty times: I shall not be vulgar" or "Stand in the hall" or "Go to the Principal". None of us kids realized how serious the situation could become, nor did we realize how useless it was to hide under a bench or a desk. When the sirens went off and you were on the street you made for the nearest air-raid shelter or hid in the vestibule of a house. Most houses in the River Quarter, where we lived, had those vestibules. The air-raid shelter locations were clearly marked on every street corner and there was one for each block of apartments in our area. Over the past two days there had been a few air raids and shooting, which I found greatly exciting, but frightened and worried my mother very much because dad was still in the army and she didn't know where he was or if he was OK.

One day, it was some time after the capitulation on May 15, the air-raid sirens went off in the middle of the day, and I heard the noise of planes. Immediately a huge racket started which was caused by ack-ack and anti-aircraft cannon. British planes had been sighted and the German guns let loose with a barrage of fire. My mother wasn't at home, our maid was somewhere downstairs, and I had been playing and reading in my upstairs room. When I heard all that noise, I jumped onto the roof-garden behind my room and stood watching the hundreds of blue and black puffs of smoke and the planes circling overhead. Other people were also standing on porches and rooftops and looking. The planes looked black and big and they had two noisy engines. They came in low and fast and you could see the big crosses on their wings. It was a magical sight and I stood there, fascinated. I didn't realize then the danger and seriousness of what was happening and just thought it was a magical adventure.

Suddenly there was a huge plume of smoke rising from the block of houses at the back of our house and nearly simultaneously a strange piercing and whistling sound, followed by a deafening explosion, a tinkling of glass and a rustling sound like a truck emptying a load of gravel. A split second later I was thrown to the floor, as if by an invisible hand, and another deafening clap of thunder assaulted my ears. That was my first physical experience of the war. A bomb or bombs had hit houses behind ours on the Vechtstraat, about 100 meters from our house, where Hans Klatser, one of my friends, lived;

When I stood up, wobbly and shocked, my ears were ringing and there was a gap in the row of apartment houses behind ours. Smoke and a cloud of choking dust were billowing up over our whole complex of apartments. It made the whole area look dark and threatening. I was standing there not believing what I had just seen, transfixed, as if hypnotized. When I awoke out of my stupor I heard more explosions in other parts of the city and could see more plumes of smoke. The anti-aircraft guns were still pounding away. A short time later, the planes left, the anti-aircraft guns stopped shooting and soon the sirens sounded the "all clear," and quiet reigned again. I could hear the bells and sirens of police vehicles, ambulances and fire engines.

My mother wasn't home yet. It turned out later that she had been hiding in an air-raid shelter near one of the shops she had gone to. Here was my chance—I decided to go downstairs and to the street and see the destroyed houses. I knew that if I waited for my mother to come home and then ask her if I could go and see, she wouldn't let me. So I quickly ran downstairs, told our protesting maid that I was going out and ran around the block to the next street. I found it covered in rubble and glass. Dust and some smoke were still whirling about. A few dazed people were standing around, some with blood on their hands and faces. The fire brigade, the police and ambulances had already arrived and two people had started to dig for victims which they thought was buried in the pile of rubble which had once been a four-story set of apartments. Two or three injured people were carried from the rubble heap on litters by the Red Cross ambulance people. One of the litters passed close by and I could hear the victim's groans and it made me feel sick to my stomach. It was the first time in my life that I had heard the sounds of someone in great pain. By now, quite a crowd of neighbors and passers-by had assembled and they were being held back by several policemen and people of the civil brigade.

On the third floor of one of the apartments, a complete bathroom, totally undamaged was hanging at an angle from the remainder of two walls. The wall on the street side had completely disappeared and we could see the toilet with its seat down; the sink and mirror were still there and towels were still hanging on the hooks. Utterly amazing, when looking at the state of the rest of the house. Some joker went around telling the story that the man who lived there and who had been using the toilet, had flushed at the same time the bomb fell. He was reported to have said something like "Oh shit!" because he thought that he had pulled the flush chain too hard. I don't know if he was amongst the casualties, but if he was, he couldn't have told his story. According to the rumors, there were about five or six people buried in the rubble and three of them were dead when they were found. It was also rumored that the bombs had been intended for the Trompenburger Garage which was used by the Germans for their vehicles. Our house was in between the garage and the house where the bomb fell—so we were really lucky.

I thought that the toilet pull story was very funny at the time and later told it (without fully pronouncing the four-letter word) to my mother. She wasn't pleased with it, and truly, it wasn't very funny. Several people had been killed in these houses and in another place, a corner house on the Herengracht, one of the famous canals in Amsterdam. There was also quite a bit of destruction and structural damage to neighboring houses. Windows were shattered over a large area, including all the back windows on both floors of our house. Only the windows in my room were undamaged because they had been open at the time the bombs fell. It now became evident how good it was that we had taped our window panes because the glass did not scatter all over the house. Apart from the windows, we had one broken vase and a very frightened dog, Julie, who had pooped and peed all over the place. One of my friend's house was not damaged severely, but it was uninhabitable and took a while to get it back in order. They moved out for several months while repairs were being made. I never played with him again because when they returned, the family apparently decided that he should not have contact any more with Jewish boys. Whether this was out of anti-Semitism or out of fear I will never know and still wonder about.

For me and the other boys in the neighborhood the bombings were an adventure. We went around and combed the streets and parks for parts of bomb casings and pieces of shrapnel from the anti-aircraft weapons. We traded them like we traded marbles and took them to school to show our schoolmates who had not been so "fortunate" to have bombs fall in their neighborhoods.

When my mother came home after the air-raid and didn't find me there, she was frantic and started searching for me. The maid and neighbors told her that I had gone to see the bombed houses and that is where she found me. When she became aware that I also had been watching the attack outside, on the roof garden, she was very angry with me, which was very unusual for her. She didn't scream, but she went red all over and lectured me for a long time and grounded me for three days. She made me promise never to do that again. I promised her, but in truth, I never kept that promise. I never wanted to be in a house and have it collapse on top of me as happened to the people in the apartments near us. That has always remained a fear with me—to be buried under rubble.

The Dutch Royal Family had escaped on May 13 in a British destroyer, together with the acting government from the port of Hoek van Holland on the 13th of May. The caretaker government was entrusted to the commander of the Dutch forces, General Winkelman. I had heard all of this on the radio, but was too young to understand the significance at the time. Grownups were devastated by the news of the departure of the Royal family and this was the first time that I ever saw some of them cry openly on the street and in shops. Everyone was very upset by the fact that Queen Wilhelmina and Princess Juliana, Prince Bernhard and the children had left, but happy that they were safe in London and not prisoners of the Germans. The Germans made use of the Royal family's escape and dropped propaganda leaflets all over Holland declaring that the Royal Family had deserted us and we might as well give up. But the Dutch felt that, as long as the Queen and her family were free, the Netherlands' spirit remained free, even though half the country was occupied. That feeling didn't go away even after the capitulation.

My father was taken prisoner but released a short time after the armistice was signed on May 15, 1940. He came home, a very different man from when he left us that one morning and had waved and smiled at us while we were cheering him on from the window. Later that same first day my mother and I had gone to see him off, in his sergeant's uniform, marching crisply with his platoon. I was so proud of him but my mother cried. But he came back so dejected. He hugged me and my mother a long time, which was unusual for him, because he wasn't a demonstrative person. Then he sat down in his chair and while I stood beside him his face started quivering and he started crying with big sobs which shook his whole body. That was the first and only time that I saw and heard my father cry and I'll never forget it. I asked him "Why are you crying, Pappie," and he didn't say anything, but took me in his arms and held me very tight and cried his heart out. I cried with him and I understood then that something terrible had happened and that it was the Netherlands's capitulation, and that now that the Germans were here, things were going to be different for all of us. I don't think my family and many others realized how different it would be and how this was especially so for the Jews of the Netherlands.

Chapter 5
LIFE IN AMSTERDAM UNDER THE NAZIS

PART 1—THE NOOSE TIGHTENS

Our family was a typical middle class family. I was an only child, a spoiled brat, who had everything a boy could want, thanks to my wonderful and loving paternal grandmother who was quite well-to-do and spent a lot of money on her only grandson. My mother apparently could not have any more children, so I had no siblings. Many years after the war I learned that she may have had a weak heart. She had been educated as a nurse before she met my father. She was a social smoker and, since she had a rich social life, she smoked quite a lot. I can still see her clearly, a beautiful, slim, pale woman with a fashionable long cigarette holder in her hand, playing cards or sitting around a seance table with her lady friends who were similarly decked out. I remember that when we went out to a café or any other social event she wore a "Voile", a very fine lacelike net, which was attached to her hat and covered her face like a veil. This veil once caught fire at a wedding party in the Krasnapolski Hotel because she was smoking a cigarette and was careless for a moment. It must have been made from very flammable material. She wasn't hurt, only shocked, but was the center of attention for a while—something she obviously enjoyed.

My father worked as a bookkeeper and handled foreign correspondence for an import-export firm which recycled used materials. He used to bring me hundreds of foreign stamps from the many countries which he had received through his correspondence at work. He and I would sit for hours putting the stamps into albums. He would show me, in the world atlas, where each country was and explain the country names on the stamps. "Hellas" was Greece; "Suomi" was Finland; "Böhmen und Mähren" was Bohemia and Moravia, "Sverige" was Sweden, "Norge" was Norway and so on. I learned geography by collecting stamps.

We were not observant Jews. We rarely went to the synagogue as far as I can remember, except once or twice on high holidays to the Esnoga (the Sephardic synagogue). We were not active members of any congregation as far as I know. If we had been, we would probably have belonged to one of the Sephardic synagogues because my father's family originated in Spain, from where they were driven in 1492, compliments of saintly King Ferdinand and Queen Isabella and their religious Inquisition. The family apparently fled first to Portugal and from there to Saloniki in Greece. According to the information I have they must have reached the Netherlands sometime around the 1700's. The family was quite religious at that time, but some lost their orthodoxy and I was part of the non-orthodox branch. As a result, my family always felt that we were Dutch first, Jewish last. In that, we were not different from most of the Jews in the Netherlands.

Since I was Jewish, I bore the consequences and from 1940 onwards and during the war I hated being a Jew. Even long after the war I hated my Jewishness, especially when my mother's sister and her husband forced the Dutch Social Service Authority to put me into an ultra-religious orphanage for war orphans in Hilversum, the "Rüdelsheim Stichting", taking me away from the people who had saved me, Karel, Rita and my two little sisters Berna and Helga; the people I had come to love. Why did this have to happen to me? Why did my parents make me a Jew without asking me? Why did the rest of the world around classify me and brand me? I was a very angry young man and didn't trust anyone and thus did not make real friends easily. Before the war I wasn't conscious of being Jewish. I went to a regular school with non-Jewish youngsters. Whether my playmates were Jewish or not didn't matter. I didn't know nor care and neither did my parents. I was one of several Jewish kids who were in one of the many midget and junior league soccer teams of Ajax, a well-known Dutch soccer club. Just like everyone else, I was a member of a public playground club and a public swimming club, and had never been turned away from a store, movie house, the zoo, the library or any public transportation. I was a Dutch kid who was proud to sing the National Anthem and cheered for the National Soccer team, loved the Royal House of Orange and looked down on anything not Dutch. I was Dutch in every fiber of my being and what did this nonsense of religion have to do with me? Religion isn't nationality—or so I, and many others, thought.

In order to conform to the standards of the day and chiefly to placate my mother's family, I was sent in 1938 by my parents to Hebrew Sunday school once a week. I hated it. It was boring to read those prayers and bible stories and to learn the Hebrew alphabet. The teacher's pronunciation at that school was the Ashkenazi Hebrew instead of the Sephardic Hebrew and it sounded to me, and still does today, slightly ridiculous and old-fashioned. Together with other boys, who felt as I did, I played hooky frequently. Who needed to learn those unbelievable stories out of those old books and mumble stupid prayers, without understanding their meaning? Since attendance at the school was taken when we entered the Synagoge building in the Lekstraat, we used to hide in the toilets or somewhere else until class had started and sneak out of the building as soon as we could and no one was ever the wiser. At least I never heard from my parents or the teachers about my truancy. Only when the weather was bad did we have to sit through the boredom of religious instruction. Then we usually got kicked out of class because of rowdiness or some other devilry we committed.

I particularly disliked the religious practices of my mother's sister and her husband in Amersfoort who were always pursuing their ritual, morning, noon and evening, mumbling prayers in Hebrew, a language they didn't even understand. When I spent a weekend with them, I had to go to the synagogue on a Saturday and had to sit through the interminable service. My aunt professed to be religious but I knew that she was a liar and a hypocrite. I had once seen her shortchange (I was good in math) a customer of their bread-and-pastry bakery cum cafeteria which was located on the Lange Straat, the main street of Amersfoort. That was clearly dishonest and you shouldn't do that, especially when you're religious, I thought! She saw that I had noticed and winked at me with a conspiratorial smile. Then she gave me an extra large ice cream cone from the cafeteria and told me to go and play outside. Until then I had been led to think that religion was supposed to make you God-fearing and honest!

Then came the occupation and the laws. How I hated the Dutch Nazis and the Germans! They made me wear that despicable yellow star with the hated epithet "Jood" (Jew) embroidered on it. Why me? I was convinced that I wasn't really Jewish; I was a Dutch boy who happened to have a Jewish mother and father. Was it my fault that they were Jewish? When the Germans overran the Netherlands and anti-Jewish propaganda began, my non-Jewish playmates deserted me one by one. First some of their families forbade them to play with me, come to my house or invite me to theirs. Some families may have been anti-Semitic all the time and now could show it openly but others forbade the contact because the anti-Semitic propaganda told them that Jews were a bad lot and some were afraid of the consequences if they showed friendship to a Jew. For some people it was a chance to act out long hidden, ignorant prejudices. There always had been much of that going on under the surface in the Netherlands. The libelous church indoctrination, that the Jews were the murderers of Jesus and used Christian baby's blood to prepare the Passover bread, didn't whip up the frenzy of a pogrom in the "civil" Netherlands as it did in "uncivilized" Poland, the Baltic countries or the USSR, but it made tacit bystanders and cooperators out of many "devout" Dutchmen. In the end it didn't matter what the reason was because the new laws forbade social and commercial contact between Jews and Christians at any level.

The day came when I was kicked off my junior league soccer team, although I was one of their best backfield players who sometimes doubled as goalkeeper. There had never been a mention of my being less for being Jewish and I always participated in the games which were held on Saturdays. But I was the only Jew on this team and one day, which I will never forget, before a practice game, two of the boys came to the dressing room in the field house on the practice field in the uniform of the *Jeugdstorm (The Dutch Hitler Youth)*. They went up to the coach, gave him a note and talked to him. They pointed at me. The coach called me out of the group of youngsters, saying, loudly, so that everyone could hear what a good Dutchman he was, that there could be no more Jews on the team. "*Get out of here, Joodje (little Jew)*", he said, and I was sent away under the scornful eyes and smirks of my former teammates. It hurt so much and it hurt even more when I heard my former teammates snickering and making remarks behind my back "*yea, run jewboy......and don't let us catch you*". I started to walk away, slowly at first and then I started to cry and I ran. I ran as if my life depended upon it. I didn't even think of taking my street clothes. I was furious, shaking and boiling with anger, shame and mortification, my insides were churning and I felt a bitter hatred towards the whole world, including those damned lousy Jews who had made me one of them. I wanted to run away from this rotten world. What had I done that I deserved such treatment? How could they do this to me?

And so it went on, weekly, step by step, the Germans restricted our freedoms. Notices were posted in the municipal pools, on billboards and in the newspapers, that Jews were no longer allowed to go to public swimming pools, playgrounds and parks. Street benches carried notices stating that Jews were not allowed to sit on them. There was the day, when we had somehow missed reading or forgotten the announcement on the swimming pool prohibition in the newspapers I went there for a swim. It was a stupid mistake on our part, but when I arrived at the municipal pool where we had a membership, the attendant, after looking at my badge and checking his list, said "*We don't want people like you dirtying the water for the other swimmers*". He pointed to the notice—and there it was: "Verboden voor Joden" (Forbidden for Jews) in big letters. Some of the kids who were behind me in the line snickered and sneered, "*Go home dirty Jew, we don't want you here. We don't want to swim in your shit. Go to Poland*". They apparently knew more about our intended fate than I did. It was doubly painful because the attendant knew me well and had always been friendly. So much for trusting people whom you thought that knew and liked you. Just because you were labeled as a Jew you became an outcast.

Wearing the hated yellow star, we couldn't visit the Kalverstraat (a famous shopping street) or the Dam (the palace square), both in the center of Amsterdam, because there was always a chance that you might be beaten up or yelled at and teased by the non-Jewish kids. Paul Frank, who was a friend of mine and who lived nearby, went there one Saturday with another Jewish boy and was kicked and severely beaten by two older Nazi youths who came out of a café unexpectedly and after he accidentally bumped into one of them. Not a single bystander lifted a finger to help him. He wore the star! We could be picked up, imprisoned or deported during one of the *"razzias" (roundups)* which became more and more frequent. We were not allowed to take the tram (trolley), bus, or taxi, and later on couldn't go for walks in the evening because of the curfew for Jews.

I often had ridden my bike to visit other Jewish friends who were restricted in their movements for the same reasons as I was. I used to spend many hours with my boyhood love Anita Grünewald and her family. I also played many games of Chess and Monopoly with Paul, who lived close enough to us so that it was safe for me to go there alone. His family had come from Germany in the early thirties and they may have been somehow related to the family of Anne Frank. I am not sure, because Frank is a very common name, but in fact, I met Anne Frank and her family a few times at Paul's house but never got to know any of them well. Anne was two years older that we were and at that age it makes quite a difference. She was also a very self-assured young lady, which became clear later from her writings in her famous diary, while we were still a playful 10-year olds. She used to tell us what we did wrong when we were playing games, whether it was monopoly, chess or cards. We, the little boys, didn't like that at all, especially since she was usually right. Her sister Margot, though older than Anne, never talked down to us like that and we liked her a lot better than Anne. I really don't remember much about the parents. I was introduced to them, but that is about all I remember.

Adjacent to our block was another whole block which was dedicated as a "speeltuin" a fenced in area which was dedicated solely as playground for children. It was set up by the local neighborhood group in 1921. There were organized sports and games and you had to be a member. I regularly played there. But in November or December 1941, the playground was closed and made into a market for Jews only. There were apparently two other such "markets" in Amsterdam. The Germans encouraged the Jewish population, who by then were prohibited from buying in non-Jewish establishments, into setting up their stalls and to sell their wares and for others to come and buy. It was an obvious trap, but people still could not believe how morally degenerate the Germans and their Dutch collaborators were. So they came and bought and sold and the Gestapo came and brought some trucks and rounded up everyone inside the fenced in square and sent them eastward to their destruction.

As time went by, playing or walking outside became more difficult and often hazardous. Non-Jewish kids went sometimes "Jew-hunting" and ganged up on Jewish kids. It was easy to find us. We were marked—we wore a star. At best, they yelled insults at us, threw things at us, pushed us out in the road when a tram or a car was coming, harassed us, or worse, beat us. Our parents didn't dare complain to their parents or to the police. There was generally no help from bystanders. Who dared complain? We were the dirt of the earth! We were outcasts from society! When a few schoolmates and I were beaten up [see page 60], I remember grownups standing by and watching, one even seeming to joke about it—*"the Jews are finally getting what they deserve; it is about time!"*

The pain of the blows and kicks were soon forgotten but not hurt of the insults and the hurt of grown-ups' indifference or consent. That feeling of resentment remains with you forever. It destroys one's trust in people. I still feel that the majority of the Dutch, while not active participants, didn't really mind that some of their countrymen were methodically abused and annihilated, because, after all, they were sort of strange and inferior and hadn't they killed Jesus Christ? Postwar research has more or less confirmed that the Dutch did not stand behind their Jewish countrymen like the Danes or, for that matter, many other European nations. This partly accounts for the fact that more than seventy-five percent of Dutch Jewry was killed. Just think about it for a moment—that is three out of every four people! The Dutch, of course, do not acknowledge this blemish on their good name and point to the very unique and accurate civilian registry system as the culprit. However, the official Dutch position, even several years before the war, was quite openly anti-Semitic. As an example, a camp was built near the town of Westerbork in Drente (a Dutch province) where German Jews who had fled persecution in their homeland were initially interned under very uncomfortable, if not downright terrible, conditions. Dutch Jewish citizens were ordered to pay for the upkeep of the camp. Not a penny from the Dutch government! The humanitarian Dutch government refused all financial support! On the instigation of one of the ministers, a devout Catholic, a law was passed in 1937 or 1938 that no more German Jews would be allowed to enter the country at all. This did not stop the border crossings, which now became illegal. Many of those illegal immigrants were caught and ended up in that camp. The camp was later taken over intact by the Germans and used as the main transit camp for Dutch Jewry to feed their hungry gas-chambers. The Germans in fact received from the Dutch a well-prepared place to concentrate the fodder for their ovens. As a further example of the official attitude the following fact is also illuminating. The camp was at first supposed to have been built on the Veluwe, a beautiful wooded area in the center of the Netherlands, but that plan was objected to by Queen Wilhelmina, because it was only seven kilometers from her summer estate and might have spoiled her summer vacations. So the camp ended up in one of the most remote and desolate areas in the province of Drente. But enough about the Dutch attitude to the victims of persecution.

Not many children my age had their own bicycles in those years, for they were quite expensive and were considered a luxury. Only when you entered middle or high school did young people begin have their own bicycles. Generally, if you wanted to ride a bicycle, you rented one for a whole afternoon for ten cents. I received my bicycle from my doting and well-to-do grandmother, Oma Francien, who absolutely spoiled me rotten. My bike, with drum brakes, a dynamo, lights, a bell, a luggage carrier, was stored in the bike rack in the downstairs hallway of our apartment building, since it was too difficult to lug it up two flights several times a day to our apartment which occupied the third and fourth floors of Gaaspstraat 36 in South Amsterdam.

One day a brown-shirted Nazi, accompanied by a Dutch policeman rang the bell. My mother opened the door and they came up the stairs. The Nazi was a neighbor, who had lived around the corner from us for many years. He saluted with a loud *"Hou-Zee* (the Dutch equivalent of *Heil Hitler)"* and proceeded to confiscate my bike, which he gave to his fat, freckle-faced, red-haired son. Jews were apparently not supposed to have nice bicycles and in fact a few weeks later an edict was issued to that effect. The boy had always been jealous of my good fortune and I had, in the past, refused to let him ride my bike because he was the big neighborhood bully. Neither I nor anyone else on the block liked him or played with him. But the Dutch fascists had suddenly obtained power and now they could have their revenge. Whenever he saw me outside, he would also come outside and circle around me in his *"Jeugdstorm"* uniform, on **my** bike ringing **my** bell, grinning from ear to ear and yelling his dad's Nazi slogans or singing anti-Semitic ditties. One of them was something like: *"Stinking Jew your father is* a *Boer* and your mother is a *Hoer*". (A *"Boer"* was a farmer—someone who was considered backward by city slickers; a *"Hoer"* was a prostitute).

Those were the times that I had a feeling of helpless rage, at being **so powerless**. I swore and day-dreamt that I would, one day, take my revenge on all of those sons-of-bitches. I did take revenge sometime later, but that is another story (Chapter XIII). I felt this same anger and need for revenge when we lost our dog (Chapter II, Part 3) and my beloved friend Anita (Chapter V, Part 4). These feelings of helplessness and impotent rage were repeated time and again over the next few years.

It must have been at the end of 1941 or the beginning of 1942 that the company my father worked for was taken over by the Nazis because the owners were Jewish. Immediately after that my dad was fired and had to start looking for other jobs. He and many others who were similarly without work had a very tough time finding anything, because non-Jewish businesses were not allowed to employ Jews and Jewish businesses were taken over by non-Jews. He was lucky to get, through an influential business contact, a job at a large Jewish bakery, which was allowed to continue operating because it supplied food for a large part of the population in Amsterdam. I can still remember the day my mother took me to see him at work. I still see him—covered with flour in a huge bakery (at least it seemed to me that it was). He waved and grinned at us and brought us a big flat cookie, which was called "Baumkuche" I think. Strange that I can still remember that scene very vividly and have not forgotten the name of the cookie.

PART 2—TO THE SEGREGATED SCHOOL

During the first year or so of the occupation I continued attending my regular school, the Vondelschool in the Jekerstraat. The school was named after the national poet of the Netherlands, Joost van den Vondel. The street's name came from the Jeker river. All the streets in the area, including the one where I lived, were named after rivers and the area was known as the "Rivierenbuurt" or "River Quarter". Joost van den Vondel was considered the Dutch Shakespeare, although his plays, being in Dutch, never became as popular as those of the Bard. Still, we were proud of our school's name. It was a fifteen to twenty minutes walk from my home in the Gaaspstraat, depending on how much I dawdled on the way. After we were forced to wear the yellow star and anti-Semitic posters appeared on the streets, some depicting the "Eternal Jew", others anti-Semitic slogans, it became a daily torture for me to walk from my house in the Gaaspstraat through the Trompenburgerstraat, across the Rijnstraat, through the Lekstraat to the Waalstraat; then on one side of the Merwedeplein, where Anne Frank lived, and finally the Jekerstraat and school. I felt that everyone was looking at me and that they were wondering how this worm of a human, this Jew, dared share the streets with good clean Aryans. For a very short time Margot Frank (Anne Frank's elder sister) also attended the Vondel school, but she was in the highest grade and left shortly after that to go to a Jewish High school. I only knew her because I had met her at my friend Paul's home. I can't remember that we talked much besides an occasional "Hi", but I thought she was very pretty and therefore she was OK in my eyes.

Sometimes non-Jewish kids and older teenagers, if not shouting insults out loud, would mouth words or try to push me off the sidewalk or into a wall of a house. When walking alone it could become difficult, always unpleasant and sometimes dangerous, so I usually tried to walk with other Jewish schoolmates, such as Paul Frank. Sometimes I cried when I came home, and tried to feign a headache or stomach-ache so as not to have to walk to school. I learned what the term "running the gauntlet" meant. I am sure the other pupils suffered the same humiliation, but we never talked about it. Once, when I was looking at some books in a store widow, I was suddenly pushed through the plate-glass window. This was at a bookstore on the corner of the Waalstraat and Zuider Amstellaan (the same one where Otto Frank bought Anne Frank her first diary). The kids who had pushed me ran away laughing and yelling "Jew" and we had to pay for the damage. My head bled profusely but healed quickly, but I remember the humiliation and the anger.

Before the wearing of the star became mandatory, I had always enjoyed school and was a very good student, although often naughty. After we were singled out as pariahs, school became a torture. The first day I had to wear my star, one of my classmates, who lived in the Lekstraat and with whom I often walked to school and who, I thought, had been my friend, said loudly in class so that everyone in class could hear: "*Keep away from me, you dirty Jew-bastard*". One of the teachers severely rebuked and removed him from the class for half an hour, for using the word *"bastard"*. That wasn't done in civilized Dutch society. His remark on my Jewish uncleanliness was of no importance. We suffered also a lot of abuse at the hands of some our schoolmates who came from Nazi families and often wore their khaki *"Jeugdstorm"* uniforms to school. They were constantly punching and pushing us; tripping us up, and spitting on us, tearing up our schoolbooks and generally making our lives miserable. The teachers did not interfere. Was it indifference? Was it fear?

It was actually a relief when the day came that I had to leave the Vondelschool because all Jews were to be concentrated in separate schools. I now went to a school for Jews only—the Michel de Clerq school, located adjacent to the Vondelschool in the Jekerstraat. We all felt actually better about being there after a very short time. We were among fellow sufferers who were all equally baffled in understanding the reason for our plight. I quickly acquired a large bunch of nice friends, Bobby Winnik, Sjakie Paes, Paul Frank, Joop and Bobbie Montezinos, Henny Klein, Fifi Parser, Jossie Pereira and others whose names I can't remember. All were Jewish, all had to wear stars, all in the same boat. It was a bright and unruly bunch and we gave our poor Jewish teachers a tough time. Some of the strange and disturbing events were the periodical disappearances of some of our classmates. No explanation was ever given to the remaining pupils by the teachers. We never talked about it amongst ourselves. We just made believe that this was some natural thing. We all knew it wasn't, but none of us knew exactly what it all meant and what "deportation" or "going into hiding" signified. Except for a few, most of us didn't know or understand about concentration camps and therefore were not really afraid of what would happen when one went to the transit camp in Westerbork. The teachers never talked about any of this with us. When, at the start of the school-day, attendance was taken by calling out names, the teacher would just look up for a moment when there was no answer and gaze at us. Then he or she would mark their attendance ledger and continue reading names. When I told my parents that someone we knew didn't come to school, they usually gave some noncommittal answer such as *"Oh you'll see them again"* or *"They must have gone away on vacation"*. In fact, they themselves did not want to believe the horrible and terrifying stories which were going around in the grownup world and of which we, their children, heard only snatches.

Even if they understood what was planned for us Jews, how could they tell us about it—about what might be the fate awaiting us all? Can you believe or tell your kids that you all will be shot or gassed? This attitude of denial is not so strange. People never want to know or to accept that the worst is going to happen or believe that it will happen to them. Even if such things did happen, it was done to someone else and somewhere else, in backward and antisemitic Poland or the Baltic states or barbaric Germany for instance. It just couldn't happen here in civilized Holland. The Dutch would never allow it. They were far too civilized.

I am reminded here of the story of the Jews in Eli Wiesel's [1] small town, who didn't believe the tales of the sole survivor of a massacre in another town and ridiculed him. It was too beastly, too ghastly and inhumane to contemplate. Human beings didn't do such things. But they soon found out that Germans and

Humans had only 4 letters in common, that they did perform the beastly, ghastly and inhumane acts and the people of Wiesel's village lost their lives as a result of their disbelief and innocence.

What happened to all my classmates? Where did they disappear to? Why did they have to go? Where is pretty curly-haired Fifi Parser and my beautiful, wild, blond Anita; what happened to tall, buck-toothed and pigtailed Henny Klein? To Bobby Winnik? To Sjakie? I can tell you where they went. Up in the sky!. Fodder for the ovens of the German extermination machines which were built to protect Die Deutsche Kultur (The German culture)! The gold from their and their parents' teeth to German accounts in Swiss banks! Their hair used in blankets and insulation! Little lovely, vibrant innocent kids. My great and wonderful schoolmates.

PART 3—A LESSON FOR US "JEWBOYS"

In late 1940 and in1941, small groups of members of the *NSB* [Dutch Nazi party], often roamed the streets harassing Jews and damaging Jewish property. The NSB members were mostly lower class people with limited education. They were disliked and feared by many of the ordinary Dutch population because of their coarse behavior and their movement recruited many younger kids who became members of the *Jeugdstorm, (Youth Storm)* which was the Dutch equivalent of the Hitler Jugend in Germany. They all loved marching like their German counterparts and were extremely proud of their uniforms and merit badges, which were given out for the smallest efforts—such as "protecting" property against Jews. In the beginning they mainly attacked and damaged stores which belonged to Jews, but in 1941 many Jews became targets for harassment because of the yellow Star of David with the word *"Jood (Jew)"* which we were forced to wear. Calling names, pushing, shoving or beating became their trade mark. And their way of having fun and showing their superiority. This happened all over Amsterdam and probably in the provinces as well. I didn't know much of what went on in other parts of the city or the country, except through rumors. Grown-ups generally didn't talk about it when children were present. When the street attacks began to occur more frequently in our area, I was seldom allowed outside our area on my own and was usually brought or taken by an adult to my friends who lived nearby. Often, when we knew that some of those groups were in the area, I just stayed at home.

The infamous propaganda posters of the "Eternal Jew" were by now plastered all over Amsterdam. They showed an ugly, scowling, hook-nosed old man with a skull cap, and a star of David carved on his forehead. Sometimes he was depicted with devil's horns and sometimes the horns were drawn on by graffiti artists. Another poster depicted a big, fat, hook-nosed, cigar smoking man in a fur coat paying some poor—looking individual, who was accompanied by an emaciated wife and hungry looking children, a few pennies for slave work they had done. The man looked at his watch which had a Star of David on it and said something derogatory—I don't remember what the slogan said. Anti-Semitic slogans were also chalked on walls, sidewalks and bulletin boards by young Nazis, especially near places where Jews were known to live, near synagogues and close to our school. Jewish shop windows were a favorite target for those notices. I physically cowered and my stomach tensed up when I had to go past those pictures and notices. By now the Nazi propaganda had convinced me that I was a dirty Jew first of all and not even a real Dutchman. After a while I became convinced too that I looked somewhat like the old man in the skull cap and all the other caricatures who were Jewish like me, and I was ashamed of belonging to such an ugly people.

Many years later I was shocked and dismayed to find the exact replica of the eternal Jew on the front page of a newspaper which was printed and distributed by an ultra-right religious prayer group at the University of Nebraska in Lincoln where I was on the faculty. I immediately complained about this to our administration but Dr. Martin Massengale, who was the chancellor of the University at the time, didn't think it was even worthwhile to issue a condemnation. Several of the righteous and religious colleagues in my department scoffed at the fuss I made over this incident. So much for what the world has learned from all that has happened—including some of our, so-called enlightened, intelligent academics!

Sometimes groups of young hoodlums not affiliated directly, but wanting to imitate the Nazi boys took encouragement from the Nazi groups and the indifference of their upright Dutch parents. Those youngsters went out to do their own bit of mischief and to show that they were also good Aryans. In the beginning they didn't do much more than yelling: *"Hey dirty Jew, get of the street"*, or other "slogans" which ridiculed or insulted us or our parents, but sometimes they became physical and pushing us into the road or threw things at anyone wearing the Jew's star. There was little restraint by the general public, the Dutch police or the German authorities and they became more daring as time went on and the harassment often got out of hand, especially if a victim of the abuse tried to defend himself or got some friends to help him. Jewish kids and older people were singled out by the younger Nazis because they were easier targets. They would be pushed, kicked or beaten, sometimes quite severely. Some of the more severe attacks were reported to the police, but little was done about them and it certainly didn't merit a mention in the newspapers. Only when someone resisted and hit back successfully, would an article appear in the paper, condemning the "unprovoked" attack by the mean Jews on the poor Aryans.

I will never forget the day of the beating I received. It was in March or April of 1942. Three of us boys were walking home together after school. We had just come out of the school building and were walking up the street toward the Merwede square when four big boys appeared from around the corner. I suppose that they were about fifteen to seventeen years old. They had apparently been waiting for our school period to end. Two of them wore the uniform of the Jeugdstorm. When we saw them, we turned around and ran away to get home another way, but our path was cut off by two other boys. They yelled to each other: *"Hold the Jews and teach them a lesson"* and *"Stop them"*. They grabbed us and pushed us into a recessed hallway in one of the apartment blocks. We yelled for help but none came. It was fairly dark in the hallway. We could not escape because they were bigger than we were and there were six of them. They were calling us Dirty Jew and other names and cursing our parents and they said that they were going to kill us right then and there:

"Dirty Jews (Vuile Joden), you are going to get it" one of the uniformed ones told me. *"We will clean Holland of you dirty rats and teach you a lesson."*

We continued to yell for help and try to defend ourselves, but in vain. They started punching us with their fists in the face and stomach. Two boys held Bobby's arms and a third pulled his pants and underpants down and they jeered and laughed at his circumcised penis. Bobby tried to pinch his legs together, but they forced them apart and one of them pinched his penis between his nails, drawing blood, and then took his scrotum and squeezed his testicles very hard. The poor boy was howling with fright ans pain. They hit him in his face and told him to shut up, kneed him in the groin and left him crumpled, twisting and sobbing on the floor. When he tried to crawl away they kicked him again and told him to stay there and keep quiet. He stifled his wails and laid there sobbing and tried to cover his nakedness while they kicked him. The two of us, Sjakie and me, continued yelling for help and struggling as they tried to shut us up by beating and kicking us wherever they could. They hit us in the face and in the belly and they slammed our heads against the brick wall and the wooden apartment doors. All the time they were insisting that they were going to kill us.

Finally one of the doors opened and a woman's face peered out to see what was going on. When she saw the Nazi uniforms the door closed again. There would be no help from her. Two or three bystanders had gathered to see what the commotion was about but no one interfered because these were big kids in Nazi uniforms who were doing the mischief, and people did not interfere with the Nazis unless they wanted trouble. One seemed to be wanting to interfere, but was held back by one of the others. One bystander just stood there with a smirk on his face, clearly enjoying the spectacle. I'll never forget that smirking face. Oh, how much would I have given to punch that face into a bloody mass.

The bullies tried to pull Sjakie's pants down. They didn't succeed because he was wiry and very strong and he managed to lash out and hit one of the bullies, drawing blood with his nails. The boy was furious and took Sjakie's hand and bent his fingers back, forced him on his knees and made him lick his shoes *"Clean my shoes, you filthy pig"*. Then something awful happened which I could never imagine being a witness to and certainly had never imagined. While two of his buddies held Sjakie on his knees, this boy opened his fly took out his erect penis and pulled the foreskin back, took Sjakie by his hair and forced Sjakie to kiss his penis. *"Kiss my prig,"* he ordered. Sjakie didn't and the boy pushed his face hard against his penis; he was apparently very much aroused and suddenly ejaculated over Sjakie's face and then Sjakie threw up over the boy's uniform. That angered the bully even more and he bent Sjakie's fingers back until they broke. I'll never forget the sound of that crack over all the other noises and I'll never forget Sjakie's high-pitched, god-awful, horrible scream "Aaw…Aaw…Aaaaa…ww". But the scream frightened the bullies apparently for they suddenly stopped their onslaught and ran away giggling and laughing.

During all this time none of the grownups had come to help us. Only after the boys left, did one of them take pity on sobbing Sjakie and Bobby and helped them to get up. I am not clear about what happened next. I pulled myself together, staggered out of the hallway and ran home, crying, with a bloodied face and mouth, bleeding knees and torn clothes. I was very angry and felt humiliated and ashamed that I had been unable to defend myself better. I don't think any of us felt the pain of the bruises, except Sjakie with his broken fingers. I ran straight up to my room and wept angrily and uncontrollably on my bed. My mother came and saw my bloody face, broken tooth and torn clothes and I haltingly told her what had happened and she started crying too and tried to hold me in her arms, but that made me even angrier. I shouted at her to leave me alone and struggled free of her embrace. I know that I wasn't really angry at her but I just didn't want her to be sad and to cry for me. Her sorrow was making me angry at

myself for having taken that beating and making her cry, for not being bigger and stronger like the heroes in my adventure books and the movies, so that I could have beaten those bastards to a pulp, swept the pavement with them and have them scream for mercy when I broke **their** fingers. For a long time afterward I used to squirm and ball my fists in frustration whenever I remembered. I have always wondered what the grownups who witnessed this disgusting spectacle were thinking and feeling and how they later felt about themselves for standing by and doing nothing. How could they justify their indifference? What were their excuses?

I later discovered that I was also angry because I felt guilty. But it wasn't only because I couldn't beat those guys. I now think that I was glad that it wasn't me who was forced to my knees and that someone else's fingers were broken.

After that day, parents of other kids in our school became organized so that at least one grownup was always present when we walked to and from school. Later in 1942 that became also dangerous for them, because people could be arrested at any time if they were caught out on the streets without a special exemption pass (Ausweiss). But by that time my parents and I had already gone into hiding.

PART 4—ANITA GRÜNEWALD

This is the way I remember her—the most beautiful girl in the world with a mop of long, wavy and often unruly blond hair and a laughing, freckled, oval face. I loved Anita Grünewald, this classmate of mine with a real deep young boy's love. She is only a memory now, but still an amazingly vivid one. I can so clearly see her skipping rope with her girlfriends in front of our school, her skirt and hair going up with every hop, and singing (with a German accent) *"Mijn man die vaart op zee, al met de marine mee [My man he is at sea, serving with the marines]"*. I close my eyes and can see the two of us climbing trees in the park and I can still feel us sitting together in my dad's big chair near the fireplace in our living room, listening to a radio program, arms around each other. I can see us wrestling on the deep-shag carpet in our living room, that determined-to-win face of hers, with the blond hair partly covering in her face and tickling mine. She was pretty strong and sometimes won her matches, especially when she managed to get a hand free to tickle me. I will never forget her. She was my classmate at the Michel de Clerq school in Amsterdam, which we both attended after the Germans ordered the segregation of all the public schools in order to cleanse them of Jews.

Her full name was Anita Maria Grünewald, born on the 7th of February, 1931 in Duisburg, Germany. She had arrived in Amsterdam with her family sometime after Hitler came to power in Germany, and came to my class during 1941. I don't remember ever meeting her father. I remember her mother and her older sister, Lieselotte, or Lies as we called her. They were all tall, beautiful, blond people—the real ideal Aryan type. Nothing like the ugly, swarthy, evil looking Eternal Jew depicted by the German and Dutch Nazi propaganda posters. But they were Jewish and therefore somehow inferior.

She was a few months older than I was and she never let me forget it, but I was so in love that I didn't mind. We were inseparable outside of school. In school there existed, of course, a voluntary segregation between boys and girls. The girls had their games and the boys played theirs and teased the girls. Because of her German accent and shaky grammar, which I found very cute, Anita was sometimes the butt of some teasing although there were quite a number of children from families who had fled the Nazis living in the neighborhood. Anne Frank's family was one of those. Sometimes the teasing was rather cruel, such as: *"Why don't you go back to Germany—we've got enough Germans here in Holland."* [It sounds much worse in Dutch]. When that happened I always protected her fiercely and defended or revenged the honor of my little goddess. A torn shirt, scraped knees or knuckles or a scratched face were the result of a fight and I displayed those "medals" proudly. My mother always shook her head, but with a smile, when I came home messed up after such a fight and told her what had happened. Nearly every day after school I would walk Anita home, sometimes I would eat at her home, which was one block from Anne Frank's home, sometimes she ate at mine. We would then sit together and do our homework. We lived less than a 15-minute walk apart and I could run it in half that time. After we finished homework, and weather permitting, we would go out and roam the riverside or the parks, at least those we were still allowed to enter after we had to wear our stars. We tried to catch fish, or row or sail my canoe on the Amstel river—until that was forbidden to us Jews too. Then we played games such as chess or monopoly, or we read books together. Other times we went to see friends or went to see a movie, when Jews were still allowed in certain theaters. At times I slept over at her house or she slept over at mine. Sometimes we even fell asleep with our arms around each other on the couch in the living room.

We understood each other so well that we didn't have to talk very much. We were like one mind with two bodies, one male one female, but sex didn't enter at all into our relationship. I don't remember exchanging many kisses, although we did walk hand-in-hand and with our arms around each other. The kisses we did give each other were only pecks on the cheeks. Kissing on the lips was unthinkable then for kids in our age group. We would have said "Yech" had anyone suggested we do such a thing. We often went for walks along the Amstel river, picked up acorns and polished them for making a necklace, or we collected flat stones for skipping over the water. Sometimes we both would break into a run at the same time to get to a clump of trees and start climbing. We'd try to outrun each other and reach the tree or a bench and sit together holding hands. We didn't have to look at what the other was doing. We often read books together at the table in my house or while snuggled in my dad's chair. In the beginning I read faster and would wait for her to finish, but later we would finish reading the page nearly together and turn to the next one. Quite often she asked me to read to her—I was a good reader and used intonations well. I loved helping her with her homework—she did have a bit of difficulty because of the language and it made me feel very important in her life. It seemed that we always knew what the other was thinking and feeling. I have never been so close with anyone since. It must be similar to that special something which identical twins feel.

There was no doubt in our minds that we were going to be married when we grew up. I used to say to her, especially after she had been teased by other kids: *"Don't worry, I will always take care of you and we will be married when I make enough money."* She would smile as if she knew better (she was definitely more mature than I was) and say: *"Oh Louis, I know—I love you very much and always want to be with you"*

I will give you an example to show you how naive I was in those days. One day my mother had taken us both to see a matinee of a fairy tale movie and in that movie, I can't remember the name, the hero had knelt and asked the king for the hand of the princess in marriage. That was at the time in 1941 when Jews were still allowed in movie houses or maybe it was one of those "for Jews only" places. Anyway I thought that this scene was beautiful and I sure wanted to emulate that prince. When we brought Anita home, I did just like the hero in the movie and asked Mrs. Grünewald: *"Mrs. Grünewald, will you allow me to marry your daughter because we love each other and want to be together forever".* Both my mother and Mrs. Grunewald looked at each other and burst into tears when I said that. They stood together and held each other and us for several moments and then hugged both of us again. I did not understand why they acted like that. I asked: *"What did I say?"* Then I turned to Anita and asked again *"What happened to them?".* She didn't answer immediately and I continued to look at her with a question in my eyes. She regarded at me with a look which I could not understand and put her finger to her lips, came over and hugged me hard and long and kissed me on the cheek. She apparently knew more than I did but she couldn't or wouldn't tell me what it was.

Then fateful day when she disappeared from my life is still one of the worst I can remember. I had come home from school after walking her to her house which was about two blocks from school. The weather was drizzly, typical Dutch late fall weather, and I had stayed at home that afternoon to do my homework. When I had finished, the weather had cleared a bit. My mother sent me to a store and so I did not go to Anita's home immediately. It was later in the afternoon, about 5:30, when I came to her house. As usual, I bounded up the outside stairs and rang the bell but there was no answer. I didn't see a tape or sticker on the door, indicating that they had been taken away by the Germans. There was a note on the door but it was too dark in the vestibule to read what was written; the light bulbs had been removed because of the blackout. Something panicked inside me; I felt that there was something very wrong and I pounded the door and rang again and again. I yelled and screamed her name over and over: *"ANITA,   ANITA,   WHERE   ARE   YOU—OPEN   UP—IT'S ME—PLEASE......OPEN THE DOOR"*. Then, a neighbor lady poked her head out of her door. She said: *"Go home quick, kid. I think that the Grünewalds were picked up this afternoon by the German police. Go quick, before they pick you up too, because they will probably be back."*. Then she closed the door quickly.

I stood there, stunned, paralyzed, speechless. Even today I can feel the horror and pain of that one moment. I don't remember how I reached home. I was crying bitterly, deep sobbing cries, tears were running down my face; I was shaking with anger and pain of losing her, losing this girl friend who had become such an important part of me. Next day, she wasn't at school. I was inconsolable for many days. There was nothing my parents or Oma Francine could do for me. I felt very guilty and was furious with myself because I had been unable to protect her. I told myself that I should have taken her home with me that afternoon and thus protected her from deportation. But I wasn't there when she needed me. The Nazis had taken one half of me away. Actually, they might have gone into hiding without telling me, but that never occurred to me. If they did, they were somehow picked up and transported to Sobibor via Westerbork. Even today, after so many years my heart still aches, and I still pray that she did not suffer too much in that concentration camp where she was taken together with her mother and sister.

After the war I searched for her but never found her nor any news about her. For a long time I lived with the hope that she would be alive, somewhere in Europe, married, with children and that she was doing well. I never forgot her and finally, in 1993, when I mustered the courage and felt the need to visit the infamous transfer camp in Westerbork in the north of the Netherlands, I received my answer. I came there with my wife, Rose, and two good friends who lived in Wildervank, a small town in the province of Groningen. I asked to see the records. I wanted to look for the names of members of my family and see if Anita's was there too. I found them all in the records and I found when and where they had been murdered. There were Anita's name and those of her mother and sister. They had passed through Westerbork and were exterminated in the Sobibor concentration camp in 1943.

I pointed my finger at her name and uttered something like:'There she is, that is her—oh my God" and then I broke down and cried bitterly just as I had cried when I was ten years old. Sorrow and anger and guilt is what I felt again. Why did I survive and not she? Thank God for my dear wife Rose and my wonderful friends, who were with me to cry with me and share a little of my pain. I still feel this terrible loss when rewriting and rereading this—sometimes I do lose it and break down in the solitude of my little office in the basement at home. Part of me must have died that day when I lost her. Sixty years later I still cannot forget her; it still hurts and I still don't understand the reason for it all. Why? What had this lively, wonderful girl done to the German and the Dutch people that she had to be dehumanized through incarceration, inhumane transport, and then to be tortured and murdered in Sobibor together with her mother and sister on the 11th of June, 1943?

What torures and misery she went through! The world stood by and let this happen to her. The German people had the gall to say: *"Wir haben es nicht gewust* [We did not know]". But with few exceptions, they all cheered their Fuhrer on with their arms raised when he told them what he was going to do to the Jews and cheered the SS guards when they drove the Jews out of their houses so they themselves could move in and steal their property. The boys and girls who stood along the railway tracks when the cattle trains with their human contents passed—they knew. They laughed and made the sign with their hands as if they were cutting their throats. They all knew! And you know—I still get this pain inside me when I read Anita's name in the book "In Memoriam" which contains the names of all the Dutch Jews who perished in the Holocaust.

PART 5—WE LEAVE AMSTERDAM

One day, the time had apparently arrived for us to leave Amsterdam. For the last several months I'd had an inkling that something was in the wind. Three or four months earlier, I can't remember when exactly, my father had been taken to a "work camp" in Ommen in the eastern part of the country. My mother explained to me at the time, that he was working there, because first he lost his job when the Nazis took over the company he worked for and then he had also been laid off from the bakery where he had worked temporarily, because the bakery was taken over by the Nazis also. He went to the camp because he was promised "financial support for the family"—or so he was told. While dad was gone, friends and acquaintances of my parents had been visiting our house and had departed with packages and boxes and even some of our best furniture pieces. My mother told me that we would be going on a long trip and that people were going to keep those things for us until we came back. She swore me to secrecy and, surprisingly, I didn't tell any of my friends. Most of our beautiful antique furniture pieces, special antique dishes, the fabulous carved armoire, which I loved, and the thick Persian carpet, all of which I remember to this day, went to neighbors around the corner in the Trompenburger Straat. Their name was Koster, and Mrs. Ada Koster was a good friend of my mother's. At least that was what my mother thought. After the war the Koster family denied ever having received anything from us, although I had seen the furniture and dishes in their house. They didn't even let me, my uncle and a detective from the police department into the house. We didn't expect to have to produce a warrant for our former friends. Before I and my guardians could make a legal issue out of it and unbeknownst to us, they had already made preparations to emigrate to Canada. But we didn't know that at the time and when we came back to the house a few weeks later with a warrant they had gone. The older Kosters are probably dead by now and I wonder if their heirs ever realized where all those beautiful things came from.

It was on a warm, sunny day in May or June 1942 that my teacher, Mr. Beuzemaker, received a note from the headmaster after morning recess. He read it and told me to take my books and papers and meet someone in the hallway. With some trepidation I went out of the class and into the hallway. There stood a gentleman who had come in after morning recess and when we met he showed me a note from my mother in which she wrote that I should go with him to meet her and do as he would tell me. He was a friendly looking gentleman and I didn't hesitate to go with him. He took my hand and we walked out of the school and into the street. He led me into a dark hallway of an apartment building and told me to remove my jacket quickly. I did as he asked and he gave me one of my other jackets from home to wear. This jacket did not have the star of David on it and I had never worn it on the street. We left my old jacket behind and started walking away from the school. He told me to call him "*Oom*" (Uncle). He also told me his name, in case we were stopped by police and they asked me who he was. He also gave me a name to tell police if we were stopped. I have by now forgotten what it was and I had also forgotten his name until many years after the war, when I was reminded of it while talking to Karel Brouwer. We walked to a trolley stop and took trolley line 25 to the Amstel station, a railroad station in the south of Amsterdam, not far from where we lived.

By then, Jews were not allowed to travel on any type of public transport and I felt very conspicuous going into the station and waiting there while Oom bought tickets. I didn't dare look around and I felt as if people were watching me and that everyone knew that I should be wearing a star, because I was one of "them" on those posters. Since we were not far from my home, I was very afraid that I would meet someone who knew me. A Jew, found on the street without a star, would be in a lot of trouble. After my guardian bought the tickets we had to go through the ticket control gate, where one member of the Dutch Black Police and a German *Grüne Polizei* (Green Police), armed with a submachine gun (a Schmeisser), were stationed and were checking the identity papers from anyone who looked suspicious in their eyes. I though that I would die going past them, holding Oom's hand, but they let us through. Would they change their minds and call after us? By then I was shaking from fear and Uncle could feel it and took me into the station's restaurant, where he bought me a cold chocolate drink to calm me down while we waited for our train. He was a friendly, bespectacled and elderly in a long brown coat and he sported a little grey mustache, similar to the one Hitler had. He kept me talking by asking questions about what I had learned this morning at school and what books I liked to read. We both had read Karl May so we could talk about the books and time went by fast.

When the train's arrival was announced, we walked to the platform, where more police were patrolling, as well as some people in civilian clothing who stood talking to them. They probably were Gestapo (German Secret Service) looking for wanted or suspicious persons. We were never challenged although my heart was beating so loud in my chest that I was afraid everyone could hear it. After a few minutes, which seemed like eternity, the train came; we boarded it and were soon on our way. In the beginning I didn't know where we were going, but it soon became clear that we were going toward Amersfoort, where my mother's sister and her family had lived and where I had often visited them. They were still there at that time because they had not yet gone into hiding. During the trip Uncle asked some more about the books I had read and since I was an avid reader, I could tell him about them and so I became quite relaxed.

I never saw any of my schoolmates again after the day I left Amsterdam. I am, as far as I have been able to ascertain until this writing, the lone survivor of that whole class of about 20 to 30 wonderful kids, and it is a terribly lonely feeling even today, whenever I think of them. There will never be a class reunion for us. Their faces are so clear to me. They became fodder for the grandiose super-efficient German extermination machine and the *Deutsche Übermensch Kultur* (German Superman Culture) which still appears to be alive and well today in many parts of that society.

Photographs

The "Mijlpaal" during WWII
My "room" was in the attic in front of the little window
and on top of the water tank.
The master bedroom is below and the sitting/dining room
is on the groundfloor

My mother and me in 1940

My father in May 1942. Photo taken in Arbeitslager Ommen (Workcamp Ommen)——part of a Nazi propaganda photo to show how well people were treated.

Sunday in Camp Ommen in May 1942—No survivors
Nazi propaganda photo. My father is third from left on the bottom row

An often seen Nazi Poster

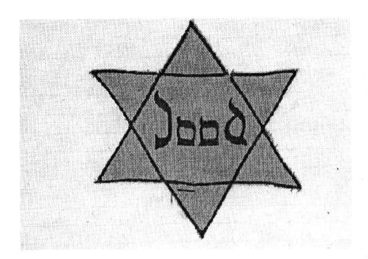

The Dutch Jew's Star of David which was to be worn
on all outer clothing—not wearing it resulted in severe penalties
and generally lead to direct transportation to the death camps.

A typical Nazi Cartoon depicting Jews in newspapers and on posters

Satanic Symbol

Nazi poster from the Netherlands depicting "the Eternal Jew"
This photograph, with the subtitle, was used in the
"UNL Good News——a Conservative Christian Newsletter"
issue of October 1988. On this photograph
one can still see where the star of David on the forehead was erased
by the publisher of this rag, indicating that they were cognizant
of its Nazi origin and anti-Semitic nature but were a bit "sensitive" about
publishing it in its original form

Leusden's Town Hall in Hamersveldt ca. 1944.
Karel Brouwer was the second highest county official here.
Many illegal actions with ID-cards took place here.

Sietske Hoekstra
The nun who saved the little boy from Aalten
by hiding him under her nun's habit

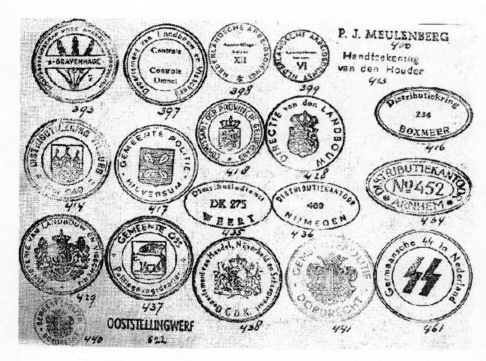

Some of the many stamps which often had to be falsified by
the Underground workers, such as those in Karel Brouwer's house.
Most of the stamps in the picture above were issued by municipalities on
ID cards belonging to people who, supposedly, lived in that location.
The stamp in the lower left is from the "German SS in the Netherlands".
Above it is a stamp of the office which distributed ration cards and
identity cards in the city of Arnhem.

De eerste deportatietreinen vertrokken
vanuit Hooghalen

The first deportation-train from Westerbork in 1942——my parents may
have been on that transport? These first ones were not cattle cars.

Kort voor het vertrek uit het
kamp Westerbork

Shortly before departure from Westerbork (transl)
These were the infamous cattle cars

A woman collecting food during The Hunger Winter of 1944–45
Note that he bicycle she is pushing does not have any tires—
those were only available to Germans and Dutch Nazis.
This photograph was apparently taken on an exceptionally
nice day because that winter was one of extremely cold and
miserable weather conditions.

A non-Jewish victim of the German occupation of the Netherlands
The little boy, inadequately dressed for the winter is out begging
for food on the streets of Amsterdam. This was a common and very
painful sight during the Hunger Winter of 1944–45.
It was repeated all over the still occupied part of the country.
Note the shoes, which are too big, the lack of socks
the short pants and the woeful expression on his little face.

Chapter 6
HIDING IN HOEVELAKEN

PART 1—ARRIVAL

During the trip from Amsterdam to Amersfoort Oom engaged me into conversation, but I was still a bit tense and during that trip and thus I didn't talk too much about the books and other things we talked about. I was a bit too preoccupied with my situation despite Oom's well-meaning efforts. I was afraid that at any moment a person in uniform or black boots would come over to us and ask for our papers. The dreaded ticket inspection happened only once during the trip, and we arrived safely in Amersfoort. We got off the train and had to walk a long way to the exit where a number of Dutch police and German soldiers were posted. I immediately suspected that they were waiting for me. I would have run away if Oom had not grabbed me by the shoulder and steered me calmly through the control area. He showed the police a badge [it turned out later that he was actually a plain-clothes detective in the Amersfoort police] and one of them even saluted him and we walked to the bicycle rack where he had parked his bike that morning. He calmly unlocked his bike and I told me to get on the luggage carrier, which had been padded with a rubber covered pillow, put my feet on two extensions for extra riders [those were required by law]......And off we went. I had no idea where to, but I was so glad to be away from that train station and all the police that I didn't worry about that.

"*Je ziet, alles is in orde Loek* [You see, everything is OK, Lou]", Oom Piet said. He was so calm and gave me so much confidence that I really relaxed. In those days in the Netherlands, and even today, the bicycle was a normal mode of travel so it did not arouse any suspicion to see a man with a child on a bicycle. Still, I felt a twinge of fear knotting my stomach whenever I saw a policeman or a person with leather boots. Boots were favorite apparel with the Dutch Nazis, who tried to copy their German masters as much as possible.

We rode through the old city, through the Langestraat, where my uncle and aunt's bakery and pastry shop used to be. It had been closed by the Nazis. We rode past the social club, Concordia, where I had played in the past, with Rita Brouwer's youngest sister, Greetje de Vooght, and out through the lovely old city gate, the Kamperbinnenpoort. We continued toward the east and then suddenly there were no more houses. We had gone through the city and we were in farm country. The weather was nice, sunny and cool, the grass a deep green. Black-and-white cows, fluffy sheep and brown-and-black horses were grazing in the narrow strips of pasture land which were separated by small, straight intersecting drainage canals. Crows, magpies and an occasional heron were busy gathering food for their families. We rode past beautiful farmhouses, topped by red tiled or brownish-yellow thatched roofs, with big oaks and weeping willows in front and flower boxes in the windows. By now I was relaxing and enjoying the ride and had lost most of my fear and tension. Then I noticed two cows doing something I had not seen before. One was on top of the other with her front legs over the rear of the other. What a strange thing. I said : *"Did you see those cows, Oom? What were they doing?"*

Ome Piet did hesitate a moment and then said:

"They are in heat and one of them needs the bull"

"Why? What for?"

"Well, you'd better ask your Mamma. I have to watch where we are going and don't have time to explain because I think that we are nearly there."

As he said that we turned off the main road near a village called Hoevelaken and onto a country road. After a few kilometers, during which we turned several times right and left, we came to a small farmhouse with a thatched roof. Ome stopped the bike and let me get off. He said:

"We have arrived. Your mother is inside waiting; go see her".

I jumped off and ran towards the front door but he called me back and told me to go to the side door because the front door was used only for important visitors on Sundays. There is a lesson to be learned every day! Before I went inside I looked to see if Oom was coming in too, but he had turned his bicycle around and was pedaling away already. I rushed through the side door and found my mother, pale and worried, inside. She cried and we kissed and held each other as if we hadn't seen each other for a long time, although we'd been together that same morning before I went to school. A lot had happened in those few hours and it had seemed ages to both of us. She had arrived early in the morning with a lot of luggage, which included some new books for me from Oma Francine.

When I did ask my mother later about the bull and being in heat she did not give me a very satisfactory answer but I was too tired from the day's adventures to insist. She did talk to me about our new situation and made it very clear that I should do nothing to make any of the farmer's family angry at me, to do everything they said at all times and to help them because they were taking a great risk by hiding us from the Germans. Mother said to me:

"If they ask you to do something for them or to help them with anything, you must do it. They are angels to help us hide. Will you promise, Loek?"

"Of course Mammy, will the farmer let me go to the horses and the cows?"

"You will have to ask him first, OK?"

She also said that Pappie might be here soon and that until then I could sleep with her. That was a wonderful first night in the warm bed with my mother. It was the first time, at least that I could remember, that I had ever been in the same bed with her. We talked in whispers about the other family members, Oma Francine and Oma and Opa ten Bosch, Uncles and Aunts; about Menno, Berthie and Hettie, my first cousins and about all the other relatives. When would we see them again and visit them? And of course I cried again about Anita Grünewald and where she might be now. About Paul Frank and other classmates and how long we were supposed to stay in hiding and......Many more things we discussed, but we were both exhausted from the adventures of the day, and I fell asleep, nestled safely in her arms.

The very next day, at about eight o'clock in the morning a face poked around the corner in our eating area and asked for a morsel of food in a plaintive voice, paraphrasing one of my Charles Dickens books: *"Please good people, would you have a crust of bread for a hungry man?"* He grinned in his old grin. *"Max—Pappie"* Mother an I both cried together and ran to him and hugged him. All of us were crying from pure joy and relief. We hadn't seen him for several months. He had escaped from the labor camp in Dalfsen and had traveled on foot and by bike through the nights to reach us. He looked tanned and tough, but thinner, older and greyer than a few months ago when I had seen him last, but for the rest he was my old Pappie, with jokes and games and stories. Henceforth, I slept in my own quarters which were located on "the hilt" above the cows, behind stacked sheaves of straw and stacked hay. The straw was used for bedding for the cows which lived below me under the planked storage area. I had to climb up on a ladder. It was warm, cozy and a bit smelly, but after a few hours I did not notice the smell anymore. My mother did though. She wrinkled her nose every time I came close to her and teased me that I smelled like a farm boy.

It was fairly dark in my sleeping area. The only light came through a small dirt covered window in the thatched roof. I could read only with the window open, which was fine as long as it didn't rain. But reading inside was difficult anyway when outside there were all those wonderful things to see and experience on the farm: the animals, machines, the green fields, the crops and the vegetable garden and the water in the canals which were teeming with frogs, tadpoles and fish. So it took very little encouragement from the farmer to make me leave my books and go outside with him to look at something interesting or to help him.

The first time I saw him he made a great impression on me. He was chewing a big wad of tobacco, which gave his thin face a very lopsided look, he was unshaven, in dirty, smelly clothes and a bit bent over. He was a lot taller than my father—so he was very tall to me. He totally astonished me when he spat an great gob of brown liquid to an enormous distance. I had never seen anyone spit like that. The boys at school used to have spitting contests standing on the canal bridges in Amsterdam and there were some real champions, but that far......never......At that moment he gained a lot of respect in my eyes. When I told my mother about it she shivered and my dad roared with laughter until he encountered a warning glare from my mother.

PART 2—LIFE ON THE FARM

I enjoyed accompanying the farmer on his daily routines. He was a bit gruff and poorly educated and more ignorant about the outside world than I was. He had seldom been in any of the big cities in the Netherlands, which astonished me. He was very religious and would talk in a way that I had not heard except on the Sunday church-radio programs. He invoked the Lord, Jesus Christ, the Holy Ghost and Mother Mary frequently. I didn't understand this Holy Ghost business and I decided that I'd better not ask about that. I did ask my mother once but her information wasn't very helpful. I don't think that she understood the concept of three gods in one herself. As it turned out later, this farmer did not take us in wholly out of the goodness of his heart or out of religious conviction, but because he was poor and needed money.

I helped him with all kinds of chores around the farm, such as bringing in feed for the cattle, cleaning out the cow manure from the milking stable and spreading it on the field. I often smelled of manure, something my mother didn't like at all, but I wanted to help and my helping was something we could do for the farmer. It also kept me, an active kid, from driving my parents nuts. They were confined to the house and came out only after it was dark enough so they could not be seen from the road or neighboring farms. If someone came I was to say that I was a far cousin from Aalten. I knew the local dialect there pretty well and so I could pass as someone from there. Since the farm and the land were rented, the farmer often went to work elsewhere. His wife and two daughters took care of the farm while he was away and I used to help them as well. The daughters were older than I was and to me they were as remote as the older girls at middle and high school in Amsterdam. The daughters were not very bashful about answering the call of nature when it came to them and would hunker down unconcernedly in the field. I was curious enough to steal a peak now and then. When one of them caught me peeking she would wag her finger at me and grin. Working together made us into a team and we got along fine. Sometimes we had wrestling matches, which they always won. I liked those encounters because they gave me a good feeling of camaraderie. We always made sure that no one could see us from the farm, because the girls said that their parents would not allow them to wrestle with boys.

I was then barely 11 years old and had experienced the usual crushes on movie stars such as Shirley Temple, Gloria Jean, Deanna Durbin, on some of my female schoolmates, and of course my girlfriend Anita. I was however very inexperienced sexually and had no idea what a woman really looked like, except from the paintings I had seen in the museums in Amsterdam and from pictures some of the older boys brought to school and showed around during recess. The porno pictures, mostly from Denmark or France, gave us boys lots of thrills and giggles, but I think that it was because it was something that was forbidden. I did enjoy hugging and kissing, but that was all. Nor did I know what my penis could be used for except doing a pee and some inklings from the dirty stories going around. In our uptight, puritanical Dutch society of those days, talk of the body and its functions was frowned upon and many parents let little kids find out by themselves about sex. On the other hand, it was not unheard-of that an "enlightened" father would take his son to a woman in the red-light district who specialized in "educating" young boys, but that happened only after they reached the age of eighteen or so. I had never had a wet dream or anything like that on the subject of the opposite sex. My dreams were mostly daydreams. At school there was no sex education of any kind and pollination of plants, with their male and female parts, was touched upon very gingerly at best. In fact, at home we each had two wash-cloths and towels. One set was used for the "uppers" and one for the "lowers". You were not supposed to mix those up!

Like most boys my age, I was of course interested in looking at those forbidden pictures of nude people, especially women and sometimes I got an erection, which was a strange experience since I didn't understand why I had one. I also woke up occasionally with a "tent" and thought that there must be something very wrong with my nether parts. That caused me to worry, but the worry disappeared when little John went limp again. When we lived in Amsterdam we boys, would sometimes go to town on a nice Saturday to eat ice cream and then wander to the red light district in central Amsterdam to see the women in the windows and maybe talk to them, but I never really figured out what it was all about. We used words only few of us understood the meaning of, but you didn't let on that you didn't know what it all meant and you didn't dare repeat them to your parents or ask about their meaning. We sometimes found used condoms in parks, but again I didn't know exactly what they were used for and I am sure there were other innocents like me among my friends. Some of us probably knew more and I knew the words for what men and women were supposed to do, but the technical intricacies were not clear to me. We just liked to see them in their professional "uniforms" in the windows. I remember that some of them were extremely well-endowed. We stood looking at them and giggled about their scantily covered breasts and thighs. Yes, I was very naive at the time but living in the same house with the two farm girls soon made me grow up and get wiser. I still remember their faces and figures. If I knew how to draw, I would be able to sketch their portraits. The oldest one, Riek, was about sixteen and solidly built with a smiling round face and light wavy blond hair, which she wore shoulder length, and I thought that she was quite pretty. She was about a head taller than I was, but then I was a little guy anyway. Riek was already out of school and worked part-time at home and part-time at the landowner's house some distance up the road. The other one, Stien, about fourteen I guess, was thinner with an oval face, and she looked more somber and serious, partly because she wore glasses which made her look a bit owlish. She was also taller than I was, but not as tall as her sister. She still went to the nearby nunnery school. The two of them also went to a special Sunday school after church. They both became regular visitors in the hayloft where I slept after we had become better acquainted and after we had wrestled with each other in the fields or the haystack. They never came together—it was always either one or the other—but sometimes, unfortunately for me, they came during the same evening when it had gone dark and I didn't get to sleep until late.

I was a virgin and very ignorant with regard to sex. I was only eleven years old then. That first evening Riek, and Stien later on that same evening, came to my sleeping place in the loft. My parents' room was upstairs at the other side of the farm house. I was sound asleep when Riek crawled over the straw to my bed and shook me awake. It was pitch dark and I didn't know what happened and was startled: *"WHA......"* I began loudly. She put her hand on my mouth and said: *"Shhh......Be quiet"* and she stuck her hand in my pyjama bottoms and felt my penis and scrotum. I was shocked and tried to pull her arm away and said "No, No I don't want that—what are you doing!" I tried to move away, but she told me to be shut up and let her do what she wanted. She slid in beside me under the sheets and kissed me on my cheek and held my penis and scrotum in her hand and fondled them. I must have overcome my fear surprisingly quickly because in a very short time I got my first erection due to the actions of a female and a strange feeling in my loins, and then I understood a bit more about the mechanics of my body. She whispered: *"Put your hand on my breast and feel my nipple but do it softly"*. She was dressed in one of those long nightgowns and it took me some time to find her breast and then her nipples and to massage them to her satisfaction. I remembered what my mother had told me that first day: *"Do whatever they tell you to do"*, and so I did, despite the strangeness and unfamiliarity of the whole situation.

I still was a bit frightened and, as a result, a bit clumsy but, since I wanted to do as I was told, I was not an unwilling pupil. Nature will have its way......Her nightgown was in the way for what she wanted me to do next so she took it off and made me kiss and lick her nipples and her belly and stroke her body. I liked touching her body and I became naturally more aroused. Her nipples became erect also, just like my penis. I asked her: *"Am I doing it right?"* And she answered: *"Yes, but use your tongue more. I will tell you what else I want you to do, and be careful with your fingers"*. Then she took my hand and directed it under the elastic of her bloomers towards her pubic area. I could feel her pubic hair, which was nice and soft, but when she opened her legs wider and made me feel her clitoris and vulva, which were moist, I pulled my hand back and said: *"Oh no"* pretty loudly. I thought she had urinated on my hand because I didn't know what that wetness was and it frightened and disgusted me. I also didn't like the way my hand smelled when I brought it up. She hissed in my ear: *"If you don't do what I tell you to do and if you tell anyone, I am going to the police tomorrow and have them pick all of you Jews up."* The tone of her words is etched in my memory and I did what she wanted.

To make a long story short, after a while it wasn't so unpleasant and strange anymore. She became more excited and started to breathe quicker and held me more tightly while, under her tutelage, I gently massaged a little knob, which I later learned was called a clitoris. She called it her "button". She started to breathe quickly and suddenly clasped her legs together tightly on my hand, her body shook several times and she groaned like: *Ahh—Ahh...Ohhh......* and then she relaxed. She roughly took my hand away and said: *"Enough, no more"*. I had absolutely no idea what had happened and wanted to kiss her breast again because I enjoyed that softness against my face but she pushed me away, put her nightgown on and disappeared after warning me again to tell no one or else......Her abrupt departure really worried me, because I thought that I had done something wrong.

I don't know how long she had been with me. Probably no more than half an hour. My penis was still erect and when I touched it. I shivered from the strange feeling which ran through me. It was like an electric current. I touched myself some more and then I suddenly jumped up because I felt dizzy and thought that I had to pee. Before I had time to run to a place to relieve myself, I ran into a body in the dark. I nearly jumped out of my skin. What a shock that was. I hadn't heard any noise because I had been moving in the straw myself and at first I thought that Riek had come back, but it was the younger sister, Stien. Her coming and the fright it gave me interrupted my run for a place to relieve myself and my urge to "pee". I didn't know yet about ejaculation. She told me to go back to my bed and laid down beside me. She was less aggressive and domineering and, although I was very tired, I was happy to have her more quiet companionship. At first we only hugged and kissed. Her kissing was different from what I had done before with Riek. She kissed me on the mouth and, though I didn't like it, thrust her tongue in my mouth and wanted me to put my tongue in hers. Again I had to learn, but she told me how to do it and I did. After all, my mother had told me so, hadn't she? Stien was also dressed in a nightgown. She said: *"You take my nightgown off and I'll take your pyjamas off"*. First she took my pyjama top off, stroked my body and kissed my chest and nipples and then, when she dropped my bottoms, she held my penis very gently.

I shivered when she touched my penis. It was still hard from its previous adventure and I still felt as if I was going to have to pee. She sensed that and said : *"I won't rub you hard and if you come, it doesn't matter"*. *"What do you mean by 'come'?"* I asked and then my world collapsed, a whirlwind took hold of me, I heard myself make a funny sound and stuff came out of me. I had ejaculated. I was crushed and so ashamed that I had "peed" on her hand, but at the same time the feeling had been so awesome, so indescribable. It was like an earthquake went up my back and down my legs and was nothing like any experience I'd ever had before. I shakingly apologized to her *"I'm so sorry......"* and started to cry. But Stien appeared unperturbed and I felt her wiping her hand on my blanket.

"Don't you know anything, silly boy? Coming means that your seed comes out of your penis. You just came" She answered *"and I don't care that you came in my hand."*

She giggled *"You are such a baby; you don't know anything yet"* and let go of my penis and hugged me tightly. That was the first time I heard that I had seed in me, and right then a few more pieces of the sex puzzle (flowers have male and female parts, don't they!) suddenly fell into place and I understood a bit more of the facts of fertilization, of sex and all the giggles and jokes I had heard at school, and of the dogs mating and the cows and the bulls and the women in the red light district. It was a revelation and I laid back utterly amazed at the realization of all these new facts. I felt good—I am a man now, I thought to myself.

I liked Stien better than her sister. She explained that she could "come" too, but that it was different for men and women. She also said that Riek had told her that I had made her come, which cleared up the "Aahhs and Ohhs" from my earlier encounter. I asked Stien: *"When you come, do you also have seed?"*. *"No, silly, women have eggs but they come out only once a month."* and she explained the facts of periods and ovulation to me, all the while stroking my body, while I was kissing her breasts and nipples, her lips, her neck and wherever she directed me. Another piece of street lore had fallen into place. There had been whispers at school from some of the more "educated" boys about so called 'monthlies' and 'bandages' which made some girls blush and others burst into tears, but I had never understood exactly what that was all about. Here in the span of two hours of one evening I was receiving quite an education. And yes, I even kissed her vulva and clitoris at her request, although I did not like the smell. During all of our later encounters they both wanted me to do that. I became used to it and after a while it was not so disgusting to me anymore and it excited both girls. I thought that as long as they were happy with me, they would not betray us to the Germans. That night while my mouth was on her clitoris, Stien started moaning and shaking too and had her orgasm. She had clamped her legs tightly together around my head and it took her a while to relax and release me.

Although they had been strictly brought up and educated at a religious girls' school by nuns, they were farm girls and had seen their animals mating and were very familiar with the sex life of animals and people. In any case Stien knew quite a bit more than I did and was willing to tell me what I wanted to know. And I was willing to learn. Now I finally learned what that erection was for and that the terrific feeling of the ejaculation was part of the relationship between a man and a woman. I wondered if my parents had done the same thing. I couldn't really visualize it, but they must have. I was born to them wasn't I?

My first ejaculation had surprised and shocked me because it had felt as if my insides were coming out. It wasn't painful, just terrifying and so surprising that first time. I was left shaking and a bit dizzy and had to take a rest. I'll never forget that first time even though I thought then that it was icky. Stien, being the farm girl she was, had just dried her hands and my body with my blanket and that was it.

Stien was really nice, I thought. She told me, she had experienced "it", the orgasms with the help of her sister and a school friend, but she said that it was nicer with a boy. She held me in her arms and stroked my body. I liked her. She made me do more or less the same things I had done with her sister, but I was more relaxed (more experienced?) and it was therefore more pleasant. It was a revelation to me that these actions could generate such upheavals in a human body. I was really tired by the time she left, but she did not forget to warn me not to tell anybody, or else......

I liked Riek's breasts better. They were larger and softer. They felt wonderful against my cheek. She made me lick around and on top of the nipples. Stien's nipples were larger and would very quickly become erect when I touched them. I think that I managed to become a pretty good toy lover for both of them. I didn't have much choice really. Between what my mother had said and the girls' threats, there wasn't much else I could do. The encounters went on for as long as we hid out on the farm. There were some nights when I had only one visitor but some nights they both came. Not one of the grownups ever discovered us. I still can't understand that. Maybe my parents did suspect and didn't dare talk about it for fear of being evicted, but I doubt it. Did the farmer or his wife know? I don't know that either.

It was always very dark in the loft where I slept and Riek said that she wanted to see what my circumcised penis and the ejaculation looked light in daylight. I really didn't want them to see my circumcised member. I was still bashful about that, but she said: *"If you don't......"* she didn't have to finish the sentence. So now occasional surreptitious daylight encounters began. We used to go behind the barn or into a field and there, after I opened the buttons on my fly (in the Netherlands there were no zippers yet on pants at the time), they used to hand-stimulate me and I would try to oblige them with a big splash of my semen. Luckily, they tired of that very soon and so I did not have to "perform" very often. As it was, in the first few days they used to make me come more than once! Riek used to become impatient sometimes if it didn't come off fast enough for her. Their rough hands made the skin of my penis sore and I used to "treat" that with udder salve, of which there was a big pot near the cows stables.

I had of course never seen their "things" because of the darkness and I asked each of them to be fair and to show me theirs. Riek flatly refused but when I told Stien *"You have seen mine, but I haven't seen yours. I want to see it."* Stien agreed. *"I'll let you see, but we have to be very careful".* So, one afternoon we went to the top of the hay stack and under its thatched roof. First she showed me her breasts and then she let me pull her underpants down. She was bashful at first and kept her legs locked together. I had never seen that part of a woman's body in the daylight, except on paintings and statues in the museum, which did not show any pubic hair, and the pictures some of the boys brought to school, which did, and I thought that her breasts, her belly and the little triangle with the blondish hair were beautiful and I said so and kissed her breast and her pubic mound.

We stayed for a while up in the stack and looked and explored each other's bodies. We were both nice and gentle with each other. I had learned by now that it was easy to hurt a girl if you were too rough with your hands. In a short time I became thoroughly aroused and I asked her if I could stimulate her clitoris again. She agreed and that is the first time I saw on a girl's face what she must feel like when making love and when climaxing. We were actually foolish taking such risks in broad daylight. I hate to think what would have happened if we had been caught.

During this time I had been unaware of what was happening between my parents and the farmer, but suddenly there came an end to this phase of our hiding. After about two months being there, my dad told me one evening that the next evening we would be moving to another place. I was disappointed, because by then I was really enjoying myself and deeply in love with Stien.

"Why can't we stay here? Why do we have to go, Pappie?"

"I don't want to tell you now, but we'll talk about it when we come to our new place. You really liked it here, didn't you?"

"Yes pappie. (If he only had known!) Are we going to another farm where there are animals and where I can do things in the garden?"

"No Louis, I'm sorry, but we are going to a house in Amersfoort and we'll have to stay inside and be very quiet during the day"

"For how long?"

"It won't be long now. The Germans are going to lose the war soon and we'll be free. Probably no more than a few months now" [the poor optimist! This was in August 1942!].

"Will I be able to see Berthie and Menno [my cousins who used to live in Amersfoort] *and Greet de Vooght?"* (I thought that maybe Greet and I could continue the forbidden games I had learned)

"Not yet, they have gone away in hiding too, but after the war is over you'll see them again"

I was disappointed and sad, but had no choice. I couldn't tell the girls, because they had gone to visit relatives for a day with their mother. The next day, in the late afternoon, two gentlemen on bicycles arrived at the farm. Each had an extra bicycle in tow. One was for my father and me, the other one for my mother. She had never liked to cycle and was very unsure of herself when she rode one. We loaded our few cases and me on the four bikes and took off. It was getting dark by then and you were allowed only to have blue "blackout" lights on the bikes. Visibility was therefore limited and, moreover, there was an after-dark curfew in the city we were going to. So we had to hurry.

During the trip, my mother fell off the bike twice and each time both the bike and she made a terrible racket. If any police had been nearby we would have been caught. I remember being very angry at her clumsiness. My dad and the people leading us were both anxious and furious and dad used some choice language which I had never heard from him. However, we managed the unpleasant trip in about two hours without being stopped and arrived at quarter past seven at our new hiding place in Amersfoort. My mother and father didn't talk for a couple of days because of dad's reaction to mother's mishaps during our bike trip. It was an unpleasant beginning for our stay in the house of the Romeijn family on the Puntenburgerlaan.

A few days later my dad told me the reason for our sudden departure. The farmer had suddenly increased the price for hiding us significantly and told my parents that he would give us all up to the Germans if he didn't get what he asked for. The underground people found us a new address, and made it clear to the farmer that he would be severely dealt with if he or his family ever betrayed us to the Germans.

Chapter 7
HIDING IN AMERSFOORT

PART 1—IN HIDING, THE RAID AND MY ESCAPE

Why does someone, who is suddenly faced with great danger behave and react in a certain way? What is it that makes you perform acts which appear, in hindsight, to be impossible, incredible, unexplainable, cruel or gross? How is it possible that people suddenly have the strength to lift a car off an accident victim, jump into a raging river to save someone from drowning, or perform other acts of heroism and bravery, which they never would have considered doing, if given the time to reflect? Someone once said [I think it was it Rene Descartes], that *"Bravery is a lack of alternatives."* A similar saying could be applied to most of my actions during the war years. I don't think that I ever acted out of bravery—it was always out of fear or a sense of self-preservation.

I, and many others, have searched many times for answers to these questions. Neither the other people nor I ever found a real satisfactory explanation. That is one reason why I never wanted to tell the story of my experiences during the war. I felt that some of them were so unreal that I could hardly believe them myself. I had no precedent of heroism or being particularly daring, except for climbing trees or defending my girlfriend Anita from grade school bullies, but when circumstances presented me with a choice of life and death, I instinctively knew to make the choices which saved my life. I've always been thankful for those instincts.

We went into hiding in the spring of 1942. It was now towards the end of October of the same year, and we were in our second hiding place in Amersfoort. The city is about 50 km east of Amsterdam and we were hiding in a multistoried apartment building adjoining the huge railroad switch yards in that city. The house belonged to a coachman and his wife. I remember that the coachman took me out a few times in the evenings to see and pet the horses in the stables[1]. The house was on the Puntenburgerlaan and had four floors, including a ground floor and an attic. We never met nor saw the family who lived on the ground floor. The first floor, up one flight of stairs, was occupied by the coachman and his wife. We lived in two rooms on the second floor. The front room looked out over the street. There were heavy curtains, which were drawn at night, and thin lace curtains, which were partially drawn during the day. To keep curtains totally closed would have aroused suspicion, because people did not keep their curtains closed during the day in the Netherlands. The Dutch climate is too gray and dark for that. My parents and I slept in the front room. The back room was our "day room."

The two rooms were separated by a pair of sliding doors which disappeared into protruding enclosures. In the day room, two other glass-paned doors, flanked by windows, opened out on a veranda (a balcony) on the rear of the house from where you could look over the huge railroad switch yards directly behind a small backyard and shed. The latter two belonged to the family living on the ground floor.

All the apartment units in the huge block were more or less identical. The apartment building block was curved and we were approximately in the middle of the curve, so we could see the porches of many of the other apartments on both sides. The double doors between the front and back room were kept closed during the day so that from the apartments opposite the front room no one would be able to see us move in the apartment which was supposed to be empty. We also stayed away from the windows in the back, because, just as we could see the windows of many of the other apartments, they could see us. When the weather was nice the back doors were kept open, as they were on all other porches and we could see and hear the locomotives puffing and the banging of switching the rail cars. Of course, with the doors open, we had to be quiet so that the next door neighbors would not hear us and start asking questions. Remember that people felt that they could not trust anyone. During the war, the switch yard was

---

1. Horse-drawn coaches were used for weddings, funerals and other festivities in those days in Holland. Apart from that much of transportation and furniture moving was still done with horse and wagons. The coachmen and horses were always outfitted in uniforms appropriate for the occasion, which would be a beautiful sight for wedding processions. For funerals, the coachmen and horses were dressed in somber black with plumed top hats (the coachmen) and plumed harnesses (the horses); the mourners were preceded by the stately coach carrying the coffin and some sort of procession leader, also clad in a somber black uniform and top hat.

a frequent target for allied attacks and many of the houses around it, including the one we were hiding in, were destroyed during some of the bombardments. I loved to look at the trains, but I had to make sure at all times that none of the people on adjacent porches, in backyards or in the switch-yard could see me. Only once during our time in the house was there an attack on a train and it was fascinating to see the planes peel of from their formation and shoot with their guns at the train standing there. We could not hide anywhere and it was actually quite dangerous with the planes coming in low over the houses and the train wagons exploding. I thought it was sort of wonderful even though we were too close for comfort but at least the Germans "got theirs".

Thus we had to stay indoors and quiet all day, but sometimes when the night was very dark, we would be allowed to venture outdoors onto the veranda to catch some fresh air. First the coachman or his wife would come out to the porch and open the doors of our back room. If he didn't greet someone when he was seated, he would give a hand signal and then it was safe for us to come outside. When suddenly neighbors appeared on their porches, we would go through an elaborate charade of saying goodbye to our hosts and go back to our rooms, while the wife made a big display of showing us to her front door and opening and shutting it. We tried not to make any noises when we were out so that nosy neighbors would not hear us and come out to see who we were. Do you know how difficult it is to be quiet all day? Not to make any noises? It was hell and we often got on each other's nerves, especially me not being quiet enough.

Here, away from the distractions of the farm, I would finally hear one night, the story of my dad's escape from the work-camp. There were several of those slave labor camps in the Netherlands, in towns such as Ommen and Dalfsen, where Jewish men were given *"productive work in agriculture and forestry"* and a nominal wage since most of them had become unemployed and unemployable because of restrictive Nazi laws. The camps were in reality a deception used by the Nazis to lure Jews to places where they "would be safe from the razzias (roundups)" as they were told and where they could be put to *"useful* and *healthy"* work. People did believe those lies in the beginning, because they did not want to, nor could they, believe rumors about the truth. It turned out that the real German plan was to have an easier time to herd the men into trains, hence to depart for unknown places in German factories to work as slave labor or to Poland for extermination. Except for a few, the occupants of those transports were never heard of again. Staged photographs showed healthy looking workers cheerfully clearing the land, sitting and having lunch, or standing and leaning on their shovels in a clearing in the forest, where they had been digging out tree roots. No soldiers or policemen were visible on those photographs. Another photograph showed a group of smiling and happy men in their best Sunday's clothes in front of their barracks. I still have some of those photographs in my possession. They were hidden in a hiding place in our old house in Amsterdam and retrieved by me after the war. None of the people in those photographs returned from wherever they were sent.

My dad somehow heard of an impending transport when he was eavesdropping on some of the camp guards. He spoke German fluently, but had not told anyone about it. He had also noticed that certain guards did not always make a headcount of the people in the work detail at the end of the day, as they were supposed to do. They were more interested in getting back to camp and going on the town with "Die Mädel" (the girls—Dutch collaborating tarts). Somehow he managed to get word of this to my mother and close to the day of the transport he made his move. That day, at the end of the long shift, when it was already quite dark and the groups were on their way to the camp, my father jumped into one of the trenches the men had been digging and waited until the group of workers was out of sight. None of the guards noticed his absence. He waited for a while in order to make sure that they were out of earshot and then started running in the opposite direction and because he was in good physical condition, managed to cover quite a great distance. After walking, hiding and running all night, he stole a bicycle, which was unlocked leaning against a shed wall on a farm. He continued bicycling and avoiding main roads and rode in the direction of the farm in Hoevelaken, where he knew my mother and I were hiding. I was so impressed by his tale that I forgot to ask him how he knew where we were and which direction to take in the middle of the night. He left the bike somewhere near the main road at another farm not far from where we were and walked the last few kilometers, arriving early in the morning. It was wonderful to have him back with us, especially now, when we had to stay inside. We played a great deal of chess and I managed to beat him a number of times. He probably let me, but that didn't matter. We also played Monopoly a lot and all kind of card games and he explained some of the passages in the grownups books I was reading when I didn't understand their meaning. My mother was of course also less tense and nervous with him being with us, which made it easier for her to cope with the whole situation. She was a rather nervous person.

I read an awful lot and when I finished the last book in the house I started over again. Since most of the books were for adults much of the material went way over my head and sometimes was downright boring, but I read them anyway. My mother helped Mrs Romeijn in preparing food and cleaning the house, but she always had to be careful not to show herself in front of a window. We all peeled potatoes, scraped carrots, sliced and snapped beans and picked peas out of their pods. One game was to see who could get the longest peel from a potato or an apple. My mother would shiver at the little caterpillars in the peas which I gleefully squashed between my fingers. We read the local newspapers, which were full of German and Nazi propaganda, and sometimes we heard stories from the coachman about what was going on in the outside world and he always told us the news he had heard from others, who had listened to the clandestine Radio Orange (news from the Dutch government in exile) and the BBC broadcasts from London. Whenever the doorbell rang we had to be absolutely quiet. If visitors came to see our hosts downstairs we could not move, sometimes for hours. The floors would creak at the slightest step. We couldn't relieve ourselves either and we became pretty adept at "holding it in". For real emergencies we kept a big covered chamber pot in the room. Mother absolutely hated that pot and made a fuss every time it had to be used. She and my dad argued about it quite a lot. The only times we could move about a little was during visits by the other coachmen and they were having a drinking party. They were "safe" and often very noisy and rowdy. But then we couldn't sleep! But that wasn't so bad since we didn't have to get up early the next day anyway! Those parties also taught me some songs which children were not really supposed to know. I thought some of them were very funny albeit quite vulgar and I soon knew them by heart, but my mother wouldn't let me sing them. We whispered at all times because the adjacent neighbors might hear us. For me it was sometimes hard not to forget that I could not laugh out loud, because the coachman and his wife were known to be childless.

It was about three o'clock on a typical Dutch fall afternoon (I later learned that it was the 1st of November, 1942) and my parents and I were playing Monopoly in the back room. The double doors leading to the veranda were closed because it was chilly and rainy. It was already getting dark outside because of the weather. The bell rang. This time I didn't hear the usual Dutch greeting *"Halloo, it's us"* or *"melkboer (milkman)"* or something similar. A male voice shouted *"Police......stay where you are!"* and we could hear steps racing up the stairway to the first floor. I was stunned for a moment. My mother said *"Oh my God"* and began to moan and cry and then she started screaming : *"Oh God, No...Oh Dear God, No, No......".* I could hear more shouting downstairs and steps were now coming fast up the stais to the second floor. My mother's continued screaming "Nooo, Oh God Nooo......" woke me up out of my shock, and suddenly my instinct told me that I had to get out of there right now!. I raced to the double doors, separating the back room from the balcony, opened them in one move (no mean feat, the lock was difficult to open) and jumped onto the balcony railing. Without hesitating or thinking, I jumped off the railing. The last thing I saw of my parents was my dad waving to me to get away and quickly closing the doors behind me. By doing so he probably gained me enough time to make a successful getaway and saved my life. The last sound I remember is my mother's terrified and continued screams. They are engraved in my memory. I never saw nor heard anything about them until I received, long after the war had ended, a death notice from the International Red Cross, telling me that they were killed in Auschwitz, my father in that same month, November 1942, and my mother in December, 1942.

My fall was partly broken by a big canvas awning on the ground floor apartment which miraculously happened to be open. It didn't break and I slid along the curve and landed on the ground floor at the feet of a totally surprised German policeman or Dutch Blackshirt—I don't remember which, because I didn't stay around long enough to see. I don't know if he was unprepared for this human body hurtling down on him or that he let me go on purpose, but I was out of his sight in no time. Being agile and a good climber I went over several sets of the ten foot fences which separated the adjacent backyards in record time.

Still under the direction of my "instinct" I now looked where to hide and decided to climb up a rain spout at another apartment in the block of houses. I ended up on a first floor balcony similar to the one from which I had just escaped. What to do next—I looked around—I was breathing heavily, my chest felt as if it would explode and my throat ached from breathing too much cold air. There it was......a big galvanized wash tub. I lifted one side up...it was heavy...I sat down and lowered the tub over myself and hunkered down. Another miracle—apparently there was no one at home in that apartment. The noises I made with that galvanized wash tub could easily have brought the people out of the house and that might have been the end of it for me. Someone, something was watching out over me that day. Lady Luck, God, Allah, Karma—whoever it was, thank you.

I was sitting there in the semi-darkness, hunkered down, cold, alone, miserable and shaking uncontrollably with excitement, fear and cold. But mother nature had prepared another challenge for me. I had to go—no doubt out of pure fear! A big one! I tried to hold it in, but it became clear that there was no escape. I had to go urgently or else......! I slowly lifted the heavy tub to search for a solution to the problem. There.... in the corner of the balcony was a good-sized empty flowerpot and in it a piece of brown wrapping paper. Not the best but it had to do. I crawled to the other end of the balcony, retrieved the items and crawled back. All the time I thought that I was going to have let go of my bowels and soil myself. If anyone of the apartment dwellers had collared me at that moment they would have had a kid on their hands who needed an urgent cleaning.

Somehow I managed to get back under the tub, got my short pants off and did what I had to do. I cleaned myself as well as I could with the stiff wrapping paper and then put the flowerpot over the whole mess. Till this day I have wondered, with no little amusement, what the people in that apartment thought and what they said to each other when they had to use the wash tub and found the flowerpot with my deposit under it!

Now that I had eliminated some of the physical discomfort and had successfully coped with this second emergency, I became calmer and was able to think about the predicament I found myself in and what my next steps were going to be. I was freezing cold, and I yearned for some nice warm place. I was dressed in a little thin sweater, short pants and a pair of felt house slippers. Not very much for a windy and rainy Dutch winter day with the temperature hovering between 35 and 40 degrees Fahrenheit. The tub wasn't very deep and sitting became very uncomfortable. The smell under the tub was also getting pretty bad so I decided to move. I suddenly remembered the wooden coal bin, which was a fixture on most balconies and crawled in there. It was about half empty and much easier to sit in. I didn't realize at the time that the bin's contents would be covering me with a layer of black dust.

After thinking about my options, which weren't many, I decided what I was going to do. I would try to get to the house of Joop Van Der Pol *"the melkboer* [the milkman]" who, I knew, was involved in helping people go into hiding. His group had helped us and my aunt and uncle and grandparents. The man who had brought me out of Amsterdam and who regularly delivered our ration cards at the farm and in our new hiding place, was associated with Joop Van Der Pol also. I wasn't too sure how to get to his house, because it was in the center of the city and I was in an outlying area where I had never been before. I had visited his home a few times, which was behind his store and where they sold milk, yoghurt and cheeses. They were friends of my aunt and uncle and Joop had been their milk products supplier and trusted friend. After the shock of the raid and the escape, I don't know how I was so clear-headed and decisive about what I was going to do next. I decided to wait until it was darker because being seen in my light clothes, without a coat, bareheaded and with bare legs in that kind of weather would attract attention. I hadn't realized that the coal dust had painted me totally black and that I therefore was well camouflaged. Apart from everything else, I was even then still afraid that someone who saw me would immediately know that I was a Jew. The Nazi poster propaganda had been very successful in my case!

I don't know how long I sat there shivering and waiting for total darkness. I had no watch and I was too far from the bells of the *"Lange Jan* [Tall John]" tower to hear the time. Luckily, darkness starts falling early in November under that rainy, lead-colored sky. I knew that I had to move, because if the people came home, they might hear me or might come onto the porch to take coal out of the bin to stoke their furnace and discover me. I lifted the lid of the coal bin and climbed up on the porch railing again, intending to go down the way I came up. I started groping for the drainpipe in the semi-darkness......and total terror gripped me. I couldn't find the drain pipe and when I finally found it, it seemed to be much farther away than before. I nearly fell down! I hadn't realized, in my rushed escape, how great that distance was when I climbed up. For a few second, which resembled minutes, I groped around in a panic. I finally got my hands around the wet and slippery drain pipe but the rest of my body would not let go of the railing. Momentarily paralyzed with fear, I hung halfway off the porch with my hands clasping the drain pipe and my feet on the railing! I was afraid to let go with my legs and held on in utter fear of falling. But then I managed to order my legs to let go. I scraped the skin on my hand and knees a bit but didn't notice it. I clambered down and hid under a garden bush on the alley side of the garden until I was sure no one had seen me or was in the area. The bush, I was hiding under must have been shaking—at least I know I was. I still remember the feeling of tension.

I crept through the alley and emerged on the street. In the semi-darkness I could vaguely see some people and a vehicle still in front of the house where we had been hiding. I had to go in that direction, but was afraid someone would see me. So I waited in the shelter of a hallway until they had gone—it probably wasn't very long, but it seemed and eternity. I left when I felt that it was safe to move. By now it was quite dark. I alternately walked, ran and crept along the dark streets. I tripped over curbs, bumped into bicycle racks and fences, and ran into house corners and light poles. When I heard footsteps, or thought I heard them, I stopped moving and hid in a doorway or behind a wall, my heart beating fiercely, trying not to breathe too loudly. There were no street lights—it was a total blackout in the city. There must have been some moon above the clouds, because it wasn't pitch dark everywhere. There surely was someone looking out for me that day.

What has surprised and bothered me in later years is that I spent so little time thinking and worrying about my parents. Throughout the years of the war I don't remember crying for them. I do not remember feeling miserable because of their arrest and deportation, but I do remember sometimes feeling lonely, because I had no one to really love me. For a long time I felt guilty about my feelings, but I suppose that I was too preoccupied with my self-preservation. After the war, I hoped to be reunited with them and was sure they were alive somewhere and would one day turn up. But even when hope waned, I still couldn't cry. I longed for them but couldn't cry.

PART 2—THE VAN DER POL HOUSE

I have no idea how long it took me to get to the Van Der Pol house nor how I found their place in the dark. It did seem to take little time. Due to the wartime blackout there were no streetlights and no lights from the taped-over and curtain-covered windows of the homes and businesses. From time to time I hid in porches when I heard footsteps in the dark, or saw the light from a flashlight, or when I heard the "mewing" of the little hand-held dynamos, which were used frequently during the war because ordinary batteries were scarce or unavailable. Because of the noise they made, the dynamos were called "*Knijp-Kat*" (Pinch-Cat) The people behind those lights could be German or Dutch police patrols—you never knew, but I sure wasn't going to take any chances. By now it was drizzling constantly and I was soaked, tense, frightened and miserable. The temperature must have been around 35—40 degrees F. I don't remember feeling cold, but I do remember clenching my teeth so they would not chatter. I was intent on finding my way and avoiding the Germans, the Dutch police or anyone else. It is amazing how I had turned from a pampered only-child into a resourceful eleven-year-old inside of one afternoon.

When I got closer to the center of the city I could hear the carillon from the bell tower and chose my directions somehow instinctively according to the tunes. I kept close to buildings and crossed over the deserted streets when I was sure that no one was near. My rubber-soled cloth slippers didn't make much noise except for the squishing due to their being soaking wet. There were a number of canals to watch out for. If I would have fallen in, no one would have heard my cries for help. The canal surface is usually six to eight feet below the road surface and it is a straight drop down. Once you are in the water, there is nothing to hold on to and you drown. No one would have come to my rescue even if they had heard my calls for help. At night everyone stayed inside.

In the end instinct, memory and luck brought me to the Van Der Pol store. First I went to the front of the store and put my ear to the door but I couldn't hear anything. The blackout curtains prevented any light from shining through as well. I therefore went around to the back of the house and listened at several windows. At the one nearest the back door I heard the murmur of voices. With my fingers I gently tapped on the window. The sounds inside stopped. Nothing moved. I tapped the window again—softly, although to me it sounded very loud. Nothing happened. Only after I repeated the third time did I hear a voice again and someone came out of the room and opened the back door a tiny crack. I went close to the opening and whispered: *"Please let me in. I am Lou Leviticus and they took my Mammy and Pappy"*. It turned out that it was then after seven o'clock. It had been about four hours since the raid. It had seemed like an eternity. A woman's voice said *"Oh my God, it's you—yes, we know about the raid. Come in quick"*. It was Joop's wife, Annie. She had a shock when she saw me in the light, because my face, and the rest of me, were black with coal dust from my earlier hiding place and streaked with rain and sweat and I had bloody knees from my encounter with the rain spout and a few falls. Also, I never noticed that my slippers had given up on me and that I was now barefoot. I must have been a sight! She had red eyes from crying and started crying again when she hugged me and I finally let go and started to cry bitterly in her arms. I don't know what I cried for—was it relief? Was it for my parents? Was it fear? She held me until I had calmed down and took me inside where the family was gathered, but Joop wasn't there. It turned out that he was supposed to have been picked up by the police in the same series of raids that took my parents and several other people, but he had been warned during the church service he had been attending and had managed to escape. The warning came apparently from "Oom" who had brought me from Amsterdam and was, as I learned later, a plain-clothes detective with the Amersfoort police. The other family members had been sitting around discussing the situation and worrying where Joop was and whether or when the Germans would come back. They often did, especially if they did not find the person they were looking for on their first try. No one knew when they would return. Clearly I could not stay there long. They made me undress and wash and put on some dry clothes from one of the family kids and gave me something to eat. I told them what had happened and they marveled at my being able to find their home in the total darkness. After that I was put to bed in an adjacent bedroom while my clothes were washed and hung out to dry in front of the fireplace.

I couldn't fall asleep immediately because I had been too excited; I was still shaking from nervousness, not from cold because the bed was soft and warm. My mind was in turmoil. I couldn't grasp what had happened or why. I worried about what would happen next. The family in the next room was discussing the situation and I could barely hear them. I crept to the door and listened. They were discussing my sudden arrival. What were they to do? To keep me there would have been dangerous for them as well as for me, but where to send me? The Gestapo could return any time. With Joop gone, no one knew where they could place me and the house might still be under surveillance with the help of some "wrong" neighbor or by the Gestapo themselves. How could they contact other underground workers to find a place for me? Finally I heard someone say, *"Maybe it is best if we take him to the police station in the morning so that he can at least be together with his father and mother"*. The suggestion was probably made out of genuine compassion and ignorance of the fate which awaited us Jews and the wish to do the best for me and for themselves. However, when I heard that I thought, *"I've got to get out of here, I don't want them to take me to the police"*, but I didn't say anything and pretended to be asleep when they looked into my room a few minutes later. I could not have done anything at the time because I didn't have my clothes.

I woke up early the next morning and knew immediately what I was going to do. While it was still dark outside, I crept quietly out of the room, found my dry clothes and got dressed. In the kitchen, I found a box of matches, which I put in my pocket, and cut myself some bread and cheese, drank some milk and took a bottle with me. I took a raincoat which must have belonged to one of the children in the house. I also stole a pair of the smallest size rubber galoshes which were there but which were still a bit too big for me. Then I left very quietly through the back door and went into the streets which were still dark and deserted. There must have been a curfew at that hour because I neither saw nor heard anyone else. I did not want to go to the main street and so went somehow parallel to the main streets and found my way to the Kamperbinnenpoort, which is the eastern gate of the old city, and from there I set out toward the east. I had no clear idea where I was going at that moment, and to this day I can't remember if I walked or ran. All I knew was that I wanted to get away from the city as far as I could as fast as possible.

I remember nothing clearly of the next period. I know vaguely that I hid in barns, sheds and haystacks during most of the day and moved further east in the evenings or early mornings. I stole eggs from chicken houses and ate them raw. I somehow managed to get milk out of some astonished cows, imitating what I had seen the farmer and his family in Hoevelaken do. Those cows must have thought me a strange farmer who tried to get milk out of their teats when it was not milking time. Several of them kicked at me to get away from me. I crept into barns to see if there was anything useful I could steal and managed to find a good scout's knife in one place, matches and a candle in another. I found hiding places in hay stacks and sheds. Farmers used to take hay out of the stacks in the morning and evening to feed the cattle. I had to be out of the haystacks during those times. I often sat and waited, shivering, in bushes nearby, and sometimes I had to run because a farm dog sniffed me out. Most of them were harmless barkers and didn't bother long with me if I didn't move, but some of them were plainly unfriendly and I had to run as fast as I could, throw stones or use a stick to keep them away. I was always petrified that their furious barking would bring out some unfriendly farmer who would hand me over to the Germans.

In the evenings, I ventured out and moved further eastward for some distance, and then stopped at another farm where I would try not to frighten the chickens with my search for eggs. If you were not careful, they would kick up a big fuss which might alert the dogs and the farm family. I found out that even raw eggs taste good when you are hungry. If there was a moon, I would go on but if it was pitch-dark, I would look for a place to spend the night, find some empty sacks for covers, crawl in a haystack and try to sleep till morning. I did do quite a bit of tossing about until I got warm, but generally I slept well, which is surprising, considering what I had gone through recently. Early in the morning the cock's crowing usually woke me up.

I remember killing a small chicken (probably a "Bantam") which I killed by crushing its head with a brick, cutting it open with my knife and plucking it as well as I could without hot water and burning its remaining feathers over a bucket with some kerosene. Where I obtained the kerosene and how I managed to light the kerosene in the bucket without setting myself and the shed on fire I don't know. I used a sharp spade which stood in the shed to split the chicken open and then used my knife for the rest of the process. Thinking about it now, that spade could have been used in manure, but at the time it didn't occur to me. I just cleaned it with straw and a sack. I ate the chicken half raw, but I really don't remember if it was good or not. I just was so darn hungry. The knife came in very handy. I used it, not only for cutting and scraping vegetables and fruits, but also as a "defense" against whatever could come up. I must have had an iron stomach in those days because I never became sick. I remember that I crept through fences and raided farm gardens for radishes and carrots and whatever else which I could find that was edible. I washed those vegetables as well as I could in drainage ditches or canals and then ate them raw. I also drank water from the canals. It was too dangerous to go to the open farmyard and pump clean water, because those pumps always squeaked and I was terrified that the farmers would hear me. There were still some apples and other half-rotten fruit under the fruit trees. Once I found an apple cellar, which is a storage place for a very special sour cooking apple (not unlike Granny Smith in taste) and which is dug in the earth and covered with straw. I ate a lot of apples during that night. That obviously affected my bowels, but that didn't bother me. I had no toilet paper available during those days, but I soon learned that grass, hay or large oak or maple leaves did the trick just as well. I would always wash my hands and my bottom with water from the little canals.

PART 3—BACK ON THE HOEVELAKEN FARM

Before the day of the raid in Amersfoort, I had never really been on my own. Until then I had been the only child, sheltered and spoiled. I had never been away from my parents for a long time except for a summer camp now and then. What happened to me when I was suddenly being thrust into a position where I had to make my own decisions in situations for which I was never prepared? At the time I didn't think that I had done anything miraculous and I always marveled at the survival stories I heard from others who had to fend for themselves during the war years and I found many of them far more miraculous than my own.

Some of the actions I took and the sudden ability to survive must have been subconsciously suggested by the adventure books I had always read. In the Netherlands, and elsewhere in Europe, popular stories of cowboys and Indians, written by a German prisoner by the name of Karl May, Daniel Defoe's "Robinson Crusoe" and many other adventure books, which told about feats of survival may have suggested to me to do the same or take similar actions the heroes in the books performed when it was required of them. I had also had a recurring dream several years before the war, which may have had something to do with my escape from the raid in Amersfoort. In this dream I was being chased by someone or something and I floated just above the hands of my pursuers out of the back window of my room and off the porch and down. I always woke up before I landed in the garden and I wasn't afraid. I have never figured out and probably never will figure out the reasons why I dreamt that dream nor why I acted later as I did. The years of WWII as well as many other wars have provided scores of examples of resourcefulness and the will to survive in young and old people, soldiers and civilians, all of whom found themselves in extraordinary circumstances.

I have discussed this period of my life several times with Karel Brouwer, the man who one day arrived at the farm where I had found refuge after my escape and who took me to his house, "De Mijlpaal," which was to be my home for most of the duration of the rest of the war. We more or less agree that it was between eight and ten weeks after the raid that he picked me up. Neither of us is very sure about that time period.

How did I get to this particular farm, which was the place where I had been in hiding with my parents before we moved to Amersfoort? How on earth did I find the way? It must have been instinct which brought me to this one place, which was known to me in the whole area. It is still a miracle that I found it. The only time I had gone there was on the back of Oom's bicycle when I rode in from Amersfoort. That was in the daytime and subconsciously I may have been observing and memorizing the route. Anyway, I did find it—somehow those few points which I had memorized and recognized led me back to that farm. I think that I reasoned that I had friends there, the farmer and his wife and Riek and Stien, and that I had always had good relations with them. I thought that I would be safe there even though the girls had threatened to betray us to the Germans if I didn't keep quiet or did not feel like complying with their requests. I truly don't know for sure what my motives and thoughts were, but I was looking for a place I knew and a place where I might find warmth and friendship. I was probably very naive, but I was desperate, alone and afraid. I cannot remember how I intended to approach or contact the farmer and I stayed hidden for two days in the area, trying to decide what to do. The decision was taken out of my hands when he discovered me the third morning in the barn, under some jute potato bags and some hay. I had arrived, tired and hungry from foraging after dark at neighboring farms, on the previous evening but had decided to wait until daybreak to go to the farmhouse and make my presence known.

Oh, memory......, I wish I could be more sure of you! But I still remember the utter terror at being woken up by his rough hand shaking me. His angry face loomed over me; I screamed out loudly.

"What the hell are you doing here? How did you get here? Did anyone see you?" He yelled while he grabbed me by the shoulders, stood me up and dragged me out of the haystack. He was very angry. I started crying and said: *"No one saw me. I came my own. The Germans took my parents in Amersfoort and I escaped. I didn't know where else to go. Let me go, you are hurting me"*

I tried to get out of his grip but he held on and continued to shake me and to yell at me in a rage:

"You cannot stay here. I don't have food or clothes to give you and it is too dangerous for me and my family".

He was obviously afraid for his safety and that of his family and may have been angry about our leaving and depriving him of income. Everyone was tense in those days and it was not surprising that he lost his temper when he found me. He was also afraid that I might have been followed.

I was very frightened and screamed and cried and begged him to let me stay with them on the farm. Between sobs I promised that I would work hard for him, and asked that he please check with the underground people in the meantime. In my panic I told him the name of the person who had supplied us with ration cards. The farmer knew whom I was talking about, but was not eager to contact that person because he didn't know if he had gotten into trouble as well as a result of whatever prompted my parents' arrest. I begged him: *"Please let me stay just for a few days. Then I'll go by myself"*. He had calmed down by then and apparently took pity on me and let go of me and said, *"OK, you can be here for a few days then, and in the meantime I'll try to contact Mr. Veer* [this was the name one of the underground worker used—it wasn't his real name. I had never seen him, but he turned out to be my "Oom" who had brought me from Amsterdam]*"*.

He ordered me to go into the back of the farmhouse to my old place above the cows and stay there. In the end, I stayed at the farm for more than "a few" days while he made contact with underground people. In fact I stayed several weeks. Again, I lost track of how long it was. I know that he was later paid handsomely for his troubles by Mr. Karel Brouwer who came to take me away from the farm.

Anyway, I felt safe for a few days and had a roof over my head and food to eat. I had the same sleeping quarters which I had on my earlier stay with my parents. Only now I didn't have sheets, just a rough blanket and some jute seed sacks. I actually "felt at home" there in my cozy little cave in the straw. I did not go into the house, so I did not see the rest of the family. I was told what work to do during the day and to tell anyone who might come by and ask that my name was Jan Bos and that I lived in Haarlem and was sent over to the farm because I was a difficult boy whose parents had decided that I was better off on a farm. When I went into the house at about noon to eat, the wife and daughters were not there. Only the farmer was there and he didn't encourage talking during meals. In the evening, the farmer brought me my food. That was unusual because his wife or one of the daughters always used to bring it to the three of us when we stayed there the first time. I went out and washed my hands and face under the pump, went to my sleeping quarters, took of my boots, pants and coat and got under the covers. I was hoping that one of the girls would come. I needed so much to be held in someone's arms. But no one came that night. Feeling disappointed, sad and very alone, I cried myself to sleep after having relieved my sexual tensions in the hay. By now I had learned to masturbate and did it frequently in order to relieve the tensions I was living under. Next morning the farmer woke me up and brought me some undershirts and shirts from Stien and told me to put them on. He gave me a few safety pins so that I could take in the shirt and pants which were too long for me. I used a rope for a belt. My rubber boots were replaced by a pair of wooden clogs which were also too big, but with a little straw added they were nice and comfortable. I dressed and went to the kitchen for breakfast. The mother and the two girls still were not there and I didn't dare show any curiosity as to their whereabouts. The farmer made breakfast of eggs, bread and fried spek (the fatty part of the bacon with the chewy rind). The farmer (strange that I cannot remember his name) did not say anything, except *"let us pray"*. We bent our heads and said the prayer.

After breakfast we went out to work again and I remember that on that day I cleaned all the cow manure from the stables and loaded it onto a flatbed farm cart equipped with a large wooden trough. Then we harnessed one of the horses and went out to the meadows and spread the manure with pitchforks and a large wooden ladle with a long handle. It was hard work for me, but I didn't dare complain or show that I was tired. By late afternoon, the farmer's wife and Riek returned. I was glad to see them. Riek gave me a wink and I hoped that it meant that she would come and visit me that night. She made me wait a long time after I'd gone to bed. By the time she came I was sound asleep and awoke with a horrible start when she touched me. Even for a long time after the war had ended, I would awake in a panic when someone touched me to wake me up. I always dreamt that I was being picked up and grabbed by the Nazis.

"Where have you been?", I asked after I recovered. Then she told me: *"We were at one of the neighbors; the wife there was going to have a baby, and mother had to help with the birth and we had to help in and around the house and the farm. I didn't know you had come back. My dad told us how he found you during supper. It was quite a surprise to us, but mother said that we should take care of you until the underground people came to take you away. Dad said that tomorrow he would contact the underground people."*

"I've been here already two days" I complained," I waited last night and tonight but I was very tired and, I fell asleep. What time is it?"

"About ten thirty. I cannot stay long. You sound as if you missed me"

"Oh, I did. Stien is not here?"

"She is staying at the neighbor's house to help out with the housework. She'll be there for a while—a week maybe, or more."

I told her about what had happened to us in Amersfoort and how I had run away from the Van Der Pol house, although I was careful not to mention their name. When I told her about the big poop I had hidden under the flower pot on the balcony she thought it was very funny. We both laughed about it. She said that she was sorry that my parents had been arrested and she said that her father had said that they probably would be deported to Poland. It was the first time that she was somehow different, nice, relaxed and patient. It felt so good and secure to be held in her arms that I suddenly started crying and she tried to console me. We spent, what seemed to me in retrospect, a long time just being close like that. Then, nature being what it is, we started to touch each other again and I became very aroused and was suddenly ready to come and then, for the first time, she let me enter her. She took my penis and guided me and I nearly came in her hand. What an unbelievable wonderful feeling it was to be inside her. We were both trying to move in unison and breathing hard and I thought that we must be making an awful lot of noise in the straw. I came too early, well before she did, and was ready to stop—a usual male reaction I learned later. I was very tired but she wouldn't let me go. She said *"Don't stop"* and climaxed shortly after. We were both exhausted, and I couldn't believe how hard I was breathing and how long it took me to calm down. I was at that time eleven years and five months old.

It felt good being there with her. The period when I had been gone had somehow caused a change in our relationship. She was much gentler. She said that she felt really bad for me that I had lost my parents. She couldn't imagine what it was like "to be an orphan" as she unknowingly and prophetically put it. She confessed that this was the first time that she had experienced intercourse with a male but that she had done other "things" before. I assumed that she was talking about her and her sister, but it turned out later that there had been a lot of playing between the girls at the convent school she had attended and had some sexual contact with an older male cousin. The poor parents; they thought that their daughters would be protected from sex when they sent them to a religious girls-school!

"You are the first one to be inside me," she whispered close to my ear, *"It felt so good; was it good for you too?"* I was still breathing so hard that I could barely answer: I managed to utter something, between deep breaths. It must have sounded somewhat like, *"It was......soo......unbelievable......I cannot...believe...that we did it......Was I really good for you?"* Apparently even then

I needed the reassurance that I was a real man. Oh the male ego! *"Yes it was"* she whispered. Surprise?......I fell in love with her that night (I changed my allegiances easily in those days—another survival tactic?) and I would have done anything she asked me. She told me that she had played a lot with Riek and other girls at the convent school and they had made each other come and "opened each other up with their fingers", but that it wasn't the same as doing it with a male. It had been much better and men and women did that only when they loved each other. *"That means that she loves me and I don't have to be afraid of her anymore."* I thought, and when I asked her if she now loved me she said:

"I think so. I was sorry when you left and I did miss you,"

"I was sorry too, but you weren't very nice to me sometimes, you know, and I was always afraid that you would go and tell the Germans about us."

"I wouldn't have. They would have punished my Mom and Dad. I was only trying to make sure that you wouldn't tell my parents or yours."

"I wouldn't have told my parents. Especially not later on when I got to like you both."

After a short pause she asked suddenly: *"Whom did you like better?"*

That was an easy one, but I decided to try and hedge my bets.

"Can I like you both equally?"

"No, you've got to love one more than the other"

"Then I love you more" (The quick learner again!)

She hugged me and we started kissing again and I was ready to repeat the previous action, but she stopped me and said: *"I have to go. I have to wash myself and Mother will start asking questions if I am too sleepy tomorrow. We have a lot of catching up to do with the housework, the farm and the garden, there being only two of us now. But you are here now to help us."* After she left me, I was laying there in my straw bed, thinking, enjoying the thought that here was someone who loved me and held me in her arms. Thinking about it today, I realize that it was very natural that I needed to be held and loved but then it was a new thought for me. I also considered what she had told me about her sister and the girls at school and wondered what she meant by "opening up." Not until much later, when I was in the "Mijlpaal" and read Havelock Ellis's books on sexual behavior (for want of other literature), did I learn about the hymen and what a virgin really was. I had the practice before I knew the theory.

After more than two weeks, her sister returned, but we never had the same relationship as we had before I left. It may be that Riek told her what had happened between us in her absence. Maybe she told her that I now belonged to her or maybe Stien had found someone during her stay away from home. With Riek

I quickly developed a more interesting relationship despite our age difference. We not only made love, but we also talked a lot. I had much to tell her even though I was a lot younger than she was. I told her about my school and Amsterdam, the electric trams, the river Amstel, the Vondelpark; the Royal Palace on the Dam, the Rijksmuseum with its beautiful Rembrandt, Vermeer, Jan Steen and other famous paintings, about the East Indies Institute with the Gamelan and the Wajang Wong Puppet Plays, about my visits to Artis (the zoo) and the concerts and opera my grandmother took me to; and about the movie theaters. I told her how they build houses on the swampy soils and that the palace on the Dam was built on over 19360 poles driven into the ground. I described for her the beautiful City Theater with its huge curtain going up in ripples, the mighty Wurlitzer organ rising from the depths and the vaudeville stage shows during intermission. I talked about the splendor of Carré, the great vaudeville and circus hall, of the magnificent Tuschinski movie theater in the Kalverstraat.(It was renamed Tivoli during the German occupation, because Tuschinski was a Polish Jewish family, which had lived for many, many years in Amsterdam). I told her about the Saturday afternoon big band, "The Ramblers," playing at tea-time in Heck's, a big restaurant on the Rembrant Square, or about the Atlantic restaurant, which my mother and her friends frequented. I told her about our vacation in the Ardennes, about the family flying from Schiphol to Paris in a noisy Fokker Tri-motor and the grand buildings, statues and avenues there. These were all things which, to her, came from a different world. She had never been off the farm except for going to school in Hoevelaken and an occasional visit to an aunt in Harderwijk, a small town on the Zuiderzee. She had only once been to Amersfoort which was not very far away. She went to see a circus there and was amazed at all the buildings, which, to her, seemed very big. It all sounded very strange and exciting to her. I hope that later in her life she did get to see the things I told her about.

She told me about her school and the nuns, and what she had heard was happening currently in the village and in the country and the rumors about how the war was going. We actually had a very good relationship considering our age difference. I had a better general education than she had and had matured a lot since going into hiding and my other subsequent experiences. I liked to describe those things to her because I appreciated them myself and it made me feel grown-up. We felt safe and comfortable with each other. She said that we were like a married couple. It was a miracle that she did not get pregnant, but then maybe she did and I never heard about it because I didn't stay there long enough to see the results of our relationship.

We even discussed religion once. The difference between Jews and Christians. She said that in general the Jews were a bad lot, but that I was an exception. They had killed Jesus Christ—it said so in the bible and the nuns had told her about it in school, and so had the local priest during his Sunday sermons.

"But that was 2000 years ago and those people didn't know any better" I protested. *"If they had known that Jesus really was the son of God, they would not have asked the Romans to kill him* (That shows you what I knew!*); and anyway, he wasn't really dead because he rose to heaven and God must have known all along what was going to happen."*

"Well, maybe you are right," she answered, *"You are so clever and that is why I love you. I hope you can stay a long time, but I know that my father has contacted the underground and maybe you have to go away from here again."*

"I will come and visit if I am not too far away and you can come visit me", I answered.

Well, we never saw each other again after I left. I often wonder what has become of her. She would be in her seventies now. I still don't understand, that neither the farmer nor his wife caught on to our activities. Or maybe they knew and chose not to talk about it? They were poor renter-farmers and very uneducated and backward. There were no books in that house except some books of bible stories and the prayer book which they took to church on Sunday, but never opened at home. I am not even sure that either of them knew how to read, very well although at one time they were probably taught at school. Most of those poorer peasant farmers left school at age twelve or thirteen and had to go to work. They never read newspapers and only seldom listened to the "official" radio stations. At meals only the parents were allowed to speak. We, the children, spoke only in answer to a question from the older people. Usually no one said a word, except the *"Let us pray"* before eating and the *"Grace"* and *"Amen"* after the meal. I seldom ate with them except on Sundays. Most of the time I ate in the back of the farmhouse. They brought me the leftover food after the family had finished their meal. But even when they brought me the meal, the farmer insisted that I say the prayers. They used to wait until I finished thanking the Lord for the food from which I was about to partake.

I worked hard during most of the day. It was mid-winter and still dark when I got up at five in the morning. I first took care of the animals and then set out to do the other tasks which were given me the evening before or that morning. Usually I worked until dark, unless it was impossible to do a job because of the weather. Rain or snow would not stop us from working outside. The two girls sometimes worked in the field, the vegetable garden or the farmyard together with the farmer and me or they helped in the house or at a neighbor's farm. One of my jobs was to take care of the one-acre vegetable garden. I did most of the weeding and turning the soil over with a spade and a hoe, both of which the farmer had shortened for me. I planted under the direction of the farmer's wife or Riek, both of whom knew a great deal about vegetable gardening; I maintained the two pits for keeping the potatoes and the sour winter apples in good condition; I cleaned the stables of manure—they had eight cows, two horses and about two dozen pigs; I brushed the two horses every few days; brought in the hay and straw from the outside haystack and learned to thresh on the floor with a threshing bat; I greased the cart wheel bearings etc. So I earned my keep as I had promised. I actually liked the work—even though I had many painful blisters, which I cured with the wonderfully effective cow's udder salve, called Peru Balsam. I was pretty reliable and the farmer left much of the routine work to me and this freed him to do paid work for other farmers or do a job for himself which had been postponed for lack of time. It was hard, simple work but I had a knack for it and I wasn't cooped up. I loved the animals, especially the horses. They, in turn, seemed to be fond of me and whinnied whenever I came and went. I always kept some half rotten or damaged fruit handy to give them—being careful not to overfeed them; their stomachs, like ours, can easily get upset from too much fruit. So between the daily chores and the nightly visitor I was kept busy and I can only admire my constitution in those days. It is only the young who have such stamina and I'm sure that the fear of the Germans and the thought that it all would be over soon gave me the strength I needed.

This was the situation when, one afternoon, I was told to clean up and come into the Sunday room which I had only seen once or twice before. Two tall men were in the room. One of them was stern looking, with rimless glasses and he wore leather boots. This frightened me and I was ready to run off. I thought that I had been handed over to the Nazis, who always wore leather boots. They must have seen the fear in my eyes because the one with the boots said that I would be going to a safe house where my uncle and aunt had stayed before they went to their final hiding place in the eastern part of the Netherlands. He knew their names and those of my cousins and also that I had fled to the Van Der Pol house. I decided that I could trust him. The one with the boots turned out to be my protector, savior, wartime father, war hero and current friend, Karel Brouwer. The identity of the other person neither of us can agree upon till this day. I think it was Sem Polak, a tall, good looking Jewish man from Amsterdam, who unfortunately took his own life after the end of the war. He was one of the many sad and troubled survivors who were destroyed by guilt feelings and who could not face the world for having lived through those hellish years while others close to them perished.

I saw Oom Karel pay the farmer and then we went out and he put me on the luggage carrier of his bike. It was a cold November afternoon and I was a bit sad to leave without saying goodbye to my best friend Riek, and to the horses and other farm animals. I had known tenderness and safety at the farm. I had no idea what lay in store for me but I put my trust in Karel Brouwer at first sight even though he wore those Nazi type boots. It turns out that he was wearing those boots exactly for that reason—to make a first impression of being a Nazi. The trip ended about two hours later at the house which would be my home until the end of the war (except for a short period—but that's another story). The house was called *"De Mijlpaal,"* which is Dutch for *"The milestone."* It turned out to be a milestone in my life.

What did I really feel at the time of my stay on that farm and my inadvertent involvement with the farmers daughters. Today I still can't really say for sure. There were many things I didn't like about my having to satisfy them. I suppose it was that sex, for which I was not mentally ready, was being forced upon me even though I learned to enjoy it. At the back of my mind I knew it was wrong. I did like the comfort and sense of security it gave me when we were together. I needed that feeling of warmth.

PART 4—I GET A NEW IDENTITY

While we were riding toward my new and unknown place of hiding, Oom Karel told me that my new name would be Rudi Van Der Roest and I had to learn that name fast in case we were stopped. He also told me my address in Amsterdam and that I was a cousin of his. So I sat on the luggage carrier repeating the name and the address and I was feeling so good. Suddenly I had lost my fears. I was finally someone else. I wasn't a Jew anymore! I was free!

This Rudi from Amsterdam came from a family whose members were also involved in underground activities. With his identity I was able to move about freely, go to school and participate in a normal daily life—as normal as it can be during a war. I even visited my "grandmother" in Amsterdam and she visited me. She was a locally famous personality, called "Tante Gré" in the central area of Amsterdam (*de Jordaan*) and I spent some wonderful days in her seventeenth century house which faced on one of Amsterdam's canals, the "Egelantiersgracht". I remember waking up to the tones of the beautiful bells on the famous "Westertoren" the famous tower of the nearby church., which always gave concerts on the hour. Of course I also fell in love with one of my "nieces", although I cannot remember her name. The real Rudy and I meet whenever I visit Holland and are still corresponding and I sign my letters to him with "Rudy II".

There is a marvelous anecdote connected to this family relationship. My "grandmother" (Tante Gré) traveled one day from Amsterdam to Amersfoort in order to go to the Mijlpaal house in Hamersveld to get some ration cards or other documents. On the way from the railroad station in Amersfoort to the house, a distance of about five kilometers, she hitched a ride with Mr. van Harte, our local milkman, with whom I was well acquainted. I often helped him with deliveries in Amersfoort and he let me drive the cart. As the horse clip-clopped along the tree lined roads he asked her where she was going. She answered that she was going to visit her grandson (me) for a day or two and told him my name. He looked at her from the side and then said, *"I thought that you looked familiar; you two have a strong resemblance. Rudy is a very nice boy"*. The old lady, who always had a great sense of humor, could barely contain herself from bursting out laughing, but she kept a straight face and said that she was happy to hear that because I had been quite a handful at home and that she had hoped that her nephew Karel could straighten me out.

Chapter 8
THE "TD-GROUP" AND THE DUTCH POPULATION REGISTRATION SYSTEM

I had no idea what was going to happen to me or where exactly we were going, but when we arrived at the house called "De Mijlpaal", I came into a center of non-violent resistance movement to the Nazi regime. I will try to explain the type of underground activity which was being developed and the reasons for the development of this mode of underground resistance. To do this it is necessary to look at the system of population registration in the Netherlands at the time.

Many volumes have been written about the activities of the various resistance groups in the Netherlands and elsewhere in Europe during WWII. Opinions on the efficiency and success of the those groups varies greatly, depending upon the conditions at the various locations, who wrote the history and what his or her sources were. I was fortunate to be part, albeit a very small one, of the activities of the TD group, which was undoubtedly one of the more successful organizations working against the Nazi regime in the Netherlands. I was part of the Mijlpaal family from late December 1942 through the end of the war and for several months after it ended.

The success of the German occupation in exterminating more than 75 percent (some say 80%) of the Jewish population of the Netherlands and being able to "recruit" many non-Jewish citizens for the work programs in Germany was facilitated by the population registration which had been developed over the years. When the Germans overran the Dutch defenses in five days between May 10 and May 15, 1940, they entered a country where precision, correctness, and respect and obeisance for authority were even more admired than in Germany itself, if that were possible. The system of population registration in the Netherlands was a prime example of love of registration run amuck. Since that country had always prided itself on its freedoms and tolerance, it may surprise many to find that every citizen's particulars were minutely documented and that individual histories were kept and updated in a carefully constructed filing system which, among many other items, included the person's religion as well as that of their parents and grandparents.

From the day a child was born, records were kept of its every move from address to address, its education obtained and where it was obtained, profession(s), marriage(s), children, divorce(s), criminal records and death. Although there was a standing order in existence to destroy those records in case of occupation by an enemy, no one in the power structure thought of destroying that documentation when the Nazis occupied the country. The bureaucrats in power were too proud of having set the system up and, in addition, many of those people were either members of the Dutch Nazi party (*NSB*) or Nazi sympathizers. They actually admired the orderliness of the Germans. Destroying the records would have been an unthinkable thing to do according to the orderly and bureaucratic mind-set of the Dutch government officials. After all, the Queen and her government had fled to England on the 13th of May, and now they, "those who had remained behind", were in charge.

One of the most notorious of the Nazi collaborators, J. L. Lentz—an evil and corrupt bureaucratic genius—wholeheartedly assisted the Germans in continuing to perfect and upgrade the system during the occupation, so that all the undesirables would be easy prey for the German extermination camps and forced labor machine. Undesirables were Jews, Gypsies, Jehova's Witnesses, Brethren, Quakers, patients in institutions for the mentally ill, physically handicapped, colored and mixed race people from Indonesia and the West Indies, known anti-Nazis and "perverts" such as homosexuals and lesbians, communists and labor activists. It was Mr. Lentz and his cohorts in The Hague who did their best to assist the Nazis in theirs efforts to keep the Aryan world "clean" and to provide slave labor for Germany's factories and defenses, from the non-Jewish population, especially in the later war years. The Dutch bureaucrats liked the compliments of the Germans so much that they continued to be protective of influential Nazis even after the war ended. A case in point is the "Menten Affair"[1]. Menten was a Dutch war criminal who was brought to trial in the late forties but acquitted because of leniency by the courts who accepted slanderous and untrue statements by the Menten lawyers. He was retried in the 1970's following a series of articles in the journal "Accent" which exposed him and his war activities, but only after the Dutch Ministry of Justice, under Mr. Van Agt, delayed taking action and allowed

---

1.   **H. Knoop, The Menten Affair. Macmillan Publishing Co. Inc. 1978**

him to escape to Switzerland. He was caught eventually and sentenced in the Netherlands. National newspapers, like "De Telegraaf", supported the Nazi criminal despite the overwhelming evidence, much of which had been available since immediately after the end of the war. Why was no action taken? Simply because the murders were committed in and around Lvov, a city far from the Netherlands, and they were only against Jews. So it did not directly involve the Netherlands.

Later in the war, this registration system was used to assemble lists of regular Dutch citizens for the "*Arbeitseinsatz*" (labor-recruitment) for the German war effort. Those same Dutch bureaucrats didn't lift a finger nor did they protest the misuse of their system.

Their countrymen were sent to Germany to work in strategic factories in the most dangerous areas, but they were "proud of their achievement". Many of those who were sent into slave labor succumbed to hunger, disease and violence inflicted by the Nazis on the ground and Allied bombings from the air. However, the bureaucrats obeyed the authorities—a well-known characteristic of the Dutch psyche. The system was also used during the years 1944 and 1945, when people were rounded up to work on the German front-line fortifications in the Netherlands itself. The inhumane treatment of those workers by "*Das Herrenvolk* [The Master-People]", as they loved to call themselves, cost many their health and others their lives and caused hardship at their homes.

The Dutch registration system specified that every citizen was to be registered in three places:

1. In the central register in The Hague. Here a so-called "OPB-card" carried a photograph, the fingerprints, the relevant history, current address, signature of the person, if old enough, and other personal data. Changes in the person's status were recorded and had to match the changes on the next two types of registration at all times. The local registrars' offices were to send in any changes in status.

2. A personal identity card (Persoonsbewijs), with the same data, which must be carried at all times by all persons over 15 years of age. To be found without one during routine street inspections or razzias (round-ups) resulted in severe punishment including jail or "*Arbeitslager* [work-camp]"—a euphemism for a concentration camp without gas chambers but deadly for many detainees all the same. This ID card was also needed later in order to receive a "Master Card" for obtaining ration cards.

3.   An index card with all or most of the above information in the munici-
     pal or local register of the place where the person currently resided.

If someone moved from one place to another, the new papers were forwarded
to the new location, while a copy was kept in the previous town's registry. The
same would happen if he or she had change of status, such as marriage, divorce,
occupation change etc. One copy of the personal data was sent to the main population registry in The Hague, where they were added to the personal file. Any dis-
crepancy was suspect, thus a stolen or falsified ID card was useless if the police
checked the fingerprints in the local register or the main register in The Hague.
In such cases, the person, whose card had been taken by the authorities and who
had been sitting in jail waiting for the answer to come back was interrogated to
find out who had falsified the card or who had supplied it. Many other people
were thus also implicated and caught. These interrogations were not gentle.

If the person survived the ordeal, he or she might be set free if nothing could
be proven, but, frequently, they were sent to a punishment camp in the Netherlands (Camp Vught. Camp Amersfoort etc.) or to Germany, where the chances
of survival were only slightly less than in the Dutch camps. The Germans and
their Dutch collaborators were not particularly concerned with that aspect. If the
victims were Jewish, they were directly shipped to extermination camps in Germany and Poland after a short stay in the punishment barracks of the infamous
Westerbork transfer camp, named after the town in the northern province of
Drente where it was located.

The Dutch registration system fell in German hands in May, 1940. In October 1941, the Jewish population in the Netherlands was ordered to register at the
offices of the Jewish Council *(Joodse Raad)* in Amsterdam. Jews who lived in
other towns were given more time. Refusal to register was punished with imme-
diate transportation to Westerbork. The Germans had learned from experience
that the Jews were apt to trust their own organizations rather than the occupier's
offices and so they decided to give the orders to the Council and let them figure
out how to make the Jewish people comply. The council members were told: "If
you can't deliver, we'll put you and your family on the next transport." The personal ID card issued to the Jews had a large "**J**" stamped on it in thick black ink.
That went together with the big yellow Star of David with the word "**Jood**"
[Dutch for "Jew"] which every Jewish person had to wear. I don't know what the
marking was on the ID cards of other groups, such as Gypsies, Jehova Witnesses,
Mormons and others.

The ID card system proved to be a major reason for the disastrously large proportion of Dutch Jews and other persecuted groups in the Netherlands being deported and massacred. It turns out that the Netherlands had Western Europe's highest percentage of Jews deported to the slaughterhouses in Germany, Austria and Poland—about eighty percent. What a record to be proud of—the Dutch efficiency in registration was very instrumental in this success.

There were many attempts at falsification of ID cards, although it was not very helpful if the data on the card did not match those in the local and main registers. However, the street inspections were fairly cursory in the beginning and falsifying an ID became rather a common practice in the early days. One way was for a non-Jewish person to declare that they had lost their ID card and the old card would then be given to someone else, who was usually located in another part of the country. Soon, however, the authorities got wise to the various schemes and developed new ways to thwart the ID-card falsifications.

Again, it was the Dutch collaborators, who invented a multi-layered ID card. Made of three layers of different paper with different water-marks, which were laminated together, the cards were practically impossible to copy. The photographs and fingerprints were inserted between the layers. When one tried to soak the layers apart, or separate the layers in some other way in order to insert a different photograph or fingerprint, the stamps and some of the watermarks would be destroyed. Because of this difficulty in falsifying, a number of underground groups started to attack and rob municipal and regional registration offices and steal unused ID-cards, master cards and ration cards. Strong punitive countermeasures by the Germans and the local collaborating police made this practice very risky and, soon, unpopular with the rest of the population which bore the brunt of the Nazi wrath. The reprisals by the Nazis were severe and totally indiscriminate. Innocent people would be rounded up in a calculated Nazi "deterrent" action and either publicly executed or sent to the concentration camps in Holland or Germany. At the school I attended, we were rounded up one day, together with some other civilians, to watch the "just punishment" meted out to three innocent civilians who were shot in order to teach us Dutch a lesson for the unwarranted wounding of a German officer in the neighborhood. It was a shocking spectacle, but, worst of all for us schoolchildren, was that no one talked about what had happened. People did not know about grief or shock counseling in those days. Everyone was supposed to cope with these events on their own. Also, any statement by teachers or others about the event might be interpreted and reported as being anti-Nazi and could expose the people to personal danger.

This was the situation in 1942 when young Mr. Karel Frederick Eduard Brouwer (Karel for short) was an undersecretary for the municipality of the county of Leusden, in the province of Utrecht. He was twenty-two years old when the war started in 1940 and he was making his career in public administration. He was married in May 1942 and had moved into his new job in Leusden where he and his 21-year-old bride had rented a house, "the Mijlpaal", in the township of Hamersveld. He had never been involved in anything illegal nor would he ever have considered such a thing. One day he found himself confronted with the problem of having to make a crucial decision—whether to save lives of people in danger or do nothing—and he didn't hesitate. He took the irrevocable step to take care of the people in danger, in this case six Jews in need. They needed shelter, food and papers. They needed protection. It all happened when he visited his in-laws in Amersfoort and found six very frightened people—four adults and two children—who were neighbors and friends of his in-laws. The people were my maternal grandparents and my uncle and aunt (my mother's sister) with their two children. They had just been notified by the Dutch authorities to pack their suitcases and go to Amsterdam the next day to register and get ready for transport, which meant Westerbork, then Germany or Poland—and extermination. On the spot Karel said that "this should not be allowed to happen", and that he would take care of them and they were to come with him to his house. An hour later he walked into his house with all six in tow, and Rita, his wife, simply accepted it as natural after Karel explained to her what he had done. Can you imagine today a twenty-four-year-old man, who has been married for half a year and a girl aged twenty-one, who would take on such a responsibility in today's world? This was real heroism and selflessness!

Karel Brouwer's position as undersecretary of the municipality, was an upper-level administrative position and he was extremely well informed about the inner workings of the Dutch registration system. He knew the ins-and-outs of the registration system forwards and backwards. It turns out that he had a genius for understanding the workings of a bureaucracy and he used this genius to aid persecuted people, both Jews and non-Jews. He still doesn't think that he did anything remarkable. "*I just could not allow this to happen*", he still says today.

Karel Brouwer developed a system, he called it "conversion", which was perfected over time and spread throughout the Netherlands with the help of a number of strategically placed people in the civil service. There were several stages in this process. The system provided a person with a new identity by giving him a duplicate of someone else's genuine Identity Card, plus a corresponding duplicate Master Card, which was essential for obtaining food and clothing ration cards. Simultaneously, with the issuance of the genuine ID card and Master Card, a change had to be made in local registers and in the main register in The Hague. A number of people were involved in this process, which consisted of replacing cards in different registries with cards from people who lived in other parts of the country or who had died many years ago and would have been of about the same age as the person for whom the new and "legal" ID card was to be issued. This had to be accomplished while Germans and their Dutch Nazi collaborators were present and without alerting them to the goings-on. A personal history was developed for each person by replacing (or extracting) the original cards with modified cards in the various local registries and the main registry in The Hague. On the basis of this "true" information, the government in The Hague issued new, genuine ID cards and Master Cards. People could even be born with the help of false birth certificates. This meant that babies born to people with false identities during the occupation, could obtain a "legitimate" identity when needed. After all, people were still people and babies were born to some of those who were in hiding as well.

All this sounds easier than it was. A network of cooperators was needed and this was slowly developed by Karel Brouwer, Dr. Dolf Hendriks, Bob van der Heiden and a few others. One problem was how to avoid that, by chance, people of the same name might cross paths. This did happen in a few cases. There was the case of the father of one of the young courier girls in the Mijlpaal group. Her father was Mr. Salomon Muys, who had the identity of a Mr. Cornelis van Rootselaar. Mr. Muys had to be hospitalized for an operation in the town of Amersfoort. When he awoke from his anaesthetic he was terrified to find that the patient in the adjacent hospital bed was the "same" Mr. Cornelis van Rootselaar! I don't remember the details but that problem was solved with the help of cooperative hospital staff. Both the real person and his double survived the ordeal. Mr Muys is not alive anymore but his daughter, Elly, still lives in Amsterdam and we do reminisce about those days whenever we meet.

In another case, two young brothers moved with their care-givers from their current township to the town of Barneveld. By one of those crazy coincidences, the "real" boys had also moved to that town. The registrar of the community found this rather strange and directed a questioning letter to the original registry which happened to be Leusden. It took some very ingenious lying, and confusing language in letters written by Karel Brouwer to quiet the suspicions of the municipal officers. The correspondence which Karel Brouwer worked up is a beautiful example of legalese obfuscation. The bureaucrats in Barneveld were totally confused and did not follow up on the matter. This correspondence is still in existence and provides fascinating reading. Another time a problem occurred when a man whose name had been used turned out to be sought by the police for some sort of crime. A warrant for the arrest of that person was issued and the police arrested the poor guy who was carrying the false identity card. Everyone connected had several anxious days fearing that the man would break during the interrogations. He apparently figured out that he was not taken as a Jew but as a common criminal for a crime he didn't commit and he didn't talk, but, sadly, he was never heard of again. The real criminal was free to go. We don't think that he ever learned who and what had saved him from arrest.

The TD group [TD stands for "**T**weede **D**istributie Stamkaart"—or "Second Rationing Mastercard"] learned to improve their system step by step. After having encountered a number of problems with the use of living persons' identities, such as those mentioned earlier, the data were taken as much as possible from deceased persons, who would have been about the same age as the person for whom the ID was needed had they lived. A new ID had to be inserted into the system with the death certification removed. Backgrounds were researched and investigated on the history of the "deceased", who had sprung to life again, in order to provide traceability of the history of the person for the new owner of the name. There were a number of instances when people were caught in round-ups by the Germans, and the subsequent investigations by the Gestapo could not discover that the person who was caught was not the person on the identity card he or she was carrying. One of the most interesting and convincing stories is that of Mr. Harry Theeboom, who ended up being released from the infamous Westerbork camp. I have included part of his story in the next chapter, titled "The Harry Theeboom Story".

If all this falsification sounds complicated, there is more to come. The governing powers were very much aware that there were forgeries on the market. Therefore, they frequently developed a new stamp or seal, or changed the watermark on the paper. New permits were required frequently in order to foil the attempts at circumventing the law. For instance, travel was restricted unless a special stamp or license (*Ausweiss*) was obtained. Cars or bicycles could be commandeered unless you had a special permit showing that you needed this for an essential service—for instance one which declared that the bearer needed a bicycle because she was a nurse or a postman. The same type of permit was needed for gasoline. The permits were only issued for special purposes and special people (doctors for instance); special medical supplies required a special permit. To be found outside at night after a curfew also required a permit. Such a permit might identify the bearer as an Air-Raid warden, Red Cross worker, a nurse, a doctor or someone working for police or a Nazi group. Later, passes were required which protected a person from transportation to factories or fortifications in the Netherlands or Germany. The false passes saved thousands of Dutchmen from transport, slave labor and, very possibly, death. All of these permits and passes were subject to frequent changes or exchanges for a new set of documents. You had to go to the registries to get the new ones and hand the old ones in. In addition, new seals and stamps were continuously developed to be added to the Master Card in order to make it more difficult for the "illegals" to obtain rations and make it easier to catch them.

The TD-group first of all had to find out in advance about the new stamps and permits, and then had to produce those permits and seals quickly. Many evenings were spent at the *"Mijlpaal"*, and other similar locations, with whittling knives and rubber blocks, trying to copy the new stamp designs. The Germans tried many tricks to confuse the counterfeiters. For instance, on some stamps they turned the head of the German eagle from one side to the other, which resulted in a small blip, the beak, being either on one side or the other. If you missed that alteration, the bearer of the document would be caught when they were stopped and checked by the authorities and the error was discovered. Tortured under questioning the person often gave away the names of the people who had supplied the documents.

It was not easy to cut a stamp on the reverse and on a bad day it took a number of attempts to come up with a good result. Our fingers often suffered from slipping knifes. But the stamps had to be done before the next day, so the midnight oil often burned behind the blackout curtains of the Mijlpaal. ID cards and Master cards also had to look used. That required a special technique which was carried out by the group at the Mijlpaal in the evenings. Dirt, house dust, spit, fat, gravy—everything was used to authenticate the documents. We called it "antiquing".

Being present and a part of all this was of course very exciting for a boy my age.

The TD-system was gradually adopted in many areas of the country, but each group operated independently. There were only a few people who knew the full scope of the operation and the various cells in the organization. This was the prudent thing to do, because mistakes, treason and bad luck happen and it was best that one group did not know whether the neighboring township had another group doing the same things. The central circle of leaders provided information and instructions and coordinated between groups when that was needed.

In the final analysis, the TD-system not only saved many Jews, but kept thousands of Dutch men from being transported to the German slave labor camps during the years of the war. Another advantage was that the system did not require raids, violence or weapons and thus did not invite reprisal measures by the authorities. Karel Brouwer and the others in his group were rewarded with knighthoods by the Queen of the Netherlands. He and Dolf, the latter posthumously, were also awarded the distinction of "Righteous Christian" by the government of Israel. Their names are engraved on a special wall at the memorial "Yad Vashem" in Jerusalem and listed in the US Holocaust Museum in Washington, DC. It is estimated that the TD group activities saved about 400 Jews and nearly 10,000 non-Jews.

Lastly in this chapter, I want to show you, the reader, what type of conscientious and bureaucratically correct person Karel Brouwer was. For two years after the war he worked, voluntarily, in order to correct, as much as he could, the falsifications which had been perpetrated during the war by the TD-group. He insisted that this should be done. It was *"a wrong which had to be righted."*

Chapter 9
HARRY THEEBOOM'S
STORY

Harry and I met at the Mijlpaal in early 1943. I knew him then as Frans Jan Berkenbosch. He was five years older. At that age, that is a tremendous gap so we were not very close during those years, but we got on well together and he was sort of an older brother to me. He was a gregarious, fun type person and had a lot of sang-froid, which saved him several times from death. He used to disappear from time to time and then turn up again. I never asked any questions. It was understood by all of us that we couldn't spill the beans if we didn't know what the beans were. All I knew was that he had another home and workplace and that he sometimes went out on some "mission". This was probably similar to what I used to do sometimes—delivering an envelope with papers or a coded message somewhere. Many young people were used for such errands because there was less of a chance for them to be stopped by the police. One of the other young people who was used by TD was a young, spindly, girl whose name at the time I don't remember. Later she became known as the actress Audrey Hepburn. She didn't impress me much at the time and by the time she was famous and beautiful she was in Hollywood and unreachable to normal mortals like myself.

Harry was, like myself, supplied with identity papers by Karel which showed that he was a fellow by the name of Frans Jan Berkenbosch, born 26 of November, 1926. At the time I met him I lived under the name of Rudi Van Der Roest, born on 27 August 1929, he was, on paper at least, only three years older than I was. When no strangers were present we usually called him Frans-Harry. I will let Harry tell the part of his remarkable story concerning his miraculous escape from the clutches of the Gestapo, which shows how well the TD-group's method of providing bogus identity papers really was. It also shows some of the remarkable survival skills of Harry, who at the time of this story was really only a teenager! Harry translated his story into English for my wife and I have kept Harry's phrasing verbatim and only corrected some very obvious spelling errors.

◆   ◆   ◆

Harry, alias Frans Jan Berkenbosch's story

I managed to hide when they came for us in our house in Amsterdam on June 20, 1943. I never saw my parents and my cousin, who was living with us, again. I fled to friends and from there to friends of those friends. I stayed everywhere for a short time only, because there was always a danger of being discovered. Most places in the city were not suitable for one reason or another for sheltering fugitives from "Nazi Justice."

I ended up in the house of "Tante Gré" an older lady who was a figure of formidable authority in the "Jordaan"[1], a section of very independent Amsterdammers in the center of the city. I was to stay there for about six weeks until proper identification papers could be prepared for me and someone would come and fetch me. Identification papers were in the form of a passport which carried your photograph and your fingerprints in addition to stamps showing the place of issuance and other details.

At the end of these interminable six weeks a man who did not provide his name came for me. He told me that henceforth I was Frans Jan Berkenbosch, to forget that I was ever anyone else and gave me the details of father and mother Berkenbosch, where they were born and when and where I had lived and gone to school, etc.. After completing my identity card I was Frans—sharing the name with a real living individual who was at that time studying at some seminary to become a priest and was therefore most of the time "out of circulation". Till this day that gentleman does not know about his double.

We were to travel by train to Amersfoort and from there by bicycle or on foot to some unknown destination. During the trip we sat in separate compartments in case of trouble with German inspections. The one-hour trip was uneventful. When we arrived in Amersfoort the Grüne Polizei [the green uniformed German police] was inspecting ID cards at the exits.

This was my first baptism of fire. My escort remained unmoved and told me to walk along some tracks and then climb a dike at a point a certain distance away. He would meet me there. When I got there he was waiting for me. I put my little case on the luggage rack of his bicycle and we set out on foot to the little village of Hamersveld in the municipality of Leusden.

---

1.   The name *"Jordaan"* actually comes from the French word *"jardin"* which means garden

The house we went to was called "de Mijlpaal" or the Milestone. It was the home of Karel Brouwer, who was, it turned out, my silent companion on the eventful trip from Amsterdam. It was also the center of operations of the resistance movement, called the TD-group. The name TD was derived from the Dutch word for the Second Rationing Master card which was one of the means by which the German occupiers and their Dutch Nazi collaborators tried to control the population and food and goods distribution.

In the house I was introduced to Rita, Karel's wife, and to three Jewish persons who had all assumed the identities of living non Jewish Dutch people from various parts of the Netherlands. One of them, Rudy, was the supposed grandson of Tante Gré from Amsterdam where I had spent my last six weeks.

It took a few weeks before I finally moved on because there were already three Jewish people staying with Karel and Rita. I spent the time learning and perfecting my story. To explain my being circumcised I would tell the story that my parents and I had lived in South Africa for a few years and that I was circumcised there for health reasons. Rudy would use a similar story, but he had been circumcised in the Dutch West Indies.

I finally moved to the town of Halle, in eastern Holland, where I was normally employed and lived with the Duitsh family who were unaware that I was a Jewish refugee. After a while I came to live with the Jansen family in Zelhem, a nearby town and worked for a Mr. Hof in his bicycle repair shop. This proved to be a pretty unsafe place for me.

Towards the end of September 1943 the Grüne Polizei and the Sicherheitsdienst [Security Police] surrounded the house. I slept with Mr. Jansen's son upstairs. The SD-men rushed in the room, dragged us out of bed and one of them pulled my pajama pants down.

"*DU BIST EIN JUDE [You are a Jew],*" was the first thing he said. I was paralyzed with fear and could only stammer that I was not a Jew. We all had to get dressed immediately and were taken outside.

There were three police vans. In the dark I could see that one of them was already full with prisoners. Mr. Jansen, his son and I had to get into the second van where we found several more detainees plus three or four Grüne Polizei guards. The rest of the night we drove around the area where more raids were conducted to capture people who were hiding. Since the Germans knew where they were going, there had to have been some serious treason by someone who knew too much. At dawn we reached the prison in Arnhem.

On arrival we were put into cells—there was no change into regular prisoner garb. I found myself in a cell with five other occupants. The stench was unbearable. It came from our public toilet—a barrel in one corner of the cell. My cell-mates wanted to know what I was in for. I told them that I had been run in that night on the mistaken charge that I was a Jew. One of them asked me for my age. When I told him I was seventeen, although I looked younger than that, he tried to coax me into admitting to him that I really was a Jew. I did not react and kept to my story. Lack of caution could only harm my chances for survival.

The next morning I was among some thirty prisoners transferred to the offices of the Sicherheitsdienst (SD) for questioning. I will not go into details here, for they were far from pleasant. I was questioned twice by two German SD-officers. One of them was Obersturmführer Bühe, a man whose name I'll never forget as long as I live. They tried to extract information from me, tried to force me into telling them the name of the person who had given me my fake ID.

I maintained my innocence and pled ignorance by saying that I didn't under-stand what they meant. I had been given my papers when I became 15 years of age and that they were wrong—I was not a Jew. However they knew I was cir-cumcised and therefore I had to be a Jew and therefore my identity card had to be a fake. I told them that I had been ill in South Africa and that I had been circum-cised in a hospital there for health reasons.

They appeared to think that they wouldn't get anywhere with me for I was taken back to the prison. Six days later I was transported to the Interrogation Center again. This time I was alone and under very strict security. I was very much afraid that this time I might not be able to stick to my story. On the other hand I had this deep trust in the genuineness of the papers Karel Brouwer had provided me with.

I was again led into the presence of Obersturmführer Bühe. He was alone this time. My ID card was ostentatiously spread out on his desk in front of him. It had been split into its three layers of paper. My fear melted away at the sight of it. I had been well informed on how the ID's were constructed and I felt that its lying there showed that they couldn't find anything wrong with it.

Bühe began in a quiet voice to tell me that the investigation had proved my ID to be a fake. I responded by just shrugging my shoulders which made him furious. He seemed obsessed with finding out who had provided me with my papers. After one hour of shouting and threats, to which I managed to give naive answers, the dispute was settled when I answered him "If the only thing which will make you happy is the name of the person who gave me my ID, call the town hall. They should know the names of their clerks—not me." He was flabber-gasted. The session was ended and I was taken back to the prison.

After fourteen days I was taken out of my cell, handcuffed to two military policemen who took me to the train station in Arnhem. On the platform a lady from the Jewish Council came up to me and informed me that I was to be transported to Westerbork (the main transit camp for Jews from Holland). I feigned amazement and asked her why—I wasn't a Jew and could she perhaps do something to clear up this misunderstanding? The lady seemed quite taken aback and told me that she would report my case—I had no idea to whom, but on arriving in Westerbork things became more clear.

In Westerbork I had to report to the administration of the Jewish Council. I told them that there had to be an error—I was not a Jew, I was Frans Jan Berkenbosch, and I wondered what steps could be taken to get me out of this. The lady in charge told me that they had already been informed (by the lady in Arnhem) about this young man who denied being a Jew. She could understand my motives for telling this tale to the SD but assured me that I could confide in her in case I wanted to tell someone the truth. I pretended not to understand what she meant. Because all inmates in the camp wore a yellow star with the word JOOD (Jew) on it she gave me one too.

At first I refused to wear it. I failed to see why a non-Jewish person would have to wear a star with the word "Jew" on it. She pointed out to me that not wearing it would set me apart from all the other inmates in the camp and that I would be asking for troubles with the Germans. It occurred to me that things would be much easier for me if I could move about as inconspicuously as possible, so I consented. She promised to contact camp commander Gemmeker as soon as possible for further investigation into my case.

My story at least yielded me a first fruit. I was not interned in the punishment block where persons who had gone underground and who had subsequently been caught were kept separate from the other prisoners by means of barbed wire fences. Those people were put on the first available transport for the concentration camps and gas chambers in Germany and Poland.

Apparently the lady was interested enough in my case to promise to keep me informed and to see to it that, as long as my case had not been fully investigated, I would not be put on a transport.

I had no idea of what lay ahead of me and, looking back, I can say that the time I spent in Westerbork was my hardest time in the war. I had, for instance, not realized that I would meet people in the camp who had always known me as Harry Theeboom. How could I convince them that I was Frans Jan Berkenbosch? I saw that a simultaneous meeting with people who knew me as Harry and others who now knew me as Frans Jan would mean great difficulties.

Although it felt as if the camp had tens of thousands of inmates, it did not take long before I met old schoolmates from Amsterdam. I did not breathe a word about my other identity to them, although I had to make an exception for an aunt of mine (a sister of my mother) whom I also met there with her husband and daughter. They assured me that my secret was safe with them—and so it was.

They did try, however, to persuade me to come with them in case they would be put on a transport themselves, for they were sure that things would turn out badly with me. *[This shows, typically, how the people persisted in not believing they were going to be exterminated—Ed.]* But I refused staunchly. I would go on to the bitter end and somehow I felt sure of my rescue. For three and a half months I was forced to keep up this game of hide-and-seek, an almost impossible task. Being all the time on the alert drained my energy.

It happened many times that when I was having a chat with someone I saw someone approaching who knew me under my other identity. At such moments I hastily invented an excuse and fled. Once I was almost caught when a boy (Lodewijk Houthakker) who I had been in the same class with, came up to me when I was having a conversation with someone who knew me as Frans Jan and laughed at the other person for calling me by that name.

He told him: "Don't let yourself be fooled, this guy is Harry Theeboom and I was his classmate at the Christiaan de Wethschool". The best was to feign ignorance, I thought, so I answered in an amazed manner that I had no idea what he was talking about: "I don't know you, I don't know the Christiaan de Weth-school either." Lodewijk seemed to wonder whether he had gone crazy or I. "But you are from Amsterdam, aren't you?" I gave him another amazed look and told him that I was from Amersfoort. Then he said: "My, I know a guy in Amsterdam who looks exactly like you." Seen in retrospect, quite a clever answer.

I never told anyone that I was trying to get out of the camp by posing as a non-Jewish person. What I did do was pay regular visits to the lady in the administrative department who had taken up my case and who on one of those occasions told me that the German camp management were considering the matter.

On 24 November 1943 my patience was rewarded. An orderly came into the barracks and showed me a paper which said that I was to report at 9.00 am next day at the administrative department of the German camp leaders, outside the camp. That night I did not sleep a wink. I tried to think of all the possible questions and the answers I should give, thus preparing myself for the next day's confrontation. However, things turned out differently from what I had expected.

I was to report at the barracks of the camp commander. In front of the entrance was a wooden step. I opened the door and walked down the corridor to inquire about where to go. However, before I had a chance to do so I was literally kicked out of the barracks by the bully of the camp—Von Eck, a highly placed SS-officer who had only one eye. He called me all kinds of names and asked how I had dared to enter the officers' barracks in my clogs and without taking of my cap. (my outfit at the time consisted of an overall, complete with yellow star, a German winter cap with ear flaps, a woolen shawl and clogs.) I was scared stiff and felt completely rattled, but Von Eck had already walked on without considering me worthy of any further attention. I went out of the barracks again to take my clogs off and with my cap in my hand I took a second venture.

This time I was referred to the room of the camp commander Gemmeker. I knocked on the door and entered in a timid fashion.

"Your name is Frans Jan Berkenbosch?".

"Yes Sir"

"You are aware that this is a special day for you?"

"Yes Sir"

"And why?"

"Because it is my birthday today Sir"

"How old did you get today?"

"Seventeen Sir"

"Well then, I have a nice birthday present for you. You will be released from the camp. We investigated your papers and have come to the conclusion that you are not a Jew. We will let you know exactly when you may leave. You will have to check out here first and we will then give you further instructions."

"I am very glad to be released from this Jews camp Sir"

"I should imagine so" He answered. (You bastard—I thought)

◆   ◆   ◆

Harry's problems were not over. He had a lot of trouble to get his ID card replaced by the Gestapo officials who had destroyed it. He was very insistent until he finally received a new identity card, in his name (Frans Jan Berkenbosch), **issued by the Gestapo**! Later on he managed to escape from a prisoner transport after being arrested during a raid on the Mijlpaal. [*see also Chapter 12 "De Inval (the raid)"*] Harry's story shows that the system of the ID card falsification system had worked extremely well. This was a great morale booster to Karel and his co-workers in the TD movement. It also showed that a person should not "cave in" when confronted by the Germans. Often they were bluffing in order to trick their prisoners into admitting to facts which they could not substantiate.

Chapter 10
"NORMAL" WAR DAYS

PART 1—HOME AND SCHOOL

There really wasn't such a thing as a "normal day" during the war. At least I cannot think of one when comparing those days to normal days in the US today. What does it mean to have a normal day in abnormal times? There wasn't a normal day for anyone in the Netherlands and in particular for people involved in illegal activities? There was always tension, expectation of an impending disaster and fear, always something happening, either inside or outside of the Mijlpaal. After I was separated from my parents, abnormal events occurred practically every day to me until the end of the war in May, 1945. The sight of a German uniform, a Dutch Blackshirt, Nazi uniforms or a stranger with leather boots would always set of an alarm in me and in many others as well and it could send people into a flurry of activities even when there was no need. If there were no worrisome encounters with the authorities, reprisal measures, roundups or arrests in the area, there were always clandestine broadcasts of news from the fronts, the coded messages from London, or having to bring ration cards or other papers to addresses in various places. My problem as I am writing this is that I find it hard to remember what happened on any particular day unless it was something frightening or unusual, like the raid on the Mijlpaal, Rita giving birth, first to daughter Berna and later Helga, or the events on the farm in Achterveld Even then I often have to rely on memory of others to fix a specific date. Always you were bombarded by some news from the fronts or events elsewhere in the Netherlands. There were still radio programs being broadcast from the Dutch Radio studios in Hilversum but they were generally filled with news bulletins about the German triumphs and conquests, the famous "elastic front", how bad the Jews and their cronies, the British and the Americans, were for the Aryan world, or about new rules and regulations which had come into effect. There was at least some classical music, especially a lot of Wagner and Strauss, but also good opera and symphonic music. There was also music from German movies, some insipid songs in Dutch which had been cleared by the authorities as being harmless or good propaganda and martial music which was supposed to inspire the masses. Clearly not the kind of programming I, or most everybody else, had much interest in, except for the classical music, which I loved. When the weather was good, there was much to do and see outside, but when the weather was bad, as it so often is in the Netherlands, one of the best things to do was reading. Because the number of books in the house was limited, I went often to the library to borrow books. I read voraciously and grabbed anything that looked interesting. It didn't matter to me if it was for grownups or not. During those years I read Guy De Maupassant, Victor Hugo, Goethe, Schiller, Louis Couperus, Stijn Streuvels, Guido Gezelle, Paul D'Ivoy, Voltaire, Greek plays and many others, including Robert Graves and Shakespeare whose books for some reason, had not been removed from the library by the authorities. One set of books, "Human Sexuality" by Havelock Ellis was of particular interest to me, considering my past experiences on the farm in Hoevelaken. Needless to say, the books aroused me quite a bit and I had to take them up to my attic in order to read them without being embarrassed by my erections, which, I thought, could be seen by everyone. Another book which aroused me greatly was D. H. Lawrence's "Lady Chatterly's Lover". One time I even borrowed the first book of Dante's "La Divina Comedia" in the original language and a borrowed dictionary to read it. I didn't finish it, but managed to read about forty pages. The librarian always asked me if I was reading those books, but I told her that they were for Mrs. Brouwer, otherwise she would never have let me take them out of the library. There were proper youth books for the likes of me, but I thought those rather insipid.

I generally managed to stay out of trouble even though I was an active kid. That was often more good luck than having good sense. As a little boy I had never been dishonest, except for the usual fibs now and then, but the events of the past and the prevailing atmosphere had made me full of mistrust and dishonest. I did trust Karel and Rita Brouwer but did lie to them when I felt it necessary. I was always looking only out for myself and didn't much think in advance if I would be hurting others with my actions. I did steal many things and I did steal often. I had become rather adept at petty thievery. Things which I thought would be useful at some time in the future I would steal and hide. It was mostly money from some of the farmhouses I visited, although I remember also stealing a fairly big knife in a sheath, which I kept with me and hid from the Brouwers. For my thievery I went mostly to farmhouses. I knew somehow where people would hide money—usually under mattresses or beds or in cupboards on upper shelves, in hat-boxes or shoes. How I came to acquire that knowledge I don't remember. I made sure never to take money from a purse which was left about on a table or elsewhere, because the owner would remember how much they had in there and might sound the alarm. They usually would not count their stashed treasures every day. I would sneak into a farmhouse when I knew that the people would be out in the field or shopping and usually didn't need more than 10 minutes to find the hiding place and take a small amount of money. I had some close calls when the owners returned earlier than expected, but managed to get away without being caught or seen. I kept the loot in a hiding place, a tin can, buried in the back yard of the Mijlpaal, but in the end never made use of it. The reason was my unexpected and hurried escape from there after the raid (See the next chapter). I would like to go back and see if that tin can is still there, but I imagine that it was found by someone or just rotted away. Some coins might still be there though.

One day I managed to get hold of an old zither which had been left in a barn at a farm which was located near a town a few kilometers from our village. This instrument later became famous when it was played by Anton Karas in the movie "The Third Man". I told Karel and Rita that I had been at a farm and found the zither and that the people had given it to me. I taught myself to play the zither pretty well and later also took up the guitar. The guitar belonged to a Jewish person by the name of Jo Polak, who often came to the Mijlpaal and sometimes left it for me to play on. I became a pretty good player despite the fact that I had neither lessons nor could read music. Berna, the Brouwer's oldest daughter, remembers me entertaining the neighbor kids outside the house. The boys in the orphanage, which I entered in 1946, remember me playing the zither and the guitar, but I have no idea where the instruments ended up after I left the orphanage in 1949.

Listening to the clandestine radio broadcasts from the BBC and its special Dutch transmission was done mostly in the evenings. We had a radio which was alternately under a false hood of a sewing machine and later under the floor in the front room. I was the only one who could crawl under the floor and so it became my job to write down the coded messages and listen to the news. First there came the sign of the BBC signing on, the famous *"Boom-Boom-Boom-Booommm"* on the kettledrums, the Morse sign of the "V" for Victory. Then came an old Dutch martial song *"In the name of Orange, open the gate"*, which always sent shivers down my spine (and still does). Then came the news in Dutch. All about the fighting at the Eastern and Western fronts, which kept coming closer and closer. Then came a series of coded messages, *"John will have a birthday on the 25th"* or *"Peter will marry Jean on…."* or *"David, the doctor wants to see you tomorrow"* and

"The baby carriage for Mary will be delivered Friday". All these messages I wrote down meticulously while laying flat on my stomach under the living room floor. The only light was a candle. Then I gave the messages and reports from the fronts to Karel, who read them and then burned them. That was also part of my "normal day".

I went to local schools on some days. Schools in many areas did not operate regularly during the war because male teachers often had to hide from German conscription raids or a school was suddenly used as a garrison for a battalion of soldiers or as a temporary prison for people who had been caught in a roundup. When the school was in session, I joined heartily in the turf fights between the Catholic School and the Protestant one. These fights were usually about insults which were shouted at each other, when someone crossed an arbitrary "property line" (did you think, dear reader, that youth gangs was anything new to the nineties?) and sometimes it was about the Protestant girls being harassed by the Catholic boys. Sometimes it was the other way around. Although the Catholic boys and girls went to separate schools, Catholic boys defended the girls' honor as fervently as did the Protestants. Most of the kids came from simple, fairly uneducated farming backgrounds and I, as a city boy, always had to be on the lookout for sudden confrontations because I was different, dressed differently, spoke proper Dutch (I did acquire the local patois after a while), had received better education in Amsterdam and was therefore ahead of the others in all subjects, but most of all because the girls seemed to like my "sophistication". I was a favorite with most of the more popular girls and that caused a number of the fights in the beginning because I soon found out which girl "belonged" to which boy. When a girl smiled at me or talked to me I usually reciprocated and some boys took offense at "that city slicker" butting in on their turf. So there was quite a bit of jealousy involved in some of my fights.

I had to run many a time when several boys ganged up on me and I would take my wooden shoes in my hand and be off in the blink of an eye. I was pretty fast in those days and had an instinct for sniffing out when an opponent and some of his friends were out to make trouble for me. Sometimes it came to a fight and then the clogs I was wearing came in handy as well. They turned out to be pretty good weapons when I was attacked by more than one boy. You were allowed to use them in such a case. A one-on-one fight was always done with bare fists, nails teeth and went on until one of the combatants gave up or until we were separated by passing adults. The scratches, black eyes, bloody noses and bumps, which I sometimes came home with, would heal after a few days and I would be none the worse. My willingness to fight when needed earned me the friendship and respect of the village boys and after a while I was seldom bothered and many became my friends.

What baffles me today is that I cannot remember the names of the boys except for Arie Ruitenberg and Wim Kas. I remember Wim's his name only because I fooled around with his older sister Dien. We always had to shoo him away or find another time and place because he wanted to see what Dien and I were up to. Dien was a fairly heavy set girl with long pigtails and she waddled a bit when she walked. But she had a smiling, sunny disposition, a warm heart, a warm body and a good sense of humor. Another girl I became very (very) friendly with was Jennie Wynands. She lived with a pair of uncles who had a bicycle repair shop on the road to Achterveld. I never learned where her parents were, but she was also from somewhere else and better educated than the rest of the kids. We got along famously, but I had to be careful to divide myself evenly between Dien and Jennie or there would be trouble. I lost contact with both of them, but did hear that Jennie had been in some legal trouble and later killed herself. I still have a nice photograph of her, sitting on a chicken coop or rabbit hutch in her uncle's backyard.

My riskiest school friendship came later and was with a girl called Lien Kieviet. She was, at least the boys all thought so, a very beautiful girl, a blonde with a freckled face and an extremely well developed body. Lien divided her friendship and her body between me and my chief rival, Arie. Arie's nickname was *"het haantje"*, which denoted more or less that he had the temper of a feisty Bantam rooster. So had I, and I can't tell you how many times we tussled over her, but in the end we were still good friends and shared Lien's ample graces. Arie's dad was a paid farm hand and they lived with a bunch of kids in a two-room hovel on the east side of Hamersveld. The poverty and filth in that house was deplorable even in those days and I did not visit them often because they clearly were the source of most of the fleas and lice which plagued all the kids at the school.

The problem with Lien was that she came from a family of ardent fascists. Her two older sisters, one blonde and one brunette, were very attractive girls and were dating SS officers (no soldiers for them). The sisters were not very steadfast and orderly in their alliances and invitations and sometimes more than one suitor turned up for the same girl, which then led to shouts and tussles inside the house, the latter often ending up in the street in front of their house so that the German MP's would have to be called in to break up the fights. What a great event that always was. The cry went out: "Fighting at the Kieviets!" and half the village would turn up to have a look and smirk at the spectacle.

Apparently, due to my being city kid, and thus better than the country "riff-raff", I was often invited after school to the Kieviet home for cookies and chocolate milk which were luxuries during the war and only Nazi party members could obtain those items. Often I would find SS officers there, who would pat my head, hand out chocolate bars and insinuate all kinds of things in German which would make the sisters and Lien, who understood German well, blush. After the war ended and before the Kieviets were able to flee the town, they were hauled out of the house the sisters' hair was shorn off and they were paraded as whores with their family and other collaborators through the village and in the nearby city of Amersfoort. They were treated pretty roughly by their captors, punched and kicked by the public, which also pelted them with all sorts of projectiles and I actually felt a bit sorry for them, but especially for Lien. I never told Karel about this liaison while it was going on because I knew that he would be angry with me about it and would have forbidden it and Karel's anger was far more important to me than anything else. Actually it was foolish of me, but she was charming and beautiful and I've always been a sucker for charm and beauty.

Teachers in the schools were strict, no matter which school you attended. Caning was the rule for disciplining and I don't think too many of us boys escaped the teachers' gym stick—a one meter long, three-quarter inch diameter hardwood—or their accurate aim with pieces of chalk and the blackboard eraser. Escaping from their grasp and running away didn't help because they would get you the next day. Our fiery red-haired headmaster's aim was fabulous and you never knew something was coming at you until it hit with deadly accuracy. We always knew when someone had been punished—just by looking at them walk after school or, if they had a bicycle, we would see them stand on the pedals and move pretty slowly. We always sympathized with the victim, even if he was from another school. But we took our punishment as men because mostly we deserved it.

From time to time we got into big trouble with farmers for stealing fruit from the trees near the farms, jumping drainage ditches between their fields, which could damage the ditch walls, or taking unauthorized horse rides. The dogs might be sent after us, resulting in torn pants, or the farmer would shoot at us with salt pellets when we ran away. Being hit with a salt pellet is very painful especially when it lodges in your back or your behind and it takes a while to heal, but it left no scars. I was hit once in my thigh and it hurt like the dickens and took about a week to heal. Later in the war when the guns had been confiscated by the authorities and powder was no longer available that danger didn't exist anymore. But the dogs and the farmers armed with a stick still remained our adversaries when we trespassed.

One of the bad memories I have was due to an experience I had to witness in late1943 or early 1944 when a group of German soldiers beat a teenage boy nearly to death before my eyes and those of another twenty or so youngsters and grownups, who were forced to watch proper punishment meted out by the German Supermen. We were all in the municipal swimming pool in Amersfoort and one boy jumped from a diving board and accidentally scratched the forehead of a German soldier, drawing quite a bit of blood. The soldiers, who were drunk and boisterous, decided that the boy had done this on purpose and that he had to be punished for this outrageous act of sabotage. The group of five or six caught him after a short noisy chase around the pool. The boy screamed for help while they were chasing him, but no one dared or could do anything. When they caught the boy they began hitting and kicking him until he stopped screaming and moving and left him laying beside the pool, with blood seeping from his nose and mouth into the blueish water, looking like a bloodied rag doll. Three of the German soldiers had forced all of us other swimmers, who were in or around the pool, to get out and stand and watch the spectacle as a lesson. They threatened, shook or hit anyone who closed his eyes. When their "lesson" was over, they got dressed and went away laughing. No matter—it was only a Dutch kid. The mighty German Reich had shown its superior power again.

We were all left standing around, paralyzed with fear, in shock at the cruelty and violence, but mostly shaking with anger and physically sick from the spectacle. Many of us were crying, some were throwing up and none uttered a word. We didn't look each other in the face. We got dressed silently and went toward the exit. The management had called the police and both the military and civilian police came, asked a few questions and took the boy away in an ambulance. I have never talked about this to anyone at the Mijlpaal. I think it was because felt ashamed and guilty for watching this spectacle, for wanting so much to do something, and not doing it. Not that I, or any of us who were present, could have helped, and it would have gotten us into big trouble. But still, this feeling of utter helplessness in the face of this animal-like cruelty is terrible......

Another atrocity I had to witness was the shooting of innocent bystanders as a "lesson" for the population. It happened in Amersfoort on the street running alongside the railroad yard, close to the station. There is still a plaque there commemorating the event. I don't remember the name of the street—it was a long one—nor do I remember how many people were lined up, but I think there were about ten of them. This German "educational" act was a reprisal for the shooting of a German. I do remember closing my eyes when the bodies fell and nearly throwing up when they twitched and jerked. They were not all killed immediately. The Germans had to use their revolvers on one or two. I couldn't watch it. Again, there was this feeling of relief and guilt after it was over. Relief that it wasn't I who was shot and guilt because I was glad about that.

PART 2—AIR RAIDS AND WING TANKS

In the second half of 1943, and during 1944 and 1945, daylight bombing raids of strategic targets in the Netherlands and, especially, Germany were a daily occurrence. That period was, in a way, a magical time for us youngsters. We didn't see it as the destruction of cities nor of the death and carnage it caused among their inhabitants. Nor did we realize the dangers to ourselves. We only saw the hundreds of planes and hoped they would kill as many Germans as possible. They, the Germans, were the enemy and the best enemy was a dead enemy—that's what we said to each other. The overflights were not without danger to the people on the ground and many a curious onlooker was killed while standing outside watching the masses of planes pass overhead and drop all kinds of hardware as the result of the dogfights.

On clear days it usually started with someone noticing something looking like a small white patch of cloud moving in from the west toward the east. As the cloud drew nearer, similar white patches would become visible behind and to the sides of it in the western sky. We would begin to hear a faint hum. The small clouds came closer, the hum became slowly louder and each cloud separated into distinct vapor trails with the plane at the front of it looking like a small dot. Steadily the noise increased as the trails and dots came slowly approached. Then we would start to see the airplane shapes clearly in front of each vapor trail. As they came nearer, the hum became louder and louder and by the time they passed overhead, it had become a deafening roar which made the air vibrate and the windows rattle. It was a sound, the intensity of which, even today, is indescribable. It's a little like the sound a large number of diesel locomotives running at full power and you standing between them. The mass of planes would pass overhead fairly slowly, because they were loaded with bombs. The noise filled the air and shook the ground and the houses—the sky was just one mass of planes, the big bombers moving ponderously and the protective fighter squadrons moving above or below them at great speed like so many mosquitos. We tried to count them and argued whether there were one hundred and fifty or one hundred and sixty five. *"You missed the ones over there"* and *"You didn't count the ones behind the church"*. *"Yes I did"*. *"No you didn't, because......"* We also knew how to identify the types of planes and on days with less visibility there were always heated arguments whether those had been Liberators, Flying Fortresses, or any of the other types. We also knew which fighter planes accompanied them; the Spitfires, Hawker Hunters, Mosquitos (used generally more for dive-bombing), Thunderbirds and the twin-tailed Lockheed-Lightnings and so on.

Most of these flights were just overflights and the planes would disappear toward the east, but quite often we would see a group of fast-moving planes coming from the East. Those would be German Messerschmitt or Focke-Wulff interceptors and fighters. They would attack the bomber convoys and be engaged by Allied escorts. Bombers which were hit would drop their lethal load indiscriminately and try to return home. Quite often we saw planes go down, trailing smoke or in flames, belching fire. We all tried to find cover when that happened because they often spiraled out of control and could hit the ground anywhere. Parachutes were often seen nearby and when that happened the whole area was overrun by Germans trying to capture the crew members. On cloudy days we could only hear the roar of the engines, but when there was a dogfight going on planes would suddenly appear through the cloud cover chasing each other or crashing into the ground. At the same time shell casings or pieces of planes would come tumbling down like a hail storm. It was quite dangerous to be watching all this but us kids were immortal and wouldn't heed the warnings of our elders.

There were many attacks on the railroads. Nearby Amersfoort had a huge switch-yard, was the center-point of railroads going in all directions and the trains were prime targets. There were rail lines from Amersfoort to Amsterdam, the north of the Netherlands, the south and locations in between, such as the railroad to Arnhem and Apeldoorn, cities further east. We were located between those rail lines and had a front seat when the Mosquitos, Hurricanes, Spitfires, Thunderbolts and Lockheed Lightnings strafed and dive-bombed the trains and bridges. Whenever a group of those planes appeared in the sky, we knew exactly what they were going to do. They would break up their formation, get in line and peel off and dive with their engines screaming. They straightened out over the target and you could see them shooting or releasing their bombs. What an excitement that destruction was for us boys.

When bombs, pieces of airplane and spent shells rained down it became quite dangerous to stay out, but stay out we did. There was too much to see. There were also projectiles from the machine guns and cannon which had missed their target. These would go into the ground with a dull thud or, sometimes, accompanied by an explosion. Without regard for the danger we would be stretched out on our backs and look up, yelling at each other and pointing at smoking or falling planes and only when the rain of lethal metal became too heavy would we seek shelter. Quite a number of people all over the Netherlands did the same thing and did get hurt as a result. One of my teachers was killed this way by a wing tank which came hurtling out of the sky, and which hit him in the chest and crushed him.

We would jump with joy and cheer at every German fighter which was shot down, and were even happier when we didn't see a parachute open. We invariably tried to get close to the burning trains but quite often we were held back by the Germans—and it was quite dangerous because many trains had munitions aboard which could explode at any time or were already exploding. I remember seeing a Hurricane pilot eject, but his parachute didn't open and we saw his body hurtling to the ground and disappear into one of the nearby forests. His plane flew on for a short distance, belching smoke and then dove into the ground about five kilometers away. We went to look for it the next day and found that it had crashed in a very soggy field and only the tail was sticking out. The engine had sheared off and traveled on and was found half a kilometer away after it had gone through a farmhouse. The Germans had cordoned off the area so we were unable to get close. I don't know if anyone in the farmhouse was hurt.

Apart from the shells, shrapnel and pieces of the planes we collected, the most coveted parts were the wing tanks, which the planes jettisoned when they were empty. You were supposed to report their finding or hand them over immediately to the authorities whenever they were found, but we used to hide them for later use and actually sold some of them to farmers.

When we found our first tank, I had the idea that we could make canoes out of them and have fun with them on the small canals and maybe have races. All the tanks we obtained, smelled strongly of fuel and we were wise enough always to be careful with them. Some tanks still had fuel in them which we carefully collected. Our first tank conversion gave us quite a lesson. We made sure it was empty, filled it with water and then carefully cut a hole in the top with metal shears which one of the boys borrowed from his dad, the local blacksmith. We hammered the edges of the hole so they wouldn't cut us. Then we emptied the water and put the tank in a drainage canal. This was going to be our first canoe!

Most of the bigger canals were about three meters wide and we tied two ropes to an eye at the nose of the tank and one to the tail end. One boy would walk on each side of the canal and tow the boat. We didn't make a decision what to do with the rope at the rear. I didn't have all that figured out yet! Since I was the clever one on the project, I got the honor of the first cruise. Anyone who has ever tried to get into a kayak has some idea of its stability and of the art of getting in. A wing tank from a plane is worse. The minute I stepped into our craft it turned around and dumped me into the water. It was summer and that wasn't too bad. But I didn't understand why it happened and thought that I had entered in the wrong way. So I told two of the boys to hold the boat steady while I stepped in, stretched my legs in the tank and sat down. Having settled and grabbed hold of the sides I told them to let go and start pulling. The moment they let go, our "canoe" rolled over, only this time I was sitting in it, my legs were caught and I ended up upside down with my head stuck in the mud. I vividly remember the panic which struck me. This was the end and I was surely going to die. I struggled, but couldn't free myself. It was just lucky that Arie, my rival for Lien Kievit's attentions at school, had the presence of mind to jump into the canal, grope for me and haul me out. I must have been a sight, because all of them were howling with laughter, while I was crying from the horrible experience I had just gone through and the foul tasting water. I was spitting mud and weeds and gagging and was coughing and wheezing. I had green scum, weeds and mud all over me. I must have looked like the green monster risen from the swamp and it was no wonder my companions were rolling on the ground with laughter.

I should have learned my lesson and left those tanks for the Germans, but I didn't. I decided that we should get ourselves another tank and tie the two together to some wooden planks which would be between them and so make a raft! A few days later we did get that other tank and, after lashing the two pontoons and some planks together with rope and steel wires, had a whale of a time playing on the small canals and small forest lakes in the area. We even drilled a hole in one of the planks and put up a mast with two cross-pieces nailed to it and tied a piece of cloth as a sail between the cross-pieces. Now we could even sail. Steering we did with the oars of an old rowboat which had rotted away behind the smith's shed. It wasn't the best steering and we often had to get out in the mud to extricate ourselves from the banks. We stayed away from the roads and moved our raft in the evenings through the fields in order not to be seen by the police or the Germans. After the raid on the Mijlpaal and my escape to Achterveld I lost track of our beautiful craft. I never had a chance to ask my former schoolmates because I never saw them again and I wonder what happened to it, and to them.

PART 3—BED BUGS, FLEAS AND OTHER PESTS

My sleeping quarter, during most of my life at the Mijlpaal was on top of the big water reservoir in the attic. The tank was about one meter high and big enough for four people to sleep on. There was a small oblong window which allowed me to look out over the fenced-in backyard and the green meadows, populated by peacefully grazing cows, behind it. I kept my clothes and books and other "possessions" in a wooden box on the floor. I did most of my reading while laying on my mattress in front of that little window. I read a lot in those days. After all, television was unknown to us then and there were few worthwhile Dutch radio programs; multi-wave receivers, with which you could listen to Radio Free Europe, were a rarity in those days and were not allowed by the authorities. Another use of the window was for "backlighting" my blankets and then searching out and killing the fleas and bedbugs which plagued us continuously during those war years. Hygiene wasn't the best anywhere in the country—even soap was rationed—and there wasn't anything like DDT or any other effective insecticide available. Apparently I brought a lot of those parasites home from school or from the farms I worked on. Public transportation was also infested and very little could be done about it. Anyone who traveled by bus or train, when it was still possible to do so, would be sure to play host to some of those parasites. So, I always had fleas and bedbugs to fight and I used to sit on my mattress on the tank and move the blanket across the window section by section to locate the bugs and fleas. In the beginning, I used to grab the bedbugs and put them in a glass jar with water so that I didn't have to crush them. I wasn't squeamish about the crushing but those bed bugs stank when you crushed them and any place you did the crushing on, including your fingers, would be smelly for quite a while. I stopped drowning them and went back to crushing after I overturned the jar one day, wetting my mattress and having to chase after some of the bugs which had not completely drowned. From then on I suffered the smell, but the bugs were squeezed properly and were 100% dead.

The fleas were also executed on the spot and they were tough customers to catch. Their execution was possible only when you caught them in the blanket and squeezed them there between your nails. I had to make sure that my nails were always long enough to do that and you had to pry the fleas from the fabric. So I spent at least one hour each day in "decontaminating" my blankets and I became pretty adept at catching and crushing.

Another one of the prevalent parasitic diseases was scabies, which is caused by tiny mites burying themselves under your skin. They were frequent visitors during the war. I can remember being infested with them twice. I had to strip naked and was then smeared with some pungent and stinging cream Dr. Bergink had given us. The clothes and bedclothes had to be washed and the top of the water tank was "cleaned" with kerosene or turpentine. It soaked into the wood and discouraged a lot of pests from inhabiting the grooves in the cover of the tank, but it made everything that came into contact with the tank, including me, reek of kerosene for a long time.

In the bathtub on the second floor we used to store wheat in sacks. From time to time when the sacks were needed, the wheat was stored loose in the bathtub. Every few days we used to grind some of it to make bread. The bathroom window was mostly left open so that the grain wouldn't get moldy, but that brought in scores of house sparrows. They not only feasted but also pooped on the grain. There was no way to keep them out when the window was open because there were no screens available. The only way was to trap them and kill them. That was my job. I'm not proud of it, but I became quite expert at killing sparrows. I would to rush in, slam the window shut and grab the panicked birds one by one. I broke their necks or slammed them to the floor and then carried them outside and gave them to the pigs. Since there were always a few birds which managed to escape before I shut the window, the word apparently got out in the bird world that this bathroom was unhealthy and after a while the bird infestation trickled to a minimum. Today when I sit looking at the activities around our bird feeders, I wonder how I could kill all those little defenseless birds with such ease. I guess that necessity made me do it and hope that their little souls will understand and forgive me.

Mice were our biggest challenge. They would get into the wheat, the hams which were hanging in that same bathroom and any other foods we stored there. Again, it was my job to catch them. I became expert at saving table-scraps and using them in the different areas of the house to set traps. Whenever anyone found mouse droppings they were supposed to leave them until I had seen them. I could tell by looking at them closely where the mice had come from and where their "roads" were, because mice don't just travel all over the place. They have certain routes. Then I would set my traps (I had about a dozen of them) in their path and I always caught them. Our pigs enjoyed eating them. Sometimes I was fast enough to chase them into a corner and catch them by hand. I used to kill them them by throwing them on a hard surface. The other inhabitants of the house sometimes looked askance at me and my mice-chasing techniques, but they worked and so everyone, except the dead mice, was happy.

PART 4—BERNA, HELGA AND GREET

We'll start with little Berna. She was Karel and Rita's first daughter. She was my first little "sister" and I loved her very much and still do today. She was born on November 16, 1943 and I thought she was the most beautiful thing I had ever seen. I could hug her and talk to her and she had these beautiful eyes. She has remained beautiful through the years and still is a striking woman., now with children and grandchildren. I sometimes played guitar or zither for her, one of the things she remembers even today. When she was still very little she had the habit of flying into terrible rages and hold her breath so long that she went blue in the face. I found that terrifying and was always afraid that she was going to die. Karel was totally unperturbed by her antics and used to grab her by her two feet, turn her upside down and sharply slap her bare bottom once or twice. That would immediately stop her from holding her breath and I used to breathe easier at the same time. Strange that I can see Karel slapping Berna's bare behind while Berna herself has no recollection of this at all. Later her little sister Helga came along, but that was close to the end of the war and I saw very little of her—as a result there was no real bond between us.

Greet was Rita's youngest sister, and she lived with her parents in Amersfoort. I had known her before the war. She was the one who taught me to play billiards in the gentlemen's club where her father was the manager. The club was directly opposite my uncle's bakery and café in, what was then, the main street in Amersfoort—the "Langestraat". Greet, my cousins Menno and Bertie and I, as well as an occasional friend, sometimes played hide-and-seek among the furniture in the different rooms which made up the club. When we caught each other, we wrestled on one of the big brown padded chairs or one of the couches. I liked wrestling with Greet. She was tall and quite strong and a good match for me. She and her parents later left the downtown of the city and went to live in a beautiful villa on the outskirts where I visited them often. Greet and I remained good friends and our friendship blossomed into more than that. We became closer and our friendship more intense. She was actually the only one I did talk to about myself and my feelings because she seemed to understand and was not judgmental like adults were. We talked a lot, mostly about daily events; what happened at school; how the war was going and about what had happened to people who had disappeared. We talked about her father, who had been in Camp Amersfoort and had suffered there tremendously. He somehow managed to survive. All this was pretty heavy talk for young kids, but it also shows how much we were occupied with what was happening around us. In time we started paying more attention to each other's moods, touching hands and, when our hormones took over, we started kissing. I don't think that anyone ever knew or suspected. Before I was sent to the orphanage, which caused us to be separated, she told me that we would marry when we were grown up. All of Greet's family were tall and Greet herself was about half a head taller than I was at the time even though she was, I think, a bit younger than I. This didn't seem to bother her at all, although it bothered me in the beginning. I was little and rather self-conscious about my height, and that was why I was in the beginning quite hesitant to be seen with her and, as a result, rather passive. I was also really afraid that, if this relationship had become known, there would be grave repercussions for me, such as separating us and me having to be moved away from Karel and his family. Neither Karel nor Rita or Greet's parents would have tolerated it, especially had they known how far our relationship went in the end.

This is why I did not instigate our greater intimacy. It was Greet, who took the initiative here. We had been meeting quite frequently and would take long bike rides or walk with our arms around each other on the moors and in the forested areas in and around Leusden and Amersfoort. One day when I was supposed to deliver an envelope, containing a message or papers, to someone in the vicinity of the "Leusderhei" (the moors near Leusden), we were out cycling together and Greet suddenly said "Wait" and stopped on the bike path. She leaned her bike against a tree. I didn't know what she was planning to do, so I dismounted also and put my bike down. We were in a densely wooded area, behind a clump of trees and shrubs, not far from the famous old medieval tower in Leusden, which was also close to the infamous concentration camp. There were never many people in that area. I thought we were going to kiss and yes, she turned around and put her arms around me and started to kiss me rather passionately on the lips. We had exchanged kisses before, but usually before we separated to go home and during an occasional cuddle. I was a bit surprised at her breathless eagerness but responded readily and happily. Suddenly she grabbed the envelope I was still holding, lifted her skirt (I remember clearly that it was a pleated tartan with red and green squares), and stuffed it in her under-panties. She looked at me with a big grin and said *"If you want it, you have to come and get it"*. I hesitated and tried to coax her to give it back to me. After all, we were out in the open and though it was very wooded, anyone coming around a curve in the bike path would have seen us. She stepped back and said again, "Take it out if you want it" and ran from the bike path in between the trees. I didn't delay and we started wrestling, first standing and then on the ground. We both were excited and I became very aroused when she let my hand slide into her panties and touch her soft bare flesh. I remember that her panties were red also. Greet was also aroused and held me very tight. From my previous encounters on the farm in Hoevelaken, I knew that I could easily hurt her and so I was careful and tender and tried not to hurry. But by now we were both excited and a bit clumsy and, while I touched her very carefully, Greet, in the process of trying to undo my pants tore one of the buttons off my fly. I had to explain that later at home by saying that I'd fallen and gotten tangled up with the bike—but since I brought the button with me I was forgiven. (Like everything else, buttons were a scarce commodity during the war). I still don't know how I could contain myself that time and not ejaculate in her hand, but I suppose her inexperience at that time had something to do with it. In fact, she hurt me a little. Later she told me that I had been the first boy she "had touched there".

That first time, behind the bushes and with a chance of other people coming, nothing more than some exploration of each other's bodies took place, although I certainly wanted more. However we managed to restrain ourselves, straighten our clothes and mount our bikes. We both knew that we had crossed a threshold and that there would be no turning back to the old relationship between us. The envelope had undergone some rough handling and had to be straightened out a bit, but was delivered duly at the correct address. There were some Jewish people hiding and I suppose the envelope contained ration cards or other needed items for them. We never delivered letters. Messages or instructions were only delivered orally. Greet and I never told anybody about our relationship and she told me to meet at her house a few days later to take another bike ride. When I came to the house on the appointed day it appeared that she had made other plans. She was, it turned out, quite a good planner. In fact, she had known that her mother would go out that day and that she would be alone in the house. I discovered that the moment she answered the door. She quickly closed the door behind me and put her arms around me and started to kiss me. I was surprised and stepped back and said "But your mother......?" She grinned and told me that her mother wouldn't be back for about three hours. She led me upstairs and we went to her room. I had never been there. Once we were inside—she turned around and quietly said "Undress me". We undressed each other, except for her panties and my underpants, she turned the bedcovers down and we and laid down together on her bed and kissed and held each other tight. It was again that wonderful feeling our bodies touching, our legs and arms around each other and we lingered like that for a while. I kissed her small budding breasts and her back and she stroked me and felt my penis through my underpants. Both of us were easily aroused, and obviously we suddenly couldn't wait and we hurried and I confess that my restraint wasn't very good on that first day. I felt that I was going to have an ejaculation and didn't want to do it in the bed and so I jumped of the bed and ran out of the room but never made it to the bathroom and, to my embarrassment, ejaculated on the carpet in the hallway. Adding to my embarrassment was Greet's surprise. She had run after me to see why I had suddenly left her. Apparently she had been "educating" herself and she was not as ignorant as I had been two years earlier in Hoevelaken but she wasn't very knowledgeable about young males and their propensity to ejaculate too quickly. She had never seen this nor known about it and stood wide eyed and looked at the mess I'd made. I told her that I would clean it and went back to her room after wiping the floor and we started caressing again and my hand made its way to her vagina and clitoris. Surprisingly she actually had an orgasm that time. She tensed up and became very wet and suddenly came with a series of short soft moans which she tried to suppress, while her body shook. After the "storm" we both said repeatedly that we loved each other and would try to be together as often as we could. We kept that promise and met quite often at her house, when her mother was away, or we went into the woods or to the Leusderheide (the moors). We also had one meeting in the haystack at the Hartman farm when I knew that both the Hartmans would be gone for a while. We never had actual intercourse because she wanted to keep her virginity until we were married. She was a very wonderful and very sweet girl. My joy and satisfaction were to make her feel good and to be close to her and sometimes, not always, feel her body given over to an orgasm. She helped me get my orgasm and became very adept at prolonging my excitement. Her being there for me was a great support at a time when I had very little love from more normal sources.

Our relationship was interrupted for about half a year by the raid (see Ch 12) on the Mijlpaal but we renewed it for a short while after I was reunited with the Brouwer family after the war ended. Ultimately our relationship ended when I was sent to the orphanage in Hilversum at the end of 1945. Once there I was not allowed to visit Karel and Rita and their family and was not allowed to write. My mother's relatives from Amersfoort, the only ones which survived the war in hiding, objected strenuously to my having any contact with the Brouwers because they had changed from Protestant to become Catholic during the war. I never understood my family's reasoning—the religion did not change the Brouwer's. Later on the relations between me and Karel and Rita were soured even more by false stories which my aunt spread around about the same people who had saved her and her family and me, stories which later turned out to be lies. I am sure Greet and I would have remained good friends when we grew up and we would have remembered our "affair" with a smile. I left Holland in 1949 and I never saw her again. She died at a very young age of breast cancer, just like her older sister Guda and her mother. Her sister Rita, her own children and Rita's children are still alive and I know that they realized during Greet's lifetime what a lovely, wonderful person she was.

Chapter 11
THE HUNGER WINTER OF 1944–45

The Hunger Winter—the winter of 1944–1945 was a memorable and probably the most terrible and devastating time in the history of WWII in the Netherlands. Most of Europe had been liberated—even the southern part of the Netherlands up to the Rhine and Waal rivers. Then a few further advances were made, but the three most populous provinces, North-Holland, South Holland and Utrecht were bypassed by the Allies and remained under the Nazi yoke. We had been so jubilant when the airborne divisions landed near Arnhem. We had been so sure that this was going to be the end. It turned out that the whole operation was botched pretty well by Field Marshall Montgomery and his staff and the liberators' soldiers paid dearly for those mistakes.

There had also been a number of delays and setbacks at the fronts south of us, notably the Battle of the Bulge, and after that fight was won, the main thrust of the Allied forces had gone into Germany itself, while the area of the Netherlands north of the Rhine, Waal and Maas (also known as Meuse in Belgium and France) rivers had been left in German hands. Food rations had been reduced again and again until they reached the bare minimum, but, until the fall of 1944, the supply had somehow been adequate to keep the population alive. The Dutch government—in—exile in London had called for a railway strike because most of the transport was used for the German war machine and this was thought to aid the Allied war effort.

When the railroads did strike, in September 1944, the German occupier, as a punitive measure, stopped all transportation by water as well to the western part of the Netherlands. As a result, food, which had been reaching the west from the eastern provinces by the way of rivers and canals, could not reach the big cities in the western parts of the country and serious shortages began in September 1944. Four and a half million people were starving, and families, many of them left without their breadwinners, who had been taken to Germany, were forced to start foraging in the countryside. The Germans relented later and allowed transportation of food through the rivers, but by then it was too late in the season because of the extremely severe winter, which resulted in canals and rivers being frozen solid. As a result no transport could take place. There were no ice-breakers, and if there was one to be found somewhere there was no fuel to operate it even for the Germans, who were by now forced to use horses to move their military trucks and ordnance. It was a normal sight to see military trucks and guns being drawn by horses.

So, literally thousands of women, children and old people wearing clothes which were too thin took to the roads looking for food. Shivering in the freezing weather and dressed in their, often wet, clothes, disheveled and haunted looking—it was an awful procession. They traded everything they had, including sometimes their bodies, to provide food for their families and they used every conceivable means of hauling them to the farms in order to trade them for food. Some used bicycles without tires, others used baby-carriages and still others had used the children's roller skates and a few planks to fashion carts. To see them made all of us, who still had something to eat, feel terrible, but it was impossible for us to feed those long lines of emaciated and hungry people. It was the haunted look in their eyes, which made me feel most uncomfortable. I felt guilty for having something in my stomach most of the time and I avoided eye contact when I met them on the streets. I, like many others, would act if I didn't see them. I can't imagine, even today, how it must have felt to those desperate people to be "invisible". These were mothers, grandmothers, grandfathers with children.

German soldiers or Dutch "Landwacht" and "Black Police" would often put up roadblocks to control "food smuggling" and confiscate some or all of their food or bartering possessions for their own use, or let them keep it after exacting payment in the form of jewelry or, if the lady pleased their eyes and was "willing", sex. There was also a problem of bands of thieves and robbers which roamed many areas. The further the winter progressed, the worse the situation became. According to research conducted after the war, more than 22,000 people died of hunger and 200,000 had to be taken to hospitals with various illnesses caused by the lack of food. This was out of a population of about four million. Those who were affluent enough to be able to buy food on the black market were not well fed either. Many people suffered after the war from remaining health problems such as bad teeth, skeletal problems or intestinal diseases as a result of the deprivation during that last year. There also were plenty of mental problems, some of which surfaced many years later. The incidence of venereal diseases skyrocketed as a result of the often forced sexual encounters between the German soldiers and the Dutch women and there were stories going around that sick Germans some-times purposely sought out women to infect them.[H. Van der Zee, "The Hun-ger Winter" University of Nebraska Press, 1998]

At the Mijlpaal the situation had become equally serious. Even with extra food coupons available to us there was often no food available from the suppliers and as a result we had to augment our food intake with non-traditional and unappe-tizing dishes such as boiled stinging nettles as a substitute for spinach. Collecting the nettles was my job and it took me only a short and painful time to learn how to pick the tender tops without being covered by painful welts. We had tea from rose pods and had a horrible sugar substitute in the form of syrup from sugar beets. We also ate suitable boiled flower bulbs. Those didn't taste very good either, but filled your stomach. I am not sure if some of the meat we ate didn't come from a dog or a cat but that didn't matter. If you saw a skinned rabbit and a skinned cat hanging side by side, you wouldn't know the difference, provided the head, feet and tail were off. Once it was cut up and cooked no one knew nor cared. We had long since slaughtered one pig and the rabbits we had raised. If we'd had a cat, we would probably have slaughtered and eaten it as well. We did have a dog, but he wasn't touched because he was Rita's pet. In addition, at the time Rita was pregnant with Helga and thus needed proper nutrition. We also had stored potatoes in a straw and earth covered heap in the backyard but they were getting pretty soft and squishy. Food supply became a problem for us also. So we had to go out and hunt for food like the others. In the beginning we were able, through Karel Brouwer's connections in the area to find food supplies from local farmers. The onslaught of foragers from the cities in the area made that more and more difficult. There just wasn't enough to go around for everyone.

◆   ◆   ◆

The following story is from Harry Theeboom (alias Frans Jan Berkenbosch) who has already been quoted elsewhere in this memoir. He went on a hunger winter trek together with Karel Brouwer. Following is his own unedited English translation of this story which he wrote originally in Dutch. The translation was made by him for my wife Rose:

◆   ◆   ◆

November (1944) had come and Karel decided he and I would go on bike to the north of the province of North Holland to get food there. Relatives of his had a farm in the village of Kolhorn there and he hoped they might be willing to provide us with flour and other foodstuffs we were now short of. We were fortunate to have a vegetable garden behind the house, and a pigstie [sic] that we had built there ourselves and in which we had fattened two pigs. One of them had already disappeared into our stomachs, the other would serve as a meal to celebrate Christmas and the turn of the year.

Through a neighbor he was able to borrow a small trailer on pneumatic tyres that had been dropped by the Allied Forces and that could easily be pulled by two bikes. As it was impossible to cover the distance in one day, also because after 8:00 pm a curfew became effective, we would make a stopover with relatives in Amsterdam.

The journey there went off as it should, although we soon heard rumours about German soldiers posting everywhere to confiscate food from people on their way back. I felt embarrassed to compare our material with that of the other people we saw. Rickety handcarts, bikes on wooden tyres and women pushing prams: a sorry sight. After our stopover in Amsterdam we departed very early, as we wanted to be back with this uncle Jo and aunt Rebecca before 8:00 pm that same day.

We encountered our first obstacle when we were just out of the city, heading for Alkmaar. We were stopped by two German soldiers who asked where we were going. Karel told them we were on our way to see some relatives and asked them politely if they would allow us to continue our journey. But no, we had to make about-turn. Then Karel got a bright idea. He had some packages of Consi cigarettes (available on coupons and scarce now) with him and he offered the soldiers two packages. We were allowed to ride on.

It was quite a tiring trip, pulling an iron cart behind our bikes, although it was relatively light due to its pneumatic tyres. The distance was greater than we had expected, but we arrived safely. We got a warm-hearted welcome and were offered a good meal, complete with a glass of fresh cow's milk. We got enough to last us for some time: some burlap sacks full of flour, cheese, butter, potatoes and so on. But once we got back on our bikes, we realized our journey back would not be an easy thing. The trailer was so heavily loaded that it was very hard to get it to move. Once set going it was okay, but getting back on our bikes after stopping was plain horror. Fortunately, the weather was very fine, a bright winter's day. We were full of hope that we would reach Leusden without major difficulties.

Then, just before Alkmaar, new problems occurred. The rope that ran from my bike to the trailer doubled up under one of the wheels of the cart and I was dragged, bike and all, under the cart that crashed the rear wheel of my bike. I only sustained some scratches, but the wheel of my bike was completely twisted and unserviceable. We uncoupled my bike and lay it on top of the trailer. Now I had to run behind the cart and push, while Karel was on his bike, pulling. Our aim was to get to Alkmaar and try to find a bicycle repairer who might be able to get us another wheel. By amazing good luck we found a repairer who let us join him for lunch, too. So we did not only get a new wheel, but a plate of pea soup as well. I do not remember how we paid him, but there we were, on our way again. In the center of Alkmaar we almost ran into a trap of Dutch black police that picked up all the men they saw and confiscated every bike. We escaped by a hair's breadth and cycled out of the town like crazy.

It was about dinner time when we approached Amsterdam. We were met by a man who warned us not to ride on, as a few kilometers further down the Grüne Polizei was posting, confiscating all foodstuffs. He told us which route we should follow instead: some four to five kilometers further down the canal lived an old man in a tiny house. He might be willing to ferry us over.

The cycling had drained all my energy. I was finished, completely worn out, but we had no choice. Karel tried to put courage into me, although he himself did not exactly look very fit either. Finally we reached the house and by good fortune the man was willing to help us get across the water, but then another difficulty arose. It was impossible to get the trailer into the boat without unloading it first. So we had no other option but to take out all the stuffs and put them into the boat, followed by the trailer and our bikes. Then the three of us got on board. Luckily the water was quiet, for it came until the rim of the boat. Once across the water, we packed the trailer again and then cycled across the polders towards Amsterdam. By now it had become completely dark and we were lucky to have a route description by our ferryman of how to get straight to the back of the Central Station. From there I knew exactly how to get to the address where we would spend the night.

It was after 8:00 pm now and we hazarded our way into the city. Nothing happened until we were just some 500 meters from the house and I got a flat tyre. By now we were experienced in loading the bike on top of the trailer and push-pulling it. When we arrived I almost fainted with exhaustion and I was unable to help Karel unload and store the trailer, bikes and goods in the storage room under the house.

We went to bed immediately, for the next day we would have to get up very early and I also had a tyre to fix. It was a good thing we were equipped to repair our bikes and that I had gained experience at the bicycle repairer's in Zelhem [See Frans-Harry's story in Chapter XI].

The journey from Amsterdam to Leusden was prosperous. No razzias [round-ups of men] and fine weather. We were out of ourselves with joy when we recognized the environment of Leusden. On passing a farmyard, Karel's eyes happened to fall on some geese and he proposed to stop and see if we could lay our hands on one. But I dissuaded him from it—we would only lose time and perhaps the farmer was not even willing to sell. So we rode on. The only thing I wanted was to see De Mijlpaal and get a good rest. It had been a hell of a journey, but we had accomplished our mission, during which it had become evident that Karel was able to hold his own much longer than I.

Chapter 12
"DE INVAL"
(THE RAID ON THE
MIJLPAAL)

It was sometime in January of 1945, during the Hunger Winter, and the Mijlpaal was unusually full of people. It was not a very large house and today I find it hard to believe that we had so many people in that little place without arousing suspicion. You entered the house from its right side. Downstairs, when you came into the front door, was a large living/dining room on the right, a kitchen on the left, a smaller den-type room straight ahead at the end of the hall as well as a toilet on the left. The stairs which led to the second floor were between the toilet and the kitchen. The den had a set of doors which led to a glassed-in sun-room in the back and a door which led into the front room. Upstairs in the front of the house was Karel and Rita's large bedroom, another bedroom on the left and a bathroom cum toilet on the right. Another set of stairs led to the attic which was partly taken up by the large square water tank for the supply to the house and where I slept on its wooden cover. Many others also slept in the attic from time to time. The upstairs bathroom was also sometimes used as a bedroom by putting a door and mattress over the bathtub. The water tank was filled from an electric pump in the kitchen. When there was no electricity, as often happened during the war, we filled the big tank with an emergency hand pump.

On that fateful day the population of the house consisted of no less than 13 people and included Karel and Rita, baby Berna (and her sister Helga on the way); a Jewish lady—Betje Polak (alias Annie Hartman); Selien Betsy Polak (alias Riekje Meerveld), who was not related to Betje Polak, (Polak is a common name in the Netherlands); Rita's sister Guda, her husband Jo and small son Wim plus a newborn whose name I cannot remember; Karel's parents—Oom Herman and Tante Floor; Harry Theeboom (alias Frans Jan Berkenbosch), who was visiting and me, under the alias of Rudy Van Der Roest. Heavens knows where we all slept—I just don't remember it all, but Harry slept with me in the attic sometimes and Berna and Karel's parents slept in the front room with Karel and Rita. There were a lot of mattresses and blankets in the house for emergencies.

Rita's sister and her family were with us because they had been bombed out of their house which was close to the Amersfoort railroad station, very near to where I had been in hiding with my parents before we were caught. Uncle Herman, who was a railroad engineer and locomotive driver, had joined a general railroad strike and since the Germans felt that this was an act of sabotage, there was a danger that he could be arrested and deported as a saboteur or worse. So he came to hide for a while in Hamersveld with his wife, Tante Flora. Karel's sister, who had lived with her parents until then, had gone to live with the family of her fiancee, who, by the way, was a Nazi.

In order to set the stage for what happened I have to explain the very serious situation in the Netherlands at that time. Many Dutch men were being rounded up and sent to work on reinforcing defense lines in the Netherlands, factory work in Germany and other places in Eastern Europe as "assistance" to the German war effort. The mobilizations and roundups occurred frequently, mainly in the more populated western parts of the Netherlands, and it was dangerous for a grownup male to be caught on the street without having the permit which proved that his presence was essential in the Netherlands. Every now and then the Germans required a new stamped document ("Ausweiss"—an exemption permit or pass) which would protect the bearer from the "Arbeitseinsatz" (Labor Pool) during that particular period. Karel, Harry, Oom Herman and Jo all had those stamps. I was fifteen by then according to my new identity (in reality I was only 14) so I had my own identity card. Consequently we were able to run errands or go to work without danger of being picked up during the frequent razzias (roundups). We knew from our clandestine radio, which was located at that time under a sewing-machine hood, that liberation was near. We had colored maps hidden showing the location of the fronts on a day-by-day basis and we were sure that the war couldn't last much longer. Everyone was impatient for the Germans to be driven out of the country. Then came a number of setbacks on various fronts including Montgomery's misjudgement of the Battle of Arnhem, which we witnessed from the sidelines, and the delays caused by Battle of the Bulge in the Ardennes. As a result and as a consequence of the railroad strike and German blockades the food and firewood shortages during the past few months had become extremely serious.

Even with enough ration cards and with one little pig hidden in the backyard (its mate had been slaughtered already and was being smoked) it was tough to find enough food and keep the house warm, but somehow we managed. Many city people who were living in the Western part of the country left their homes during the infamous "Hunger Winter of 1945", to scour the countryside on foot to buy food or to barter whatever valuables they had for food. Trains or other means of public transport were hard to find by then and were mostly used for German troops or goods transportation for the war effort, and were frequently attacked from the air. Karel and Harry also went for a week's trip and managed to bring back some sorely needed supplies, but even they nearly did not make it due to sheer exhaustion.

Much has been written about the infamous "Hunger Winter" and the devastation it brought to the Netherlands and I alluded to it in the previous chapter. We were still under the heel of the Nazi oppressor and twenty thousand hungry Dutch people died on the roads while trying to find food for their families.

A large number of those who had been picked up were used as slave labor for the German fortifications on the Grebbe-Line in the area between Hamersveld, Achterveld, Barneveld and other parts of the defense line. The ones working near us had been marched on foot to Amersfoort and housed in unused, bombed-out or neglected buildings. There was no heating, few blankets, little food, long hours of hard labor in mud, in unsuitable clothing and long walks to and from the work area in freezing cold or drizzle. Their long lines passed by the Mijlpaal every day on the way to the fortifications; hundreds of them; dirty, tired, disheveled. It was like an unending procession of men out of some hellish movie. The well-fed and armed German and Dutch Nazi Blackshirts and Brown shirts marched along beside the columns. Some of the men, who couldn't go anymore were picked up and put on a cart, but sometimes they were shot and left by the roadside to be picked up later. Your fate depended on the mood of the Nazi nearest you. It was a pitiful and painful sight and it made us all boil with frustration and anger. It was awful when they passed by and looked at you with hopelessness, hunger and pain in their eyes. The feeling of helplessness and frustration we had at being so useless! We all felt that we were cowards for not helping them and we got very angry, but there wasn't anything we could do and we swallowed our anger and went on with our lives.

That winter it became nearly impossible to keep our house warm, which caused problems with everyone's health. We were all sneezing and coughing and Rita was pregnant with Helga and therefore especially susceptible in that crowded house. The cold also made it difficult to work on preparing papers at night and to make rubber stamps, a very exacting job. If we messed up an ID-card, it was a serious loss and if we made a mistake cutting a rubber stamp, we had to start over again. During the warmer months it wasn't hard, but when there wasn't enough wood to keep the room warm, our hands were stiff from the cold and the work needed nimble hands. Karel decided that we definitely needed more wood to keep us all comfortable, but wood was hard to come by, even on the black market. It was also forbidden to cut ant tree without a permit. Only in case of official use for the occupying forces or for Dutch Nazi collaborators were those permits issued. Needless to say Karel somehow managed to prepare a permit in order to cut a tree in a nearby private forest. He found a tree with a diameter of about half a meter (at least that's what it looked like to me then), and several of us set out with big crosscut saws, ropes and axes, mauls and splitters. While we worked, Karel stood by in a leather jacket and with leather boots in order to make passers-by think that he was a Nazi overseer for a work-crew. We worked like beavers for several days to bring the tree down and cut it into manageable pieces, which were transported to the Mijlpaal in wheelbarrows and carts. Harry maintains we used wheelbarrows but both Karel and I remember that we had a borrowed two wheeled pushcart.

On a fateful morning, Jo, Harry and Oom Herman came out of our gate in order to get another load of wood. They were pushing a two-wheeled cart. Uncle Herman was the first to spot several men of the black police (SS-men) on bicycles coming in their direction. He was startled and panicked and said something like *"The Germans are coming-run—let's get out of here"*. His panicked voice startled the other two and without thinking all three left the cart and fled. They were close to the Mijlpaal and in their confusion they made the mistake of running into the gate of the Mijlpaal's garden. Luckily they didn't go into the house. They raced across the garden and pushed their way through a reed fence in back of the garden, jumped a small canal and ran away.

The Germans, who were still about 100 meters away, saw them running into the Mijlpaal's front gate but did not see where they ran to from there, because trees and bushes hid the fugitives from view. Nor had they seen where the trio had come from. They gave chase and burst into the house and there confronted everyone—*"Wo sind die Männer die soeben hierher gelaufen waren (Where are the men who just came in here?)"*. All of us had seen what had happened and all were good liars [we were well trained by now, because most of us had been in some type of confrontation on the street with the authorities in past years] and everyone played innocent and ignorant. We said that we had seen men running, but they ran past the house and we didn't know them, nor did we see in which direction they went afterwards. The Germans searched the house perfunctorily and asked to see our papers, but were really only looking for the runaways. I managed somehow to convince them to come outside with me and I would show them where they had run and how they apparently had fled through the backyard and had broken through the reed fence. I waited with my suggestion until I was sure that our men had a chance to disappear. They decided to follow me and to give up their search of the house. I led them into the backyard and they looked around the fence, but since there was nothing to be seen they seemed satisfied with what I had shown them and they left. As it turned out, we were wrong in assuming that they had believed us. We did underestimate them or the people to whom they reported. We were apparently kept under surveillance. From where or how we never discovered, but we had our suspicions with regard to one neighbor, a few houses down the street.

After several days the situation had seemingly returned to normal. Harry and Jo returned; Uncle Herman and Aunt Floor had left in the meantime and were with other relatives or back at their home again—I don't remember. Everything seemed to be fine.

It was the 8th of February 1945. We had just finished breakfast and Karel was at the front door with a courier I knew well, Mr. Moltjes Veer (My Oom, who had brought me from Amsterdam). He had just received some ID and ration cards for people he was helping and who were in hiding. Suddenly the garden gate burst open and about five or six German and Dutch Black police came storming into the house. How Mr. Moltjes Veer managed to get away, and with the ration cards, I don't know, but the Germans found all of the others there. I was so shaken that I don't remember those first minutes with clarity. As during my earlier escape in Amersfoort, survivor instincts took over and made me think and do the right things.

After the first shock, the Germans were shouting in the house and herding everyone but me and Rita into the living room. They had somehow overlooked me since I was rather small and they were not looking for little boys. I rushed into the kitchen and the first thing I saw was the steel box standing on the kitchen counter, containing new ID-Cards, Master cards, ration cards, rubber stamps and other falsification paraphernalia, and at least one revolver and ammunition. The case had just been taken from its hiding place to give the ration cards to Mr. Moltjes Veer. While the Germans were busy with Karel, Harry and Jo in the front room, I grabbed the heavy case, dragged it, somehow unseen, into the side garden, put our big wheelbarrow over it, dragged the wood sawing stand over and started sawing wood from the nearby woodpile (this was some of the wood we had brought in by carts and wheelbarrows) and piling the pieces in front and on top of the wheelbarrow. There was only one German guard and he had been guarding the back exit but he was at the other side of the house when I carried the case and hid it.

In the meantime, Karel, Jo and Harry were under guard in the living room. One of the Germans had gone upstairs and found Rita in bed because she had some problems with her pregnancy. She managed to hide some incriminating papers, which had been lying on the bedside table, under her pajamas in plain view of the German. Two or three others were roaming through the house and asking questions of Riek and Betje and looking in cupboards, cabinets and under the beds.

Karel asked if he could put on a pair of shoes. He was granted permission and in the confusion managed to escape through the backyard like the others had done a week before. I saw him flash by and go through the fence. By the time they discovered that he was gone, he was already out of sight. They never found him. I guessed he went to the town hall which was about 250 meters away. It made the Germans furious that he had escaped and their behavior changed for the worse. They started asking me a number of questions as well, grabbed me by the shoulders, slapped my face and shook me, but I played the dumb kid who cried and didn't understand German. I had seen nothing *"nichts gesehen"* (I didn't see anything—I knew that much), and when they left me alone I continued sawing wood. By now the case was well hidden, but I continued my sawing, thinking continuously about an opportunity to run away myself. By now there was a new contingent of German and Dutch police and several of them were roaming around the garden and looking under bushes. I had to bide my time before trying to escape when I needed to, but at that moment I was still safe. They didn't suspect me yet.

In the meantime, Rita, who always acted as if she didn't know what was going on, but was quite a sharp lady, had managed to convince the policeman, who stood watch over her, to have our doctor, Dr. Bergink, come and attend to her. Doctor Bergink came and checked her situation and pronounced that she needed to be sent immediately to the hospital in Amersfoort. During the examination, Rita managed to pass the papers she had on her body to Dr. Bergink, who didn't bat an eyelid when he felt her hand going into his pant pocket. Our friend the milkman, Mr. van Harte, was called over and drove Rita to the hospital with his horse and delivery cart. A Jewish girl, Thea Brandon (who had a false identity under the alias of Eefje Hasselaar) was alerted and took little Berna to Rita's parents' house in Amersfoort—all this under the eyes of the Gestapo.

I was still sawing wood as fast as I could in the backyard. I wondered later why the Germans didn't think it strange that I was sawing away at such a furious pace while they had overrun the house and garden. It wasn't long before they found me out. The Germans had been reinforced by the feared military security police (SD). They continued searching the house, straw shed and garden, breaking open floors (they found the forbidden radio which was hidden under the sewing machine hood). They found our pig in the straw shed. That was also something which was forbidden unless you had a permit or if you were a farmer, but even then you could only have as many pigs as were written on the permit. One of them was strolling around the garden and poking around in the bushes with a stick when he stumbled over one of the pieces of wood lying on the ground where I was sawing. He lost his balance and fell on top of the little woodpile I had made, and the handle of the wheelbarrow poked him in his back. Apparently it hurt because he said "Scheisse!" (Shit), grabbed the piece of wood and wanted to shake it loose. It was heavy, so he tugged some more and then the woodpile shifted with the wheelbarrow and it fell of the box, the box fell over, opened and spilled most of its contents including the handgun and ammo.

He stood there for a fraction of a second and then yelled for his comrades. Until now they did not have much on any of us because everyone had proper identification and permits but finding the papers, the weapon and the ammunition changed the situation drastically. They grabbed me immediately, yelled "Kleine Schweinhund" (little bastard), kicked and dragged me toward the house and punched me in the face and on my head and pulled me inside, ordering me to sit on the sofa in the living room where Jo and Harry were still being held. I sat on the sofa between them. By now I was crying and I shook like a leaf—I was momentarily blind to my surroundings and was only conscious of a giant ball of fear inside me. The kicks and punches didn't register with me—I was so afraid—so very afraid. After a short while, I calmed down, though about what to do next and decided that I was going to try and make a break for freedom. They could only shoot me if they saw me escape and anything was better than a concentration camp. I asked while still crying if I could please go to the bathroom. They agreed, but one of them was ordered to watch me. The bathroom was to the right of the door when coming out of the front room and in a recessed area behind the stairs. The soldier who was supposed to watch me stood in the living room doorframe to watch me, but by opening the bathroom door it hid another door just beside it, which led to the side room. I slipped into the side room and from there I quickly came out onto the back porch or sun room. By this time there were no Germans or Dutch police in the garden anymore and I grabbed my wooden clogs from the rear door and ran, clogs in hand, to the back fence and jumped straight through the reeds. By now the fence had several holes in it from all the previous escapees. I was a pretty good jumper, but the reed fence, although a bit damaged, decelerated me enough so that I didn't make the other side of the little canal which was about eight feet wide. I clambered out of the soggy mess and didn't look back while I hurried toward the town hall, which was close by. It was the only place I knew at that moment, where I could find help. By the time the Germans found the empty toilet I would be well out of sight. If I had looked back, I might have seen my ID-card floating on the water. It must have come out of my pocket when I floundered in the canal. However I'm not sure about that, because if it had been found the Germans would certainly have gone after my namesake and his family in Amsterdam. But they didn't. I came to the town hall's back door and entered. When I saw Bob van der Heyden I told him what had happened, but he already knew.

Karel had reached the town hall before me and alerted the "good" staff as to what was going on. He was hiding in the vault which was often used to hide people. Beside its door was a very narrow slit through which one could pass a key to the person hiding inside. By inserting the key from the inside in the lock no one could open the vault. The people who worked with Karel had received his instructions in case any more of us escaped. They got me some dry pants and socks and then they whisked me out of the back door of the town hall and brought me on a bicycle to a farm between Hamersveld and Achterveld which belonged to a family headed by a Mr. P.v.d.H. The farm was about three kilometers, as the crow flies, from the Mijlpaal and thus I was out of harms way in a very short time. I stayed at the farm until we were liberated. But that wasn't the end of my problems. It turns out that some of the most difficult events of my life would take place on that farm.

An afterthought

After writing this down and checking with Harry's and Karel's memories, there was something which puzzled me. I mentioned at the beginning of this story the name of a man called Mr. Moltjes Veer. He had come to the Mijlpaal for ration cards for people who were hiding. We never really understood how he got away, and with a bunch of papers as well. He was always a mysterious figure because he worked alone and we did not know his real name nor his address. I wasn't even sure that I remembered his name correctly because Moltjes Veer, even in Holland, is an extremely unusual name. However, both Harry and Karel and all the others remember him by that name. No one knew why he had that name or what it meant. Karel didn't know much about him, except that he took care of a number of Jewish families in hiding. He was the one who brought me from Amsterdam to our first hiding address and arranged for our second hiding address. He took good care of my parents and me during that time. He took care of many others among them a well known Dutch entertainer by the name of Henrietta (Heintje) Davids. Mr. Moltjes Veer is long dead now. He was an older gentleman when I knew him. We will never know the truth about his life during the war. After the war I discovered the son and daughter of Moltjes Veer. His real name was Van Der Kieft and he was a plain-clothes detective for the Amersfoort police. He therefore had a police identity card or a badge, which was probably why he was not arrested during the raid, and was able to make his getaway. He was one of the real "good Dutchmen", a hero of the first caliber. It is tragic and it makes me angry that we were not able to honor this man during his lifetime. He put himself in a great deal of danger and never put himself forward or in the limelight after the war. He was a silent and unsung hero. I am glad to mention his name as an honor and tribute to him.

Chapter 13
DEATH ON THE FARM

I didn't write this chapter on purpose at the end of this memoir in order to leave a certain impression. It just happened that this occurred near the end of the occupation. There is a saying that "Your best enemy is a dead enemy". This is not considered a very nice Judeo-Christian sentiment or principle to live by and has been condemned many times by religious and other "humanists" as well as by flaky salon-liberals and psycho-sociologists, but it is a way of life which people, who have to live under extremely stressful and dangerous circumstances, often have to adopt in order to stay alive. Soldiers have have to face the choice of "kill or be killed" in wars and so have people who live from day to day with danger and fear of being canceled out of this world by a determined enemy. It is the only way to stay alive in many cases. The moralists and bible-thumping righteous ones, who have never been in any real danger and never have had their family, friends and loved ones taken away to be murdered, or were witnesses to atrocities, have neither the background nor the right to pass judgment. Their condemnation is worthless, since it is based on academic and theoretical meanderings of minds which never had to deal with such circumstances. Their interpretations of psychological theories, written by equally inexperienced theorists, and wrongly translated biblical texts are useless. Their opinions do not recognize the real world in which we live.

This part of my story tells how I committed a murder, even though it may have been an accidental murder. I know—this sounds terrible, but I really killed two people. I'm not proud of it and have hesitated for a long time whether I should put it down at all. It will need a bit of introduction to describe the circumstances how this came about. This is the first time I have ever told this story to anyone (only my wife Rose knows about it) and I am still hesitant to put it on paper, but I feel that I owe it to my family, friends and others to let them know what I did that day and maybe they'll understand why I acted as I did. My grandchildren may be shocked to read this. Is this their grandpa? Another reason for not talking about this is that I was afraid for a long time of possible consequences for myself and the other people who were involved. But such a long time has passed since these events took place in 1945. The people involved are today either as old, or older than I am, and some will have died. I don't know if they will ever read this even if they are still alive. Except for the bible and prayer books they did not read much else at the time. I am not writing this because I feel that I have to relieve myself of a burden. I don't really feel guilty for what happened because it was so unavoidable. I haven't had dreams or nightmares about it either. This part of my life story showed me how close to the surface the animal instinct of self-preservation is hidden in me, and probably in many of us.

I was nearly fourteen (my real age) at the time of the "Hunger Winter" of 1944–1945. The farm of the "v.d. H." family was located between the villages of Hamersveld and Achterveld, but closer to the latter. The small village of Achterveld became historically important and rather famous toward the end of the war because this was the village where the Germans and the Allies discussed the food aid for the hungering Dutch population during the infamous Hunger Winter and discussed the surrender of the German occupying forces in the provinces of Utrecht, North Holland and South Holland, the last remaining occupied part of the Netherlands.

I earned my food and lodging by working on the farm, which was a fairly large one for that area. The farmer and his wife were a jolly, robust, Catholic middle-aged couple who had brought sixteen, mostly strong and equally jolly children into the world. They stopped producing them only because the last three had some slight mental or physical handicaps (harelip, clubfoot, very bad eyesight) and they apparently received dispensation from their church fathers to stop the multiplying process. Many of the older kids were "out of the house" and I never met them. I always thought that the most interesting thing about this family was that none of the children resembled either each other or the father. Several bore a resemblance to the mother, who was a hefty, healthy looking lady about a head taller than and as broad as her husband. It was always interesting to go to the early Sunday morning Mass with them in Achterveld, because usually it was a party of about eight to ten of us, clip-clopping into the church in our clogs, which had been cleaned and whitewashed for the occasion. I went to church quite often, even for mid-week services, because I enjoyed the Catholic liturgy and especially loved the organ music and choir singing. I also was prepared for and was duly baptized shortly after I came to the family. I did my "studies" of the catechism very quickly; to me they seemed very easy and as silly as the stuff they had tried to teach me at the Synagogue in Amsterdam. But I felt that it would protect me and the old priest was happy to get another soul, especially one who seemed to enjoy the services, stayed awake and sang well and would help clean the church. I suppose that he actually suspected that I was Jewish and wanted to make sure that he had a convert. I didn't disappoint him.

Being the runt and a stranger in this big farm family wasn't always easy and I had plenty of "good-natured" oral and physical abuse, although it was never really malicious and I was as often as not the instigator of the conflict. But I knew that the Allies were near and the knowledge that it wouldn't be long before all this would end and that I would then go back to the Mijlpaal and Karel's family, kept my spirits up. At the time, and also for many, many years after the war, and despite the stories of extermination, I also kept up hopes of seeing my parents and school friends again and I often daydreamed about how our meeting at the railway station in Amsterdam would go and how I would hug Pappie and Mammie and return to our home in Amsterdam with them. When I didn't hear from them immediately after the war, I always invented excuses why they were unable to contact me—one of them being that they were still somewhere behind the Iron Curtain in Poland or Russia and therefore couldn't communicate. From what I knew about conditions there, I thought that they probably had no telephone, or maybe thought I was dead like so many others. The stories which had, at first filtered through and later confirmed, about the camps and killings, did not give me much confidence that my hopes would be fulfilled.

During the first half of 1945, the farm and its inhabitants had the dubious distinction of being situated in no-man's land between fronts. The German fortifications along the "*Grebbe Lijn*" were to our west, on the dike along a canal, and the allies to our east. One day there would be an artillery barrage from one side, and then the side which had done the shooting would have its infantry and motorized brigades fan out over part of the area and occupy farmhouses, barns, woods or another location where they would dig in. The next day they would retreat by themselves for no visible reason or be driven out by the other side opening up with all they had. Our farm had so far escaped occupation by either side and was therefore undamaged. The reason for our luck may have been that we were quite a bit closer to the German lines, which stretched out along the big canal and the dike, which ran along it, about a kilometer to the west and northwest of the farm. The dike had been fortified with its trenches and many concrete bunkers with the help of slave labor, consisting of groups of Dutch citizens from the western part of the country who had been "recruited" for this purpose. We could see the bunkers and other fortified gun emplacements on the dike clearly from the farm. There was also an area along the dikes which had been flooded by the Germans. When the German guns started firing, we could clearly see the flashes and then hear thunder of the guns and at about the same time the shells would come screaming overhead. We became quite expert at determining what projectiles were being fired and guessing from the flashes where they were going to land and often we would just continue with whatever we were doing. We knew that they were targeting someplace else. When we heard mortar fire though, we knew that this was short-range stuff and that we had better find shelter quick or hit the ground, It also meant that there were ground troops from the other side in the area and it was easy to get caught in the crossfire. When the Allies fired their long-range guns, it was always time to take shelter. Their aim was usually off by a few hundred meters in the beginning and they had scouts in the area or a plane up in the air to redirect their fire. Plenty of shells missed their target and fell in the fields and on farms nearer the canal.

During the later months we spent more and more time in shelters due to the artillery duels and other skirmishes between the two sides. However, the animals in the barn had to be fed and since I was the little Jewish guy who had become part of the family but didn't really belong. I had the task of feeding the animals in between the artillery, mortar and machine gun eruptions. They would say: "Come on boy, time to slop the hogs". At other times, when there was a lot of heavy work to be done, other sons or daughters would join in to help me and get it done quicker. It was often quite hard for me to move all the hay and the silage, which was hauled on a wheelbarrow and bring in the buckets of other feed. Then the animals also needed water and since there was no electricity any more it had to be hand-pumped and hauled in buckets. It was heavy work but I had told them that I really didn't mind doing it and wasn't afraid to go out there. I liked the animals, always talked to them and patted them and they returned my affection. I found them a lot more reliable than people. It was also a welcome relief from being cooped up in the air-raid shelter under the farmhouse. I was in fresh air (except in the pigsty) and could see what was happening. I used to throw myself on the ground and crawl to a nearby shelter when a new barrage seemed to be dangerously close and then could hear the shrapnel humming overhead and around me and the sharp crack as it hit a building or the soft thud as it hit the bare ground or the hay stack. Later we would collect the shrapnel and dig around in the craters for the rear fins of the heavy mortars, which we kept as trophies and drilled out for candle holders. We knew which craters were from mortars and which were from artillery shells. They are quite different.

One morning a veritable carpet of shells was laid by the Allies. They came thick and fast and very close to the farmhouse. The earth was shaking for what seemed to be at least half an hour. In the wet soils of the polder area the sound of impact was a bit muffled but the vibrations were transmitted very well. After this barrage we didn't recognize the fields near the farm house. It looked as if they had been dug up with a giant trowel. Big holes and mounds of soil were everywhere. The vegetable garden had taken two hits and there wasn't much left from the carrot, beet and potato beds but we collected as much of the produce as we could find. Some of it was quite a distance away. Several chickens were dead and the coop had been demolished. So were most of that days yield of eggs, although we found a few unbroken ones, which was astonishing. Whatever could be salvaged of the chickens was eaten that day, or pickled or smoked, because you couldn't keep chicken without refrigeration and electricity was unreliable at best and the ice man didn't deliver his blocks during those dangerous days. But the house was not hit, which was a miracle.

When the barrage started I was outside and couldn't make it back to the shelter in the house. I threw myself down beside the haystack and crawled in as well as I could. It was a frightening barrage and it had never been so close. I don't know whether I shook from the explosions or from fear. Despite my efforts at taking cover, I was hit by two tiny pieces of shrapnel, one piece entering my right side and another tiny piece lodging in my left arm, but I didn't even know I was hit. I thought that I had been stung by some pieces of straw. Both shrapnel pieces entered at a slight angle and without much force and lodged close to the skin. I didn't notice my arm wound until later when I notice blood on my sleeve. The other wound wasn't bleeding much either and I didn't even realize that it was there until about it an hour or so later when I answered the call of nature. Since my wounds seemed to be little more than scratches, they were cleaned, disinfected with iodine and bandaged. We decided that we would try to get to the doctor in Achterveld or Barneveld later.

Miraculously, only the cow barn had received a direct shell hit in one of the corners. The round had gone in through the roof and exploded above the cows. There were numerous smaller shrapnel holes in the wooden walls of several of the other farm buildings. When we went into the barn we found that two of the cows which stood at the end which was hit had received serious shrapnel wounds. Parts of their entrails were hanging out and they stood there dazed with glazed eyes and breathing hard—obviously in pain. There was nothing we could do for them. Where could you find a veterinarian willing to come out to no-man's land? To put them out of their misery, they were slaughtered on the spot. We would have to smuggle the meat to Achterveld or somewhere else during the next few nights because the farm didn't have sufficient refrigeration available.

It was very unpleasant to see the throats being slit of animals which I had befriended and milked and on whose flanks I had warmed my hands. On regular slaughter days, the "humane method" of killing the animals was to have someone with experience wield a large sledge hammer and crush the animal's forehead in one blow, after which its throat was slit open immediately and the blood collected for making blood sausages. I was never sure if the animals were really dead when that was done and didn't enjoy the process. This time, however, killing them was an act of mercy. In the meantime the farmer's wife and the daughters got busy heating water for stripping the carcasses and for cooking the meat. While the older men were busy cutting up the meat, thee youngsters had to hold the legs or the hide. While we were working intently we suddenly heard clattering noises of approaching vehicles.

We looked up and saw several camouflaged tracked vehicles with soldiers approaching along the main road coming from the east—the direction of Achterveld—the direction from where the Allies would come. The farm was about half a mile from the road and we could see them clearly. This was the first time the Allies had been so close. Mr. v.d.H. cried *"It's the Americans"*. We all started waving and hollering and jumping up and down. The convoy stopped for a moment. They had seen us and someone was pointing at us. At that moment heavy machine guns, mortars and cannon opened up from the German side on the canal dike. All hell broke loose and we were outside slaughtering cattle in the open. We all went down flat. Those close to the house managed to get in and go into the shelter. With the Allies (it turned out that they were not Americans but Canadians) shooting back, and calling in their heavy artillery, which was located somewhere between Achterveld and Barneveld, another town further east, the din was deafening, and I remember trying to press myself into the ground. I was longing for the shelter but didn't dare get up and run for it. Shrapnel was humming like angry mosquitos and you were surely going to be hit if you so much as lifted your head.

I don't remember how long it lasted. According to the clock, we were told it was about ten minutes but it seemed like it went on for a much longer time. I wanted to crawl into the ground and close it over me. It became so bad that I was sure I was going to die and I did wet my pants; I was totally panicked and felt utterly helpless; I prayed to Jesus and Mary, especially Mary, the mother figure, my surrogate mother, to save me and make the shooting stop. And then it was all over as suddenly as it had started. We all rose, shaken but whole—a miracle. One of the older daughters, Daatje, one of the calmest people I have ever met, came out of the house. Her perennial red cheeks were white as a sheet and she was close to hysterics. They had been hiding in the shelter under the house and the place shook so much that they thought that surely all of us were killed. We stood around for a while trying to see if any of the "Americans" were still there, but apparently they had gone back to their lines.

Then Piet, one of the older sons, suddenly said : "Germans coming" and pointed to the west—two German half-tracks were coming towards the farm. The family ran to the house but I ran away from the farm—my usual get-away instinct—and hid in bushes along the farm lane which led to the main road and saw the first half-track enter the farmyard. I was hiding about a quarter of a kilometer away from the farm. I could see several Germans coming out of one vehicle and going into the house. The other vehicle apparently remained on the other side of the farmhouse—I couldn't see it. The driver and a soldier manning the machine gun stayed with the halftrack. The others went in and around the house and then came out and walked to the barn. Then the driver came out of the half-track and started walking in my direction. I flattened myself to the ground as much as I could. The German soldier stopped about ten meters away from me, undid his belt, opened his uniform, unhooked his suspenders and hunkered down to answer the call of nature. He sat there with his face looking straight at me. I was petrified and could not move, my heart was beating overtime and I barely dared to breathe during the whole time he sat there, seemingly looking straight at me, but apparently not noticing me. He finished his business, cleaned himself, stood up, rearranged his clothing and went back to the vehicle. I could breathe again and I decided to move a bit further toward the main road until I reached a spot around a curve from where I couldn't see the farm anymore. I stayed hidden for, what seemed like eternity. It was cold and had started to drizzle and I was uncomfortable because of my wet pants. During that time I also had to answer the call of nature and that is when I found that the small shrapnel wound in my side had started bleeding again. That didn't make me feel any better. It looked rather bloody.

It was by now late afternoon and getting dark. Finally, I heard the sound of engines again. I crept slowly toward the road and saw the half-tracks moving back toward the German fortifications. I made my way carefully back to the farm where I found a lot of confusion, fear and anger. The Germans had thought that some of the Allied soldiers had stayed behind on the farm and did not believe the family when they said that the "Americans" had not been further than the road. They had roughed up two of the older sons and took one as prisoner to work on the defense lines. Since the German troops in the area were a mixture of regular Wehrmacht and SS-Stormtrooper battalions, it was a miracle that they didn't rape the women. They did, however, promise to return. They had not made a thorough search but had found a lot of the meat from the slaughtered animals and said that they knew that there was more food around and would commandeer a couple of cows, so we knew they would come back when they had more time. I heard several years later that the son was later shot "while trying to escape" according to the Germans.

My wound was cleaned and bandaged and I felt a little like a hero—the family praised me for having had the good sense to run away from the farm. If I had been found there without my identity card, which was lost during the Mijlpaal raid, and if, as a result, they had pulled my pants down, it probably would have been much worse for all of them as well as for me. I don't know if I could have reacted the same way as Harry Theeboom did under questioning by the Gestapo. Moreover, I didn't have the identification he had. Most of the talk was naturally about the son who had been taken away. That evening I went to sleep in my clothes, not knowing when the SS would be back and not wanting to have to escape in my underwear. I left the small window in the roof open in case I needed to get out through there and put a crate under it so that I could climb out quick. I took a so-called "pit-spade" with a short handle as a weapon to bed with me. The pit spade was used to dig silage from the side of a silage pile. The silage is very dense and the spade is has a short handle with a Foot step and a large rounded and very sharp blade which rounds into a point. Keeping the spade close at hand, I went to my bed in the loft above the cows and tried to sleep. I'm sure that I wasn't the only one who had difficulty falling asleep that night. The "weapon" was more for my own comfort and assurance than for protection. I knew that it wouldn't account for much if I had to face the Germans with their Schmeisser submachine guns and Mauser or Walther pistols. I wasn't the only one having a "weapon; one of the sons had an old hunting rifle with five shells, which had been hidden despite the prohibition by the Germans to have any such weapon. I decided to carry my assurance with me wherever I went. I had no inkling that I would use it very soon.

The next two days were alternately rainy and clear and there was a lull in the skirmishing. Both sides were apparently taking a rest. Except for a few visits from allied reconnaissance planes and subsequent aerial attacks on the Grebbe-line bunkers by fighter planes, which elicited a flurry of anti-aircraft fire from the canal dike, nothing happened. It was absolutely quiet so we ventured out into the garden plots on the west side of the house. We were in the full view there of the German fortifications. The Germans didn't return, as they had promised, and we started to relax our vigilance. Usually we had always one person on the lookout outside to keep watch and give warning when there were Germans moving in the area.

On the third day, in the afternoon, when several of us were working on digging a new potato storage pit we were surprised. We hadn't heard anyone coming. Suddenly there were two German soldiers in the farmyard. I was working with a pitchfork, but grabbed my spade as well when I saw them. We understood German orders quite well by that time (none of us spoke it very well and they only spoke a few words of Dutch) and they said that they had come to collect food. This time they had not come with an armored vehicle. They had brought two horses and a wagon on rubber tires, which is why we had not heard them approach. The horses and wagon had probably been commandeered from some other farmer in the area. They ordered us to start loading the cart with *"Fleisch, Kartoffeln, Spek, Apfel, Eier, Brot—aufladen* [Meat, potatoes, bacon, apples, eggs, bread—load up]" and whatever else they could think of. They were in a hurry and prodded us with their weapons. *"Schnell, Schnell, Du Hollandische schweine-hunde!"* (Quick, quick, Dutch pig-dogs!).

We naturally did as we were told. The girls brought bread and eggs from the house and Henk and I started digging in the potato storage heap. Henk had a pitchfork to move the straw and I used my hands to dig potatoes and Daatje, the oldest daughter, held the sack. We knew that disobeying or working slowly would get them even more hurried and anxious to get back to their lines and they could seriously hurt us or even kill us if they became angry enough. There were plenty of stories going around about their behavior during the occupation and especially the last few months, when they knew that they were losing the war on every front, stories of their cruelty had been rampant. These were SS soldiers, the worst of the lot. We were all pretty nervous and jumpy because of tension and fear. My heart was pounding. They were in a hurry and we were not quick enough for them. They pushed us with their gun barrels. One of them kicked me hard in the back with his boot and made me fall. I started crying, while the other soldier was shouting something at one of the girls, Trijn, who was one of the younger and prettier sisters. She angrily answered him and spat on the floor in front of the soldier. He hit her in the face with his gun butt and knocked her to the floor. Her cheek and nose were bleeding and she started screaming. This "Pride of Germany" then kicked her hard in the stomach and told her to get up but she couldn't, or wouldn't, and he started dragging her on the ground toward the back of the farmhouse, kicking her and yelling at her when she continued screaming.

I was still bawling while putting potatoes in a sack and had stopped to see what was happening with Trijn and forgot for a moment that the other German stood behind me and what I was supposed to be doing. I was still looking when he shouted *"Schneller—Du [Faster—you]"* and he gave me a very hard poke with his the barrel of his weapon in the middle of my back—I suppose he hit me in the kidneys. It doubled me up with pain, but it made me boiling mad. I was hurting, I saw red and at that instant I lost my grip on reality. What happened next is still a blur in my mind. It was really as if I wasn't there, as if things happened to someone else and I cannot recall it clearly. If I had been clearheaded and sane, I would have never dared do what I did. When Iwas told later about the course of events, it seemed as absurd and unreal to me as it must have to the others who were there and witnessed it. Did I really do this? I, who wouldn't hurt any animal and who didn't like to see blood? Well, here is what happened. When the German poked me in the kidneys I bent over with pain, I screamed with anger and grabbed my shovel, my "weapon", and swirled it around in a flash with a circular motion and the spade's blade caught the German, who stood too close behind me, in the throat. The sharp heavy blade went through his throat like it was butter and opened up his main artery and his windpipe—such was the force I swung it with, combined with the inertia of that whirling spade. Blood spurted out of the gaping wound and caught me flush in the face and covered my clothes. He only managed a gurgling sound once and then he went noiselessly to his knees and toppled over on his face and bled and twitched to death right there......I became hysterical, out of control, screaming and cursing something awful and my eyes felt as if they were popping out; I was gagging and throwing up from the sight of the body and the horrible, awful taste of the German's blood which had gotten into my mouth as well. The other German, who was doing God knows what to poor Trijn, heard me screaming and yelling and came running towards us with his weapon at his side. He didn't see his mate lying on the ground immediately, but when saw me covered in blood and his mate in his pool of blood, he lifted his gun to shoot. I knew then that I was going to die and lunged toward him. But......luck was with me again.

In his haste the soldier had passed by Henk and now Henk was at the back of him with a pitchfork and when he aimed his weapon at me, Henk launched the pitchfork like a harpoon into the German's back and thereby saved my life. The soldier uttered a terrible howl and turned around, apparently to face his attacker, but the pitchfork stayed in his back and he dropped his gun and started screaming in a high-pitched voice and went on whirling, trying to get the fork out of his back. Both Henk and I must have gone berserk. When I regained my senses, as if waking from an awful nightmare, we were both standing, crying, cursing the worst curses one can imagine and screaming hysterically in Dutch and some German, *"Rotzak, klootzak rotmof Schweinehund,......and much more"* over what had been the body of the second soldier. I found myself plunging my spade again and again into his quivering body and his moaning face until he stopped moving while Henk was holding the thrashing body on its side with the pitchfork still in the back. The bloody mass didn't look human anymore—blood, organs, bone, intestines—that's all it was—worse than a slaughtered cow. I shall never forget that day, that awful smell of shattered body parts and stomach contents, the horrifying spectacle, not like anything I had experienced before or ever would in later life. My heart was pounding and seemed to want to burst out of my chest; I couldn't see anything clearly because of my tears and the blood from the other soldier and I was unable to focus my eyes; everything around me seemed to be moving; my head seemed on the point of exploding. My throat hurt from the screaming; my lungs hurt from hyperventilating; I was out of control; my mind was numb and I wasn't really conscious, but I stood on my feet. I walked away—I was gagging and crying and my legs gave out a few times and I fell, then got up, fell again; I may have fainted; I don't know......it took me a long time to calm down. Trijn, the daughter who had been beaten, kicked and apparently nearly raped and whose clothes were torn was sitting against the wall, staring ahead, crying softly, her face and arms were bleeding but otherwise she appeared unharmed. Henk, who was a big strapping twenty-some-year old, was sobbing and throwing up against the farmhouse wall. I know there were others around me, but I can't remember them clearly—it was all a daze. The usually stoic Mrs. v. d. H. was crying hysterically and running from one person to the other. It must have looked like a scene from a Brueghel painting depicting the horrors of hell. We were all dazed, not knowing what to do next. Soon the realization of what had happened and what would happen if other Germans came to look for their comrades, made us calm down and we started to think about what we were to do next. First we washed the blood off ourselves as well as we could. We looked at each other, wondering whether this had been real or a dream. But the remains of the Germans near us made it clear that this had really happened and that we were faced with the harsh facts: we had killed German SS soldiers and this was a crisis and we had to do something about it.

We left one person as a lookout and after we had calmed down and cleaned ourselves up it was already dark and we sat in the kitchen and discussed what to do. We had a grisly task to perform and I am not proud to say that some of the ideas came from me. God knows where I got them from. Father v.d.H, Piet,

Henk and I took the bodies, and literally cut them up into manageable pieces as if they were the same as the cattle which had been slaughtered a few days ago. We cut off legs and arms. The sound of the sawing, having to hold the leg or arm of another human being while another person was sawing, cutting off the already half-severed head of the one soldier, God forgive me......It was pretty awful. We put the remains in sacks. We all had dry heaves while we were doing this. We couldn't look each other in the face and only spoke a few words. We disposed of the mess later that evening in several of the deeper drainage ditches which criss-cross the fields in the polder area. We weighted the sacks with bricks, stones, old horse-shoes and pieces of farm equipment and pushed each sack into the muddy bottom with poles. We took their papers and identity cards, the leftovers of the uniforms and underwear and burned them in the wood stove in the kitchen and threw buttons and insignia and other pieces into other water-filled ditches.

Later that night we drove the wagon with the two horses as far as we dared toward the east where the Allied lines were, unhitched the horses and let them go free in a pasture away from the main road. We left the wagon at the side of the road. We returned on foot through the fields. The soldier's weapons and ammunition were left in some bushes beside the wagon. One pair of boots we filled with soil and put in a ditch. I kept the smallest pair of boots for myself and hid them in another location in a nearby forest. We didn't want the Germans to come around looking for their buddies and then find German weapons, parts of uniforms and papers on or near the farm. That would have meant the end for all of the inhabitants of the farm and probably of neighboring farms as well. That was standard procedure when German soldiers were harmed. If they would dare to venture east and happen to find the wagon without horses, the weapons and other items we hoped that they would think that their comrades had deserted to the Allies and left their weapons behind. I think we succeeded because, strangely and inexplicably as it may seem, no one from the German defense line ever came to look for them on the farm. We did see their patrols along the road but there were always some reconnaissance patrols near the area where we had left the wagon and weapons and so they may have found them and been fooled the way we intended them to be.

We never discussed what had happened that day or why and how it came about. None of us knew how to approach this type of subject. None of us had ever experienced this kind of event. Personally I know that I was simultaneously shocked, shamed and exhilarated. Shocked that I had done what I did, shamed that I had become an animal like a German and exhilarated because "I had done it—killed those two bastard Germans". I also got the distinct feeling that the family was a bit afraid of me and my crazy temper after witnessing my behavior. I don't think they respected me because of it. I had made them accessories to murder.

I washed my face, my hands and the spade compulsively many, many times over the next few days. For a long time I thought that I still could smell the blood. I felt it had stayed on me, in my clothes and on the spade. I imagined that others must smell it too. You just cannot imagine the horrible odor of intestines and blood and the sight of those bloody bodies. I would have liked to talk about it all and get some "absolution" from the priest in church but didn't dare bring it up. I actually decided once to tell the local priest in confession, but in the end couldn't get myself to do it. When I finally mustered the courage and sat in the confessional at the church, I told my confessor instead that I had been peeking at some of the daughters when they were undressing and taking a bath. That was true too, but I didn't feel bad about that. He absolved me and told me that we make those mistakes when we are young, that it was carnal sin and he gave me a lot of Ave's and a one day fast as penance. Actually I did several days penance in the hope that the all-powerful being in the sky would forgive me for what I had really done and not confessed to.

We cleaned the ground thoroughly and made sure that nothing was left to indicate the carnage which had occurred. I had the bright, but macabre, idea to let our two dogs loose on the area of the slaughter and let them sniff out and locate any places we had overlooked and lick the blood which we had not cleaned. The dogs did, in effect, find some grisly spots and cleaned them up and they had a great time sniffing and licking the area and then marking it in their usual way. After that we dug up the hides from the dead cows which we had buried and which had a very "ripe" smell by now and dragged them over the whole area and buried them again near the potato pit where the killing had taken place. Digging the stuff up didn't smell good but if the Germans would come back with dogs to look for their comrades, which they sometimes did, the dogs might think that the blood spots and smells in the area were from the cows and would dig up the skins.

It was several weeks later that a cease-fire was signed to allow food to be supplied to the occupied Netherlands and some time later the armistice was finally signed and, although the local SS troops did not give up immediately, the area was at least free of the bombardments, fighting and raids. We had seen the German convoy with white flags going toward Achterveld a few times now and were whooping and hollering with joy every time we saw them. It wouldn't be long now. When peace finally arrived and it became clear to all of us that nothing was going to happen anymore, I returned to the place where I had hidden the boots. I had left them there with the thought that I might be able to wear them one day. My clogs, the only footwear I had from when I escaped, were practically worn out. The boots were a bit too big on me but were better than what I had.

The strange thing is, that, after being reunited with Karel, Rita and their family, they never asked me how I obtained the boots and nor did any of my schoolmates, my teachers, the priest in church or my family members who survived the war. I wouldn't have told them the truth anyway. I never told anyone about it. I wore those boots for several years and had them resoled at least twice, just like many other people in those days who had found German boots somewhere. I think that I was sort of proud of them at the time. It seemed to me that this was a small bit of revenge I had extracted for my parents and family, for my dog, for my bike, for my beloved Anita, for my schoolmates, for the beatings and the shame, for the humiliation, for the kid nearly murdered in the swimming pool, for the innocent people shot on the streets and for the many other atrocities I had witnessed and for all the others we had heard about.

Oh yes, what about those pieces of shrapnel? By the time the Canadians finally took me to an army doctor at the field hospital in Barneveld, the small wounds had completely healed and no infection had occurred. A Canadian army medic thought that it might be worthwhile to take the pieces out but luckily a sensible doctor came along who saw my frightened face and decided it was better to leave the shrapnel in. They have been there ever since, wandering about under my skin in the area where they entered. The one in my left arm disappears occasionally and then reappears again, and the other is totally encapsulated on my right side.

After more than 60 years, I am still amazed how we got the better of those two Germans. I suppose they were as surprised as we were ourselves by the unexpected eruption of this uncontrollable rage; they didn't expect a small boy to go berserk. I'm glad we did get the better of them though; I would not have been here to tell you about it. Compared to many others who have gone through similar traumatic experiences, I guess I have been and still am lucky. I neither dream of the event nor do I feel that I was a monster—just a fourteen-year old under a lot of pressure......Killing that first German was really an accident, but we murdered the second one in pure rage, fear and hysteria. Of course he would have eliminated us, had he been given the chance. But still......

At the time it never once occurred to me that in Germany two families were waiting for two young soldiers who would never return. If it had occurred to me and was asked about it, I am sure that I would have answered that they deserved to die the way they did. They were SS and Nazi scum and not human except in shape. Now, having lost a son myself in the 1973 war in Israel and having felt the pain, I wish things could have been different and that I didn't have to do what I did then and cause pain and suffering to families who could not even bury their sons or visit their graves. I know now what it feels like to lose a child. But what could I tell the families of the soldiers whom we killed at the time; what would I say? What they were doing to us, a bunch of innocent farm people, and what they might have done to us if we had not cooperated? They were committing a crime when they were killed and we were defending ourselves. As I said at the beginning of this chapter—your best enemy is a dead enemy.

According to psychologists this event should have weighed heavily on my mind. I don't think it ever did. I have never felt sorry about this act, or had pangs of conscience. At the time I felt a combination of disgust, triumph and exhilaration; the latter two may have had their source in my need to get rid of the anger and frustration which had been accumulating and because of the pain and injustice which I and many others had experienced at the hands of Nazi Germany. I debated a long time whether to write about this or not. Does it serve any purpose? Should my family and the world (if this is ever published) know about it? Would they think less of me? In the end I decided to write the truth and let the chips fall where they may.

EPILOGUE

It wasn't long after the war ended that I returned to th Mijlpaal and was reunited with my family, Karel, Rita, Berna and Helga Brouwer. Life returned slowly to normal although there were still many repercussions of what had happened during the five years of occupation. There were still problems with food and supplies, clothing was hard to come by as well. Like many other kids, I played with all sorts of ammunition and weapons which had been left over from the war. We did a lot of dangerous things but luck was with me and I wasn't hurt like so many other kids.

Then I started going to High School in Amersfoort, despite the hiatuses in my schooling during the war. I really studied very hard and managed to skip from 1st year to 3rd year and so made up for some of the lost time. Then came a tug-of-war between my relatives and the Brouwer family which ended with me having to go into an orphanage for Jewish war orphans. The efforts made by my mother's sister and her husband caused me an the Brouwers a lot of pain and I never forgave my relatives for, what I considered, their insensitivity. I also felt, it turned out with some justification, that my aunt wanted to get her hands on any money I would be getting from our estate or from reparations. I had not liked her long before this, but now I positively hated her.

When I had to leave Karel and Rita Brouwer's family and came to the Rüdelsheim Institute for orphans in Hilversum, I became part of a group of children who had all been traumatized during the war in one way or another. Some had more problems than others, but everyone had lost all or part of their family and felt alone. Some had gone through absolute hell, either in camps or, unfortunately, at the hands of their "protectors". The ages of the orphans in the home ranged between five or six and eighteen. We were never helped to understand each other's problems; some of us were told about the experiences of others by the director and our counselors. However this was, in fact, of very little help in making us understand, because we were too mixed up ourselves and too engrossed in, and ignorant of, our own problems and the counselors themselves were not capable of understanding us. We were just unhappy about something we couldn't define. At least I know I was. They didn't talk at all about sexual abuse, which was one cause of the psychological baggage many of us carried, because talking openly about sex was even then considered a taboo in the prudish Dutch society. Every one of us had lived through our own kind of hell and many were still living it by day and especially at night and it often affected our behavior. After five years of harassment, hate pain, and loss, few of us were "normal" and knew the words "love" and "trust" and what they really meant. We certainly had learned not to trust most grownups.

One of our counselors, a psychologist by the name of Dr. Drucker, who came to the orphanage to interview us and "help us" overcome our problems was considered by most of us a rather laughable figure and we quite often made fun of him. We couldn't see how he could help us. We didn't think that we needed help. Dr. Drucker was a good man, but he had a very serious stutter and was often unable to start or finish a sentence without some visible difficulty. He often called the orphanage during dinner and I, being often in charge of the phone in the hall, used to answer it. Hans Muller, one of my room-mates, still remembers the time that I went out in the hall and, after waiting to hear an intelligible sound from the other end of the line (and me saying "What?...Who?...What?...") said: *"Oh, I see, it's Mr. Drukker. Wait, I'll call Mr. Kaneel (our director) for you".*

Whenever Dr. Drucker or Dr. Keilson, the psychiatrist, whom we considered to be just as useless to us in our, limited, opinion, came to the orphanage they used try to make us talk about our problems and show us those "funny inkblots" (Rohrshach tests). They would ask us what they reminded us of, and our answers were supposed to give them an idea what our problems were, how we were adjusting and how they could help us. They really didn't know what it was we needed and had absolutely no idea how to approach us and win our confidence. As a result, some of us used to make up the most horrendous stories to satisfy their questions. I never gave a sensible answer and made up things like: "That looks like underpants, this looks like a flower", when there was absolutely no resemblance. It was Leo Lindner, I think, who in one session gave the same answer to the question: "And what do you see here?" when he was shown the ink-blots. He answered "manure" or "shit" every time. When Dr. Drucker finally asked him: *"B-but w-w-w-w-why d-d-d-o you see t-t-those t-things-s in those b-b-black and white s-s-s-s-sh-sh-shapes"?* Leo answered *"I always see that everywhere".* The good doctor put his face in his hands and told Leo that the session was over. The poor guy, he was visibly upset and he wanted so much to do well by us but at that time the knowledge about treating PTSD (Post Traumatic Stress Disorder) caused during wars was still in its infancy. He himself was, of course also a victim of the Nazi persecution and experienced his own hell. I still feel a bit guilty about being so cruel to him, but I was just a mixed-up kid and didn't know any better. I wish I could talk to him now and apologize.

It is clear that all of us would have benefitted from competent analysis in overcoming our anxieties and frustrations, our distrust and fear and anger. There were so many hidden stresses due to physical, mental or sexual abuse, loss of parents, siblings and friends and home atmosphere. Some had the trauma of perceived/imagined abandonment by parents who couldn't hide together with their children in the same place. When those parents did not survive, there was no way for their children to learn the truth. All these things affected nearly all of the survivors and the reactions appeared often much later in their lives. Many of my fellow orphans had difficulty adjusting to a "normal" world and it took many of them a long time to find their way. Some of us, myself included, sought help from professionals or support groups later in life. Some were never able to live without the support of long-term analysis. For some, this did not work at all and they ended their lives in institutions or took their own lives in desperation. Sem Polak who was with us in the Mijlpaal group never overcame his problems. He married a wonderful lady but was miserable and felt the survivors guilt very keenly. He committed suicide in the 50's.

What we all needed was personalized love and care, which an orphanage system does not provide. One main reason that all of us children were brought into the orphanage was to get us out of the non-Jewish environment we were living in and give us an orthodox Jewish education. It was not intended for the good of the children, it was to protect Judaism from losing members of the clan. During the war many of us had been made to feel that it wasn't a good thing to be Jewish, and had, as a result, great difficulty accepting the authority and rules of an insensitive orphanage board, which tried to force religion upon us, especially after the first director was fired for "being too liberal and good to the kids". Many of us, like myself, came from very liberal households anyway and we were not ready to be orthodox Jews after our experience with persecution. My parents weren't religious, so they hadn't expected me to grow up religious either. So why were those people trying to force me to be something my parents hadn't wanted me to be? We kids had all survived by denying our Judaism and suddenly we were forced to become ultra-religious Jews. It didn't make sense to us.

This feeling was intensified by some of the religious education we received. Our teacher for religious studies, a Mr. Spitz, was a man who jeered and sneered at all non-Jews and their habits and beliefs. He absolutely hated everything non-Jewish and was very vocal about it To me he was just as bad as the Nazis, or even worse. We, the Jews, who had been saved by Christian families, who had mostly taken good care of us and had given us as much love as we could accept and security, were now told we should never trust a non-Jew because through the ages all Christians had persecuted the Jews. I asked him one day, when Leo Lindner and I were with him, what about people like Karel Brouwer, Dolf Hendriks, Joop Van der Pol, Moltjes Veer and so many others. His answer was so full of hatred that I still cannot believe he said it. He answered *"They made good money during the war. No intelligent Jew should ever trust a Christian"*. I should have asked him how and by whom he was saved, but I was too angry to think clearly. I got up and yelled "You are a bastard and a liar. You are wrong! You are as bad as the Nazis!" and ran out of the class and refused to return to be taught by him again. This man and the religious practices which were forced upon us without any explanation, except that "this is the way it is", were some of the reasons that I even refused to become Bar-Mitsvah at the orphanage when all the other boys did. As far as I have been able to ascertain, quite a number of the orphans have, like myself, turned away from orthodoxy after they left that orphanage and I think that the insensitive clueless regime in the orphanage has to carry much of the blame.

The one person, who was generally accepted and well liked by the kids, the first director Koos Kaneel, was ousted from the directorship because he was "too good for the kids," and because he was "not strict enough in religious matters". Kaneel and his family always ate their meals with us, although the orphanage board had asked him not to. He wanted us all to be a family and he and his wife tried to give love to all of the children, which was a very difficult task, because many of us, including me, were not trusting enough to accept that immediately. After Mr. Kaneel was fired and his replacement, Mr. Elburg, became head, the atmosphere in the institute worsened. Elburg was unfriendly, dictatorial, uncommunicative and very religious, the latter at least on the outside. He was a pasty-faced individual, dressed in black, who seldom smiled and who had no idea how to talk to us or handle our problems. His wife, as somber as her husband, wasn't much better in communicating with the kids, an ineffectual housemother without any apparent wish to, nor abilities, at handling children. Moreover, the two of them angered some of us older kids, when we saw that they took the first pick of the gifts and presents which were donated by well-wishers and philanthropists from the Netherlands and the USA. I managed one day to steal the keys of the cupboards the donations were kept in and make soap imprints of them. Then I adapted and filed keys for those cupboards and so some of the goodies came back to us. I, and some others, used to wear the clothes openly, but I was never challenged on those "thefts", which, to me were only "taking back that what belonged to us". I think that Elburg knew that I was the instigator and he bided his time to get back at me. He could not do much, because the upper management had a financial interest in keeping me. Not only did they receive funds from the government for us, but they also used funds which came from family property, if there was any, for our upkeep. He may have been afraid of my not keeping my mouth shut about their pilfering from the presents to the orphans.

Elburg, his wife and three children, ate often separately from us in their private quarters and we knew that they often received better food than we did. We learned that from the kitchen help and some of the staff members, who brought the food to their apartment on the second floor. The regular staff members ate with us in the dining hall. It all made for an unpleasant atmosphere and I was definitely unhappy there and had many discipline problems.

There came a time when some of us were planning to run away and go to Israel, but the plans were leaked by someone, I never knew who it was, and we were prevented from leaving. At one time there was a rebellion with some actual violence, which was solved after some negotiations with the Board of Directors whose members lived in Amsterdam. I was one of the rebels who, as a result, was "encouraged" to leave the institution on my own or be sent to a "Boys Home" in Amsterdam. I chose the former because I wanted to have a life of my own and not be in another semi-prison. During the last year I had also felt that the management was actively encouraging the older wards to leave the institution. The reason for this may have been that they thought that it was too difficult to control the older ones and that this had a bad influence on the younger ones. Another reason, the cost of caring for the older orphans became higher when some of them had to travel daily by train to the Jewish High School in Amsterdam, and these costs were probably not reimbursed by the Government.

Looking back to that time, I think that this particular Jewish institute, its directors and management, made grave errors and showed a near criminal lack of understanding and compassion which was inexcusable even then, by forcing the children to suddenly become religious "Jews," an epithet which many had learned to fear and despise during their formative years.

To tell the story of the rest of my life till today would probably fill another book or so. I may write that one day, but I find that this early phase of my life was more important to put in print. I wandered quite a bit in the world and had several professions before ending up today as Professor Emeritus at the University of Nebraska and volunteer Curator of a small museum. My road took me to France as part of a Jazz band, to the sea as a deck hand on a tramp steamer, to Israel as a mechanic in a kibbutz and in a private factory, to Africa as a mechanic for an

Israeli company, back to Israel as technician and later student at the Technion (Israel Institute of Technology in Haifa), to Purdue University for my doctorate and, after some more wanderings, to Lincoln, Nebraska, where I still live.

I still find it incomprehensible that my beautiful and gentle mother was, in the words of the Germans "Eine Jüdensau—A Jewish Sow", who had to be exterminated in order to save the purity of the German race. And my dad, Pappy, the smiling outdoorsman, hiker and biker and faithful provider, who wouldn't and couldn't hurt a fly? How about my beloved Anita and all my class-mates? What had they done to the German people? I ask myself—how many of those Germans, Austrians, and so many others, who think alike, are still among us today? And how many of their offspring have they infected, be it intentionally or not?

I retired from my position as a tenured professor of Agricultural Engineering in the Department of Biological Systems Engineering at the University of Nebraska and as director of a test laboratory in 1997. I live in Lincoln, a wonderful city on the Great Plains with great people who have made me and my wife Rose very welcome.

Reference Reading List

Readers may find more detailed information about the times and events mentioned above in some of the following publications:

1. **Günther Schwarberg**
   The Murders at Bullenhüser Damm—The SS doctor and the children
   Published in German as: "Der SS-Arzt und die Kinder—Bericht über den Mord vom Bullenhüser Damm".—(1980)
   Indiana University Press, Bloomington, Indiana, 1984

2. **Henri A. van der Zee**
   "The Hunger Winter—Occupied Holland 1944–1945"
   University of Nebraska Press, 1998

3. **Bob Moore**
   "Victims and Survivors—The Nazi Persecution of the Jews in the Netherlands 1940–1945"
   Arnold Press, 1997

4. **Hans Knoop**
   "The Menten Affair"
   McMillan Publishing Co. 1978

5. **Peter Lurvink**
   "De Joodse Gemeente in Aalten—Een geschiedenis 1630–1945" (in Dutch)
   (The Jewish Community in Aalten—a history 1630–1945)
   Walburg Pers, 1991

6. **Kees Ribbens**
   "Zullen wij nog terugkeren......"—De jodenvervolging in Amersfoort tijdens de Tweede Wereldoorlog (in Dutch)
   ("Shall we still return......"—the persecution of the jews in Amersfoort during WWII)
   Uitgeverij Bekking Amersfoort (Bekking Publishers, Amersfoort) 2002

7. **Hans Buiter and Ignace de Haes**
   "Geruisloos verzet—de TD groep tijdens de Duitse bezetting......)" (in Dutch)
   "Soundless resistance—the TD-group during the German occupation......)"
   De Horstink, 1982

8. **"Nederland en de Tweede Wereldoorlog"**—Volumes I and II (in Dutch)
   Readers Digest NV, Amsterdam, in cooperation with the Rijksinstituut voor Oorlogsdocumentatie (State Institute for War Documentation) 1995

9. **Stéphane Bruchfeld and Paul A. Levine**
   "Tell Ye Your Children—a book about the holocaust in Europe 1933–1945"
   (Original title in Swedish "...om detta må ni berätta...—En bok om Förintelsen I Europa 1933–1945")
   Regeringskansliet Levande Historia, Stockholm,1998

10. **Harry Theeboom (Alias Frans Jan Berkenbosch)**
    "Lest we forget"
    Private correspondence (1993) and official declaration to Yad Vashem, Jerusalem (1989)

0-595-30611-X